Michaela Boland writes for *The Australian Financial Review* and Hollywood newspaper *Variety*. She has been a broadcaster with ABC Radio and 3RRR, was editor of *Cinema Papers* magazine and has written for *Juice, Premiere* and *The Age*.

Michael Bodey is show-biz editor at Sydney's *Daily Telegraph*, a regular cultural commentator on ABC radio 702 and a contributor to *Men's Style* magazine. He was previously a film critic for *The Age* and arts editor at *Beat Magazine*.

Michaela Boland and Michael Bodey

AUSSIEWOOD

AUSTRALIA'S LEADING ACTORS AND DIRECTORS TELL HOW THEY CONQUERED HOLLYWOOD

A SUE HINES BOOK
ALLEN & UNWIN

First published in 2004

A Sue Hines Book
Allen & Unwin Pty Ltd
83 Alexander Street
Crows Nest NSW 2065
Australia
Phone: (61 2) 8425 0100
Fax: (61 2) 9906 2218
Email: info@allenandunwin.com
Web: www.allenandunwin.com

National Library of Australia
Cataloguing-in-Publication entry:

Boland, Michaela.
Aussiewood.

Bibliography.

ISBN 1 86508 971 0.

1. Motion picture industry - California - Hollywood (Los Angeles). 2. Actors and actresses - Australia. 3. Motion picture producers and directors - Australia. 4. Hollywood (Los Angeles, Calif.). I. Bodey, Michael. II. Title.

791.430979494

Edited by Jo Jarrah
Text design by Ellie Exarchos
Typesetting by Pauline Haas

Printed in Australia by Griffin Press
10 9 8 7 6 5 4 3 2 1

Contents

foreword

'Hollywood', of course, means many things to many people. In this instance, it is a catch-all phrase for American film and television, which consumes 70–90 per cent of the Australian box office, half the prime-time TV schedules and an inordinate amount of world media attention. In reality, the Los Angeles suburb of Hollywood is a tawdry stretch of cheap tourist shops, run-down apartments and derelict cinemas, frequented by tourists assembling for 'tours of the stars' homes' or posing with a Crocodile Dundee lookalike. Among the only true remnants of 'Hollywood' in Hollywood are Paramount Studios, Mann's Chinese Theatre and the Roosevelt Hotel, former home of the Oscars.

Some of the actors included in this book were born offshore, in Hawaii or the UK for example. Their involvement in *Aussiewood* is tacit acknowledgement that their story is, in some way, 'Aussie'.

The 'Pivotal Projects' listed at the start of each chapter have been selected by the authors as a means of illustrating the actor or director's journey to Hollywood, and to flesh out the accompanying chapter.

introduction

The achievements of Australia's leading actors and directors in Hollywood reached a critical mass in the lead up to the Golden Globe Awards in 2002. Ten Australians were nominated across 24 film and television categories, some twice. Even the international press began asking, 'Is there something in the water Down Under?'

Nicole Kidman was quoted saying she hoped the Australians could sit together but any plan for a 'Team Australia'-type table at the event was quashed by the mandate to assemble personnel from each nominated show or film. Kidman's excitement was infectious. It was a year after her split from Hollywood titan Tom Cruise, and the Australian media had been particularly supportive of her personal struggle. She rose to prominence for compelling lead performances in *The Others* and a US-financed Australian musical, *Moulin Rouge!*, and 15 years after decamping to Hollywood she was rediscovering her tribe.

Kidman has several high profile Australian friends in LA: Naomi Watts, Heath Ledger, Russell Crowe and Phillip Noyce, to name some, but her situation is not necessarily the norm. For Geoffrey Rush, meeting Cate Blanchett and Rachel Griffiths at various pre-awards functions before the 1998

Oscars was 'As close as anything I've had that resembles an Australian moment in LA. The rest of the time I have no connection with an Australian network.'

Whether or not a network exists, the impact of Australians in Hollywood – right through to Rupert Murdoch, Chairman and CEO of News Corporation, owner of Twentieth Century Fox – is undeniable. Hence *Aussiewood*.

The Golden Globe Awards is one of many precursors to Hollywood's premier gala, the Academy Awards, and the organising body, the Hollywood Foreign Press Association, has beyond dubious credibility. Nevertheless, the event spotlights the crafts of acting and directing in television and film. The same parameters have been applied to *Aussiewood*.

The Golden Globes ignore the groundswell of Australian cinematographers, digital artists, costume designers and other creative talent inflating the ranks of Australians in Hollywood, people whose contributions richly underpin the careers of their more famous peers. When Bruce Beresford made his first American movie, *Tender Mercies*, he recruited a cinematographer, editor and composer from Australia. Gillian Armstrong fought Canadian labour laws to import her first assistant director when making her first Hollywood movie, *Mrs. Soffel*. Peter Weir always collaborates closely with Australians, no matter where he works. A dozen of the leading cinematographers in Hollywood are now Australian. Their stories could fill another book.

There is a kindred spirit among Australians in Hollywood born out of their 'shared colonial experience', Weir wrote in 2002, and evident in the characteristics that helped them succeed. Determined, hard-working and easy-going are all adjectives often applied to Australians. 'There's something about the stamina, work ethic and the ability to have a healthy sense of the absurd which seems to distinguish Australians in film,' says Anthony Minghella, the English director of *The English Patient*. But that doesn't explain how a disproportionate number of Australians have come to fly the flag in Hollywood.

The directors, after achieving some success in Australia, were lured to the US by money, the chance to further their creative journey (whether through bigger budgets or by working with top-shelf producers) and the larger audiences the American film distribution system ensures. This situation appears unchanged after 25 years.

According to Phillip Noyce, Australians are flourishing in Hollywood because they are westernised, adaptable and don't have a distinct culture. 'We share the English language [and] we are brought up on American TV and movies but at the same time you have a different vision of the world which comes from being an Australian,' he says. 'Whether you're an actor, a director or a photographer you can easily connect with Americans but you'll always see a situation differently. That uniqueness of vision is an advantage because that's what everyone's looking for in cinema, a new way of looking at something.'

Frances O'Conner posits that Australia's isolation means 'We can develop our own sense of who we are. We look to America but we're very much our own culture.' In fact the actors' experiences of Hollywood are more disparate than the directors'. Geoffrey Rush, Judy Davis, Nicole Kidman and Sam Neill, Toni Collette and Rachel Griffiths came to the attention of the Americans because they starred in popular Australian films – respectively *Shine, My Brilliant Career, Dead Calm* and *Muriel's Wedding* (and each film propelled its director – Scott Hicks, Gill Armstrong, Noyce and P.J. Hogan – to Hollywood too).

Some actors used well-received ensemble films as calling cards. *The Adventures of Priscilla, Queen of the Desert*, led to Guy Pearce and Hugo Weaving gaining attention, although it took until *LA Confidential* for Pearce to shine through. Weaving's big break, *The Matrix*, was filmed, oddly enough, in Australia. Eric Bana and Russell Crowe proved that if your lead performance is strong enough, the movie doesn't even need to be seen by many Americans. *Chopper* and *Romper Stomper* became popular films on Hollywood's private screening room circuit. Everyone saw their subsequent efforts, Bana's *Black Hawk Down* and *The Hulk,* Crowe in *LA Confidential* and *The Insider*, to name just two.

Others had less illustrious entries. Anthony LaPaglia, Heath Ledger and Naomi Watts didn't arrive in Hollywood riding on an Australian-made film. But for their determination they might never have risen above the crowd. Ledger believes knowing he could return to Australia was a superb back-up plan that kept him unharried. Portia de Rossi agrees; appreciating she could always go home meant she didn't exude the all-or-nothing desperation of many young Hollywood wannabes. *Without a Trace* co-star Poppy Montgomery tells a similar story.

Desire rather than desperation is the driver for many Australian actors in Hollywood. Subsequently, they're more willing to take artistic risks. The careers of Watts and Kidman are cases in point; they truly accelerated after edgy, esoteric choices, such as *Mulholland Dr.*, *21 Grams* and *The Hours*, *To Die For* and *The Others*.

The Australian influx into Hollywood is not unique. The world's movie heartland has been a beacon for immigrants ever since it grew out of the desert at the turn of the twentieth century. The studios have always cherry-picked the globe. Alan Ladd Jr, the then Fox studio executive who invited Fred Schepisi to Hollywood, was surprised to hear Schepisi was the first of the Australian New Wave directors to depart. All Ladd knew was, 'I thought he was a very talented man and I'd like to work with him.'

Some of the early expats struggled with their decision to leave the publicly funded industry that had nurtured them. They also faced animosity from the community. When Weir and Bruce Beresford followed Schepisi, the Australian media decried their exit as a betrayal. Beresford responded simply: there was no money in Australia, whereas the Americans paid good fees and were experts at selling movies to audiences.

When Jack Thompson was preparing for his first trip to the US (to promote *Petersen* in 1976) his neighbour warned, 'Remember Phar Lap, son.' Thompson recounts, 'Either Phar Lap or Les Darcy, they were both considered Australian champions poisoned by the Americans. I said, "Thanks a lot".'

As Australia's self-confidence has grown the sense of betrayal has dissipated. 'Australian actors have stopped resisting going to Hollywood and thinking that was selling out,' says LaPaglia. 'There was a big feeling of that when I first went there in the 80s and 90s, that they just do crap there and the Australian industry has more integrity. When you realise you can't make a living here, you go where you [can].'

And nowadays there's so little money in the Australian industry, consensus has come full circle: those who can work overseas should. Cinematographer John Seale told *Variety*, 'The last thing I want to do when I come home is to make a low-budget film. I don't want to take a job that will be a stepping-stone for a young Australian cameraman.' Other cinematographers are known to scoff at the suggestion of working for local rates.

In 2002, Jack Thompson said, 'If you want to be a success in Hollywood you have to go and live in Hollywood.' According to Thompson, 'A lot of the industry revolves around, "Were you at the party?"' The contemporary crowd subscribes to this theory only half-heartedly.

Rush is one Australian actor who refuses to live in LA and finds his career unsullied by the decision. Crowe, Bana,

O'Connor and Cate Blanchett manage their professional lives ably from Australia or the UK. Series television actors like LaPaglia and *The Guardian* star Simon Baker don't have this choice, which admittedly is relatively new for movie actors too.

While many key industry parties are in LA, the growing proportion of movies and television being produced in Canada, Europe and Australia means there's less pressure on actors and directors to remain there. Plus the Hollywood party season, for film at least, is now an intense three months from early December until the Oscars at the end of February. The 'season' comprises a rash of laudatory events, meet-and-greet screenings, breakfasts, lunches, dinners and cocktail parties where campaigning for awards is heady and can take place in London, New York, Los Angeles and places in between.

Some Australians have assiduously worked Hollywood's kudos season and reaped the results. In 2002 and early 2003, Kidman endured a gruelling number of events designed to throw the spotlight on her performance in *The Hours*. Always looking a million dollars, she studiously attended the necessary parties and ultimately collected a Golden Globe (her second in as many years) and an Oscar. Conversely, Peter Weir has received four Golden Globe and four Oscar nominations (for *Master and Commander, Dead Poets Society, The Truman Show* and *Witness*) but not one trophy, arguably because of his reticence to press-the-flesh in Hollywood or anywhere else.

Not that there is a template for playing the game: Roman Polanski collected the Oscar for Best Direction of *The Pianist* in 2002 without stepping foot in the US. Nor is there a specified route to success. The only lesson is that there are a multitude of lessons. Nevertheless, a number of elements remain common to the extraordinary Australian influx.

The most obvious factor contributing to the success of Australia's filmmakers is the existence of a strong domestic industry. Australians have thrived in Hollywood for the past 25 years because there has been an Australian industry for 35 years. Mel Gibson, Jack Thompson, Judy Davis and Bryan Brown were all introduced to Hollywood via lead roles in Australian films in the late 70s and early 80s: Thompson in 'Breaker' Morant; Brown in the mini-series The Thorn Birds; Davis in My Brilliant Career; and Gibson in Gallipoli, Mad Max and The Year of Living Dangerously.

All those films were made in the late 70s, almost a decade after Prime Minister John Gorton moved to consolidate an Australian film industry. Upon advice from the 1969 Interim Report of the Film and Television Committee of the Australian Council for the Arts, Gorton's government introduced an experimental film fund, a film school and a publicly funded development body (later the Australian Film Commission, or AFC). As the industry grew, the AFC began marketing and distributing Australian films overseas at international markets such as Cannes, where, in 1980, Thompson garnered acclaim for his role in 'Breaker' Morant. The AFC established offices in Los Angeles in 1978 and in London. Meanwhile television quotas for Australian drama content were introduced, ensuring the presence of Australians on the small screen and protecting the training and employment opportunities of casts and crews. The government-funded Australian Broadcasting Corporation also proved an effective training ground.

The nurturing of this industry has produced Australians who can work across media. While publicly funded film schools such as the Victorian College of the Arts (nee Swinburne) and the Australian Film Television and Radio School trained directors and technicians, the acting schools graduated Jackman, Blanchett and Baz Luhrmann, among others. The schools' preference for teaching stage rather than screen craft has meant film actors such as Jackman and O'Connor are just as suited to

Broadway or the West End. Many of those who didn't go to acting school trained on the small screen, in *Neighbours*, *Home and
Away* and other soaps or dramas. The harsh economics of the
Australian industry have ensured 'Australian actors float
between mediums because they don't have the luxury of doing
one or two movies a year,' says LaPaglia.

Little wonder this versatile bunch thrived in 90s
Hollywood, which had cruelled itself by chasing models, not
actors, for lead roles. Australian men also bring to the screen a
physicality recently lacking in American male actors as a result
of Hollywood's preference for casting lithe teenage males. *LA
Confidential* is one of the great 'tough men' movies of all time.
Three Australians – Crowe, Pearce and Simon Baker – starred.
Jackman and Bana translated their physicality, honed on stage
and TV respectively, straight to action roles. Australian actors,
from Errol Flynn to Jackman, use their bodies, not just their
faces – an oft-quoted criticism of Hollywood's close-up kids.

The Australian robustness isn't merely an external trait.
According to LaPaglia, 'Australians are tough by nature.
They're much more pragmatic and not into self-analysis so
they don't over-think things. Am ericans over-think shit and it
hurts them in the end.' Director John Duigan surmises that the
toughness in the Australian psyche stems from the 'tall poppy
syndrome'. A country that doesn't tolerate swollen egos 'seems
to produce people with a complete lack of self-consciousness
and a real immediacy in the acting'.

Frances O'Connor contends that Hollywood's cosmetic
surgery culture is eating into its own talent bank. Surgery, she
says, 'undermines women's beauty, and also men now, so
women never get to feel relaxed in themselves. They
[Americans who have it] kind of die inside because they're so
worried about the exterior, whereas Australian and British
women have more of a sense of their own value.'

The Australian voice has also matured. Twenty years ago the cognoscenti in New York were surprised to learn Australians spoke English. Now, post Paul Hogan, they know. Australia, Canada, the UK and South Africa share a common language with the US but Australians find it easier to adopt US accents than the Brits and South Africans. Director John Badham who unsuccessfully tried to cast Bryan Brown in *Blue Thunder*, observes, 'There's a great charm in the Aussie accent whereas an upper class British accent can be off-putting.' The South African accent is harsher still, he adds.

But Australian accents had a slow ascent to visibility. In 1975, *Petersen* was released stateside, redubbed by American actors. The film's lead, Jack Thompson, says, 'They couldn't understand Australian voices.' Dr George Miller's road movie *Mad Max* – which was a cult hit in the US a few years later – also had a new 'American' voice track. Not long after, *My Brilliant Career* was released unaltered. Likewise the actors. Jack Thompson only ever played an Australian in his early Hollywood roles. It took 15 years until he was cast as an American (in *A Woman of Independent Means*). Some movie people, he says, 'have, by definition, limited imaginations'.

Now the reverse is true. Most Americans consider Kidman, Ledger and Jackman to be American. Little wonder that Ledger and Mel Gibson teamed as son and father in *The Patriot*, a movie about the US War of Independence, a defining event in the country's history. Kidman also underscored her red, white and blue credentials by headlining a US Civil War epic, *Cold Mountain*, a project which typifies the blurred national boundaries of modern Hollywood. Directed by a Brit (Anthony Minghella) and shot by an Aussie (Seale), it starred an American, Canadian, Brit and Australian.

Crowe, it must be said, has gone to extremes to brand himself as both a New Zealander and an Australian. Once he had enough clout, he even used his Australian accent on screen, in *Proof of Life.* Geoffrey Rush, in *Intolerable Cruelty,* changed his English soap-producer character to an Australian, with the Coen Brothers' permission. Australians are now so entrenched in Hollywood, nobody bats an eye when a slimy, sleazy producer hails from Down Under. Of that, Australians should be proud.

The exit of actors and directors to the US – once the cause of much hand-wringing – has become a source of national pride. And the picture has grown so large there are now Australians working in Hollywood who began their careers there and are utterly unrecognisable to Australian audiences. Directors Robert Luketic and Jamie Blanks leapt from film school in Melbourne straight to directing Hollywood studio pictures (*Legally Blonde* and *Urban Legend,* respectively). Newcastle-born *24* co-star Sarah Wynter returned to Melbourne in 2004 for her first Australian role, in the film *Three Dollars.* Another US television star, *Without a Trace*'s Sydney-born Poppy Montgomery, is barely known to her countrymen. The Australian industry cannot take credit for nurturing these last two. So they stand as yet another exception to the rules but nevertheless testament to the growing impact of Australians abroad.

In the future other aspirants will head to LA without considering that the stories in these pages represent but a fraction of the Aussies who have gone before them. Many, many more, some with oodles of experience and high profiles, have ventured forth and failed.

Still, the current Hollywood love affair with Australians to some degree ensures an audience. Frances O'Connor says, 'We are respected and seen as serious actors and good to work with.' International directors, including Ang Lee and Badham, speak of relief at not having to rely on the same old people.

De Rossi says, 'It is a little bit on the trendy side to be an Australian right now because casting people think they've discovered some great, untapped source.'

That rich, untapped source is finite, especially while the Australian film industry flounders. But there's hope. A 1984 Australian Film Commission report on Australia's dismal showing at the Cannes Film Festival included the paragraph: 'While the individual directors and actors like Mel Gibson are being acclaimed and adored, the Australian movie industry they helped build is suffering.'

Twenty years later Australian films are not even being selected to screen in the official selection at Cannes, but as any Hollywood studio maven will tell you: it only takes one hit. Two years after that AFC report, *Crocodile Dundee* was released, the highest grossing Australian movie ever and the second biggest film in the US that year (after *Top Gun*). And Australia has since produced many other hits, most of them starring the actors featured in this book.

01

nicole kidman

Pivotal Projects

Cold Mountain (2003), The Hours (2002), The Others (2001)

Moulin Rouge! (2001), Eyes Wide Shut (1999), The Portrait of a Lady (1996)

To Die For (1995), Days of Thunder (1990)

Bangkok Hilton (TV) (1989), Dead Calm (1989)

Vietnam (TV) (1986), BMX Bandits (1983)

nicole

During 20 years in the public eye Nicole Kidman has transformed from a gangly, freckle-faced teen with an unruly mane of ginger curls into a willowy beauty. In that time she has also evolved from a candid, happy-go-lucky actress with a bright future into a savvy, ultra-professional workhorse with the most envied female acting career in Hollywood. 'She's emerged as probably the one genuine movie star in the world,' says the man who directed her in *Cold Mountain*, Anthony Minghella. 'She's an icon everywhere now ... And what's fantastic about it is it hasn't been bestowed on her, she's earned it. She's done this succession of parts that's demonstrated she's the real deal, from a place of some skepticism in the sense that she's had to work harder to emerge from being part of a celebrity couple to being viewed as a really significant actor in her own right.' Being part of that celebrity couple – Christmas 1990 she married Tom Cruise when he was the biggest movie star in the world – has had its costs. Her life was, and continues to be, significantly scrutinised by the tabloid media.

In interviews Kidman generously shares her thoughts about how her career has developed and her incredible pride in being Australian. She is grateful for the point of difference it gives her in Hollywood and 'would like for my country to be proud of me'. But she is coy when quizzed about the specifics of her journey from the Sydney suburb of Longueville to Hollywood and she doesn't like to discuss the movie industry. 'I am reluctant to ever get too aware of that sort of stuff,' she says. 'I don't have a production company, I purposely don't have involvement in the business.'

Kidman's decision is at odds with some of the powerful younger actresses who've added a producer's feather to their caps, such as Drew Barrymore and Reese Witherspoon. Kidman's former husband Tom Cruise is another who produces movies, both his own and others', such as *The Others*, which starred Kidman. 'I'm not looking to be a producer. I'm not interested in the business side of it. I think if you get too aware of that stuff it actually *'I don't even know what the definition of a movie star is'* imbalances [the acting],' she says. As an actor, 'You're there to support your director'. She is also incredibly busy being a movie star, though she says, perhaps a little disingenuously, 'I don't even know what the definition of a movie star is. What is it? Just a funny couple of words.'

They weren't funny words back in 1989 when movie star Cruise and his famed *Top Gun* director and producers, Tony Scott, Don Simpson and Jerry Bruckheimer, invited her to meet them in LA. Kidman's Australian agent, June Cann, had circulated her showreel among American talent agents, producers and directors. Her Australian credits were now worthy of consideration, although one brash New York agent had apparently expressed some doubts: 'I don't know about the girl but I'd love to represent the hair,' she exclaimed. Kidman's most recent film, *Dead Calm*, Phillip Noyce's high-seas thriller in which she starred opposite Sam Neill had not been popular at the box office but it had become hot property on the Hollywood Hills private screening room circuit. In *Days of Thunder*, the thinly plotted *Top Gun* follow-up, in which high-octane NASCAR racing cars replaced

Top Gun's high-octane fighter planes, Kidman was to play Cruise's girlfriend, an Australian neurology intern (no need to tackle the accent just yet). When Kidman met with the principals she was just twenty-two. Knee-knocking stuff.

Cruise was white-hot after hits including *Cocktail*, *Rain Man* and *Top Gun* (the biggest movie of 1986). His Oscar-nominated performance in the Vietnam vet movie *Born on the Fourth of July* was next. *Days of Thunder* reunited at Paramount the *Top Gun* team, plus Oscar winner Robert Duvall and *Chinatown* screenwriter Robert Towne. Paramount intended to use the movie as its big 1990 summer release, or 'tentpole', and was prepared to spend to meet the high expectations of it. Tony Scott is of course the less famous brother of *Gladiator* director Ridley Scott. Bruckheimer is the workaholic producer of movies like *Coyote Ugly* and *Flashdance*, TV series *Without a Trace* and the *CSI* franchise. His producing partner from that era, Don Simpson, led a life of excess until it killed him in 1996 at the age of fifty-two. Simpson's gargantuan appetite for cocaine and hookers is Hollywood legend. He was at the peak of his power going into *Days of Thunder*; by the end of production his career was in tatters.

Nicole Kidman, in stark contrast, had just played an Australian schoolgirl in John Duigan's *Flirting*. It was her third project with the director, whom she counts as a good friend and one of five key mentors during the early years of her career. 'I was incredibly fortunate to have Terry Hayes, [Dr] George Miller, Phillip Noyce, John Duigan and Chris Noonan,' she says. 'All these very protective and smart people around who were able to advise me. I was still very young and able to lean on them for an enormous amount of advice.' This posse worked at that time with Miller's production company, Kennedy Miller, the same production company that gave Kidman a dream run of early opportunities.

Flirting was Kidman's fourth Kennedy Miller project. The series elevated her from previous youthful, inconsequential performances in films like *Windrider* and *BMX Bandits* to significant dramatic heights. The collaboration began in 1986 with the bumper TV mini-series *Vietnam*, continued with *Dead Calm* and another mini-series, *Bangkok Hilton*, then *Flirting*. All four stories featured characters who had the same sort of left-leaning, middle-class preoccupations of the 1980s Sydney milieu from which Kidman hailed. The former North Sydney Girls High School student was in familiar territory.

After *Vietnam*, Duigan advised her to eschew drama school, specifically National Inststute of Dramatic Arts (NIDA). She'd done acting classes at the Australian Theatre for Young People and he surmised workplace experience would be more valuable. She followed his advice but acknowledges she was lucky to have been able to. 'Having the opportunity to do that is rare,' she says. 'It is also slightly frightening because you're making all your mistakes on celluloid and that's what happened to me.'

Some mistakes. As early as 1986, after *Vietnam*, Hollywood picked up on her. 'I had a number of agents calling me in Australia and wanting to represent me,' she admits. 'It was a terrific showcase,' says Duigan of the series. '[On screen] she went from a schoolgirl, preoccupied with the usual teenage things, to a young anti-war activist who was at university and had to [articulate] her views against the war. The role had some great set pieces and she revealed the marvellous range she already had at the time.' After playing the girlfriend in *Windrider* she was grateful to receive a role for which she would eventually earn an AFI nomination. 'It really made a big difference to work with a three-dimensional character and flesh out the comic and dramatic aspects of the role,' she says.

But the 19 year old rejected the invitation to head to

America. 'I ran away from it at that stage,' she recalls. I was working with Kennedy Miller, they were preparing *Bangkok Hilton*, and I had *Dead Calm* being talked about and was very happy. As an actor you want complex roles with interesting people, good directors, good writers, it's that simple. In Australia, in America, in Timbuktu, that's what you want. If you really love what you do then the satisfaction comes from the exploration and the process, not from the magnitude of it.' So she stayed in Sydney to star in an Australian mini-series during an era in which local miniseries actually had big budgets and even bigger audiences. Hollywood would have to wait.

'As an actor you want complex roles with interesting people, good directors, good writers, it's that simple'

When Kidman eventually decided to work in the US, she didn't face the work permit difficulties other Australian actors have had to grapple with. 'I grew up in Australia but I was born in Hawaii [when] my father was studying at the University of Hawaii,' she says. '[After I was born] we moved to Washington DC and then back to Australia, when I was three. I actually have a US and Australian citizenship.'

Her initial recollections of visiting the States as a professional are vivid. She went to Los Angeles to promote the US release of *Dead Calm* with Noyce and Sam Neill. 'I thought, I don't want to live here, I don't want to be eaten up by this business,' she says. 'I want[ed] to maintain my individuality and not conform to what they expect.' It was a resolution that would require considerable fortitude; Hollywood can be an alluring town. 'Everything glows because everyone is smiling. Everyone is saying this can happen and that can happen,' she says. Agents and managers, eager to sign fresh talent to their books, can fill impressionable young minds with grand promises that fail to bear fruit and dash hopes. 'The opportunities are abundant and "Oh, isn't it wonderful?" [they say]. You can be lured and corrupted very, very easily. It's insidious the way it happens.' According to Kidman, remembering why you chose acting in the first place is one way of keeping an even keel through this period. She steeled herself with the thought: I have to stay very true to my commitment to my art, and the reason I wanted to act in the first place.

On this trip she met with some agents who were impressed by her solid body of work despite her tender years. According to Duigan, 'If *Vietnam* was the series that established her as a dramatic actor, then *Dead Calm* was the film that really announced her.' *Bangkok Hilton* confirmed her star status in Australia and *Flirting*, which became her last ever Australian-financed film, was fun. It starred Noah Taylor and Thandie Newton as teenage lovers; Kidman was a secondary lead. 'I asked her if she wanted to play a schoolgirl for the last time,' Duigan recalls. Kidman wasn't necessarily an easy fit for the film as she had just finished playing a twenty-something mother grieving the loss of her child in *Dead Calm*. Duigan was unperturbed. The Nicola Radcliffe character was 'a sort of ice-princess. She liked the role a lot and I think she had great fun making it,' he says.

The chasm between playing a head prefect, but nevertheless a stand-out role, in *Flirting* and portraying the girlfriend of Cruise's character on *Days of Thunder* was significant. Duigan recalls the facilities for *Flirting* were primitive. 'In that period of filmmaking we still couldn't afford to have things like honey wagons so all the make-up and costuming was done in one big bus with everyone together.' On *Days of Thunder*, honey wagons, or 'trailers' to use the more common term, were plentiful. Kidman cancelled an appearance in the Sydney Theatre Company's production of *A Midsummer Night's Dream* to join the balmy Florida set of *Days of*

Thunder. Principal photography began late 1989 on the US$40 million movie, US$7 million of which was Tom Cruise's pay packet. The budget quickly rocketed to US$70 million and stories of hedonistic parties on the set abound. One night the crew rented an entire bowling alley and threw a party. Another night they hired a Daytona Beach nightclub for a party at which Tone Loc performed. Simpson is always at the centre of reports of these shenanigans but Cruise, Bruckheimer, Scott and Towne are also implicated to varying degrees. Despite the rocketing budget, Paramount expected *Days of Thunder* to be 'Top Gun 2' or 'Top Gun on Wheels' and as such, a safe bet.

But was it? The script wasn't finished by the time cameras began rolling at the end of 1989. Each day the cast would receive new pages of script. At one point Cruise crashed his car because he was reading his lines off the dashboard. After that, his lines were fed to him via headphones under his helmet. *Top Gun*'s budget had been US$17 million, US$2 million more than the average of the day. At US$70 million, *Days of Thunder* was in another league and the mounting pressures reflected that. It soon earned the nickname 'Days of Plunder'. Paramount complicated matters by fixing the movie to release on the Memorial Day holiday, tradtionally the last weekend in May. So, no sooner had the cameras begun rolling than the release date loomed. There was little margin for error.

Kidman may have been unaware of the pressures swirling around her. But the delays due to rain, cars that continually broke down and accidents on the track could not have escaped her notice. Paramount's co-president Sid Ganis is quoted in the Don Simpson biography, *High Concept*: '*Days* was so difficult, so painful, all the way. There was almost no story, and there was no ending. It was just cars, going around a racetrack. We shouldn't have started without a script.'

The project holds mixed memories for Kidman, although the good fortune of getting to know her future husband far outweighs the bad. But when the film released critics pounced, almost without exception. Luckily for Kidman most of the bile was directed at Cruise and what critics considered Simpson, Bruckheimer and Scott's rather crude filmmaking formula. Roger Ebert's review is typical: '*Days of Thunder* is an entertaining example of what we might as well call the Tom Cruise Picture, since it assembles most of the same elements that worked in *Top Gun*, *The Color of Money* and *Cocktail* and runs them through the formula once again. Parts of the plot are beginning to wear out their welcome, but the key ingredients are still effective.'

Of Kidman? 'Kidman has little to do as the love interest and doesn't make much of an impression.' *The Washington Post* wrote of her Hollywood debut, 'Women – in particular, Nicole Kidman, who plays the brain specialist who supervises Cole's recovery after his crackup and eventually becomes his lover – are used for decorative purposes only.' Tough stuff, especially given the recent huge success in Australia of *Bangkok Hilton*, a mini-series written for her, in which she played the central character, a naive Australian tourist imprisoned in Bangkok for unknowingly trafficking heroin.

During 1990 Kidman fell in love with her on-screen beau. By the end of the year he had divorced his wife, Mimi Rogers, and married Kidman. She was just twenty-three. The union would affect her career in ways she couldn't have predicted. 'I wasn't that interested in becoming an individual after I got married,' she says of that time. 'I enjoyed being somebody's partner, so my struggles were later.'

She is almost apologetic about her second Hollywood role as a gangster's moll in the Dustin Hoffman mob movie *Billy Bathgate*. It was her first attempt at tackling an American accent. 'It's embarrassing when you first start doing an accent, you feel, Oh, my gosh, I'm not doing this well, but suddenly it clicks and before you know it I'm not even aware that I'm doing an accent. At first everyone's scrutinising it, more so than anybody's normal accent – it's too scrutinised.'

Ebert's review said of Kidman, 'we never feel her as real'. Without doubt, Hollywood wasn't giving her the kind of scripts she'd been used to in Kennedy Miller productions. Kidman is adamant her career simply was not a priority during this period: 'Nothing mattered, I just wanted to be near him.' But in an interview with *The Age* to mark the release of *Billy Bathgate* in April 1992, she expressed some frustration about the lukewarm welcome she had received in Hollywood. 'Over here it just looks like I married Tom Cruise and became an actress. It's not the way it happened at all and it pisses me off,' she told Jim Schembri.

Kidman told *The Age* she had a strong desire to retain her identity despite making movies with her incredibly famous husband: 'I don't want to deny that I'm with him (but) even when presenting an Oscar they asked us to do it together and I said, "No".'

As Kidman settled into life with Cruise press reports from the time are filled with pregnancy speculations and eventually the couple's adoption of Isabella. In fact, the level of reporting on the couple's every move was intense, and remained so for the duration of their marriage.

Frustration with her career began to niggle, she admits. 'I went, Am I never going to get to do anything but play the girlfriend occasionally in a blockbuster, a formulaic movie that has no depth? That [thought] was upsetting, disturbing because I felt things inside me were never going to be accessed or expressed.' Her roles in Harold Becker's *Malice* and Joel Rubin's *My Life*, didn't help matters; both promised much but failed to make an impact. Her next project with Cruise, *Far and Away*, an epic tale of Irish migrants, also flopped despite its obvious marketability. Media outlets paid it little attention other than endlessly replaying a scene in which the young woman furtively peeks at his manhood. Kidman's drought lasted five years.

She was fortunate never to have to suffer the indignity of making money movies − projects to pay the bills and keep agents, managers and others who collect a percentage of her pay cheques from the door. Cruise's professional status continued to rise during this period with *A Few Good Men*, *The Firm* and *Interview with the Vampire*. Kidman says, 'I was happy being a mother and a wife and to have a quieter profile.'

She failed to nab the lead role in at least one movie which would prove to be the breakthrough for its leading lady: *Ghost* for Demi Moore. Hollywood was initially skeptical that because she was Australian she couldn't perform as a regular American. She says, 'A common reaction from casting people and directors was: "She can't do an American accent," or "How's she going to understand the American mentality?"' Kidman says. 'Now it's almost a plus to be Australian, people are intrigued by it, they have seen we can do accents, we can take on personas, and we can embody characters.' When presenting the Best Actor Oscar early in 2004 Kidman's accent sounded more Australian than it had for many years. She has obviously seized it back with gusto.

People such as Russell Crowe, Cate Blanchett, Naomi Watts, Rachel Griffiths, Radha Mitchell and Heath Ledger are 'now very easily working in the industry,' she says. 'But when I first came over there was Mel [Gibson] and Judy [Davis]. It wasn't like any sort of ground had been forged.' Kidman doesn't take credit for forging that ground but she could. 'Also Bryan Brown and Rachel Ward, I connect[ed] with them; they are very warm. And Jack Thompson was working as well. It was interesting to see they were balancing a life in Australia and being able to work as actors all over the world.' For Kidman that wasn't an option. 'I fell in love with an American and moved to America because he wasn't going to move to Australia and that was that for me. I wanted to be with the man I was in love with and the country didn't matter.'

During the early 90s meaty roles continued to elude her. She auditioned for the lead in Jane Campion's *The Portrait of a Lady* but that project was postponed for a year when Campion fell pregnant. Then she agreed to another 'girlfriend' role, as Dr Chase Meridian in Joel Schumacher's *Batman Forever*. The job was, Kidman says, 'fun and short'. It was stunt casting; Elle Macpherson played a similar role in Schumacher's follow-up, *Batman & Robin*. Schumacher was even famously quoted saying, 'I know, I know she doesn't look anything like a criminal psychiatrist but it's my Gotham City and I can do what I want!'

Kidman's beauty is an undeniable factor in her success. Schumacher was one director honest enough to say as much. 'I've had my eye on her since *Dead Calm*,' he says of casting her in *Batman Forever*. 'You meet a lot of beautiful people in this business but there's something almost luminous about her.' As with her acting, Kidman has applied a strong work ethic to her looks. Her once so-called 'unruly mane' is tirelessly maintained and her impeccable presentation during red carpet and public appearances is impressive. She has worked hard on her public profile.

When Kidman read the script of the black comedy *To Die For*, due to be directed by independent cinema darling Gus Van Sant, she knew she wanted the role. Meg Ryan was pegged to play the conniving cable channel weather girl Suzanne Stone and Kidman, according to Van Sant, was merely 'one of the actresses we'd met'. Van Sant didn't even realise she was married to Cruise and when he discovered this later, he says he didn't care either way. 'There were a couple of other actresses we were considering. One was worried about the obvious things, like, "Why do we like this character?" The other one had scheduling difficulties.' Van Sant was happy to wait six months for the other actress's schedule to clear but then 'Nicole called and said she knew she wasn't my first choice but that she was destined to play the part. She convinced me on that phone call . . . I realised [Kidman] probably would have put the most work into it. She seemed interested in working very hard,' Van Sant says. 'I started to think maybe because she was married to Tom she needed to carve out her own side of the family and I thought that's going to be great.'

Van Sant was grateful Kidman didn't want to imbue the conniving Suzanne with redemptive qualities. 'She already knew the character,' he says. 'We very quickly decided to go with her mostly because of her conviction . . . She just laid it on the line and made me believe she would really work on it,' he says. And she delivered. 'She did exactly what I hoped she would do – she worked very hard and always the best thing for a director [is] that they feel somebody's going to work hard rather than walk through it or have a lot of questions.'

Five years after arriving in Hollywood, *To Die For*'s Suzanne was her breakthrough role. She'd done more high-profile, more expensive films but this was her knockout performance. Roger Ebert again: 'Nicole Kidman's work is inspired. Her clothes, her makeup, her hair, her speech, her manner, even the way she carries herself (as if aware of the eyes of millions) are all brought to a perfect pitch: Her Suzanne is so utterly absorbed in being herself that there is an eerie conviction, even in the comedy.' Others, including US *Rolling Stone*'s Peter Travers suggested the 'volcanically sexy and richly comic performance' deserved to make her an Oscar favourite.

She didn't earn an Academy Award nomination but she did collect a Golden Globe award – her first taste of Hollywood kudos. It would be another five years until she again came to the attention of the selectors with her roles in *Moulin Rouge!*, as the courtesan Satine, *The Others*, an Alejandro Amenabar thriller, and later *The Hours*, for which she collected an Oscar for playing Virginia Woolf. While Kidman shrugs off the importance of awards – 'everyone's aware of you winning worldwide but otherwise it doesn't change anything' – she concedes that from Australia she has always felt pressure to succeed. 'There was all this expectation on me to have a career in the US, which originated in Australia; it was like, "Well, she's done this here and is America going to offer her the same opportunities?"' Awards are the most obvious validation of her career but not the only one.

While Phillip Noyce and Sam Neill pursued high-profile Hollywood careers after *Dead Calm* (Dr George Miller was already working there), Kidman says Hollywood was not really her passion. 'I was more interested in an international career. I wanted to be able to work in England, Sweden, all over the world. Part of the reason I became an actor was to see the world, understand different cultures and to understand people from different countries. By being an actor you get to play all different nationalities and you get access to these countries on a very, very rich level. So it was never directed at America.' To wit: Kidman has worked with legendary Danish director Lars von Trier on *Dogville*; Brit Jez Butterworth on *Birthday Girl*; and Chilean Alejandro Amenabar on *The Others*, arguably the film that flagged her current renaissance.

Her biggest adventure beyond Hollywood was, however, her decision to decamp with the family to the United Kingdom to work with Cruise on legendary auteur Stanley Kubrick's laborious sexual thriller *Eyes Wide Shut*. Cruise had just completed the huge action film *Mission: Impossible* and made the critically acclaimed *Jerry Maguire*. *Eyes Wide Shut* was an experiment for Kidman and Cruise in submitting themselves to the master, Kubrick. The release was greeted with, again, excessive scrutiny, from which neither Kidman nor Cruise emerged unscathed. Many critics said their love scenes were cold. Kubrick died just before the film's release; it stands as his epitaph and an unusual insight into the couple's marriage. He submitted all his actors to intense direction, indulging himself with more than 100 takes on some scenes. To that end, he chose his leads well, as Kidman's strong work ethic has been one of the foundations of her career. It's not something she publicises but she has continued to study acting.

Her preparation for roles is intense. John Duigan recalls casting her for the first time in an episode of a kids' series called *Winners*. 'She played a young athlete,' in an episode called 'Room to Move'. She was only fifteen or sixteen and 'already a very focused and poised actress, she knew she loved acting so already at that stage one never had any problems with her focusing or concentrating. She was still having her social life as an active teenager but that was always after we finished shooting ... At one stage she twisted her ankle. It was a small TV film and we didn't have a lot of money so this was very alarming. It looked as though she wouldn't be able to run the big race which is the dramatic finale of the film, so we bound her ankle and she soldiered through it. That, I think, is very characteristic of her as a performer, she has show-must-go-on staunchness which I can imagine got her through *Moulin Rouge!* [after breaking a rib].'

Her work ethic comes from both her nature and her experience. 'I know it doesn't last,' she concedes. 'I've seen how this industry is very, very hard on women, particularly as they get older, but I would like to be able to leave some works of integrity.' Some of cinema's greatest beauties such as Catherine Deneuve, Lauren Bacall and Sophia Loren continued working into their forties and beyond. Hollywood is less forgiving of women's age than European and world cinema. Kidman's hard work during her thirties is partly driven by her acknowledgement it won't last.

'I understand there [are] other parts out there for me, other lives. I don't see myself doing this for the rest of my life, I don't feel like I have the strength. It requires an enormous amount of emotional strength, dedication, and I have children [Isabella and her son, Connor]. I have a huge desire to have another child ... I'd like to be able to gracefully slip away,' she adds. 'It would be wonderful to become a great charity worker, a philanthropist, and be able to take care of people. I'm always accused of being motherly so I suppose I would like to still maintain that but on a bigger level of social conscience and political conscience.'

'I know it doesn't last. This industry is very, very hard on women, particularly as they get older, but I would like to be able to leave some works of integrity.'

Just as Kidman's marriage to Tom Cruise appears to have ushered in her creative drought, her divorce at the end of 2000, a decade after her marriage, signalled her creative renaissance and unleashed a voracious appetite for work. The day after she won her Oscar in 2003, her mother, Janelle Kidman, had just one wish for her daughter – to slow down and take a break. But Kidman is unstoppable: she has *Birth*, *The Interpreter* and *The Stepford Wives* opening in 2004.

Personally, she's attempting to stay out of the spotlight, saying 'it's my quiet time in my life'. She's been burnt by the excessive scrutiny. 'I certainly won't be going into a marriage of [such] magnitude, I could never withstand that again,' she confesses. 'I don't want to. So it will never be discussed or dealt with in that way, put it that way. I'm not going to be standing there holding hands on red carpets smiling, taking photos with my partner.'

Sounding every inch the 20-year showbusiness veteran that she is, Kidman says, 'It's so strange the journey of life, the way things play out, because I would never have ventured out [had it not been for] my divorce – which at the time seemed the most devastating, horrible thing to occur.' In the year preceding it she delivered two fine performances, in *The Others* and *Moulin Rouge!* After her divorce, both films released to great acclaim. Soon after, her performances in *The Hours* garnered Kidman her first Academy Award. 'Out of [the divorce] strangely came my work and my passion for my work. I don't quite understand it because it wasn't a choice, it was almost a magic carpet that picked me up and flew me along,' she says.

One project sidelined by her divorce was the film version of Susanna Moore's novel *In the Cut*, a sexual thriller to be directed by Jane Campion. Kidman retained an executive producer's credit but backed away from starring in the project and Meg Ryan, looking a lot like Kidman, took the role opposite Mark Ruffalo. 'I wanted time off, I didn't want to work,' she says. She also explained that a serial-killer thriller just didn't appeal at that difficult time in her life.

'I would still choose a happy marriage, a happy relationship, a happy family life over a career of this magnitude. I don't mean to sound unappreciative but I come from a strong family where it's all about the connections between family, and that to me is more important than any of those other things. But that is life and I've have been given enormous blessing. To have the opportunity to express all these things – darkness, lightness, thoughts, ideas – through my work, that is a very rare thing and one that I appreciate enormously and, I suppose, cherish.'

In career terms she has climbed beyond the peak she had envisioned. 'Far beyond. I would never have thought I would be in a position to work with the greatest directors in the world, the greatest writers in the world, and [have] an abundance of choices,' she says. And those choices have made her perhaps Australia's most distinct cultural export since Paul Hogan.

'I do have a strong sense of being an Australian contributing to the world,' she says. 'I hope that when I'm older it will be seen as a good contribution and I would like for my country to be proud of me. I don't mean that to sound corny or superficial, but I do feel a huge part of my success comes from the uniqueness of the country that I come from, the way in which we view the world, the way in which we laugh, the way in which we cry, they way in which we Australians experience things.'

02

geoffrey rush

Pivotal Projects

The Life and Death of Peter Sellers (2004)

Pirates of the Caribbean: The Curse of the Black Pearl (2003)

Intolerable Cruelty (2003), Quills (2000)

Mystery Men (1999), Shakespeare in Love (1998)

Elizabeth (1998), Les Misérables (1998), Shine (1996)

geoffrey

In 1993 Geoffrey Rush was an acclaimed theatre actor at the top of his craft. He was in his mid-forties and his wife, actress Jane Menelaus, had recently given birth to their first child. Going to Hollywood wasn't a consideration.

With their baby daughter the focus of home life, Rush decided to take it easy. He performed in just two plays that year, David Mamet's *Oleanna* at the Sydney Theatre Company (STC) and John Marston's *The Dutch Courtesan* at the Melbourne Theatre Company (MTC). He persuaded the STC to pay him the princely sum of $1200 a week for the ten-week run of *Oleanna* (including rehearsals) opposite a recent drama school graduate named Cate Blanchett; his MTC fee was similar. Then, after 22 years in the theatre, roles in four ABC TV series and three movies, he was offered the lead role in an Australian movie. *Shine* was his tilt at the big time, if an Australian movie could be called 'big time'.

Adelaide-based director Scott Hicks wanted him to star in the biopic of a little-known, largely eccentric Jewish pianist from Perth called David Helfgott. Rush, who was to play Helfgott as an adult (Noah Taylor portrayed him as a teen, Alex Rafalowicz as a child), stood to earn $50 000 for ten weeks work. He considered it 'an extraordinary amount of money'. Jan Sardi's beautiful script, the chance to tackle a lead role in a relatively unfamiliar medium (film), the 'unusual' nature of the character and the lure of a large audience were all undeniable enticements. He wanted the role. 'A film playing a long run in an arthouse cinema is still seen by more people than saw, for example, the entire season of *Cats* in Melbourne,' Rush observes. But the shoot kept being postponed. 'I thought, I've got a daughter, I'm happy, [but I also] remember thinking, how am I going to pay for my child's education?'

The mid-90s were the twilight of the era of mammoth, long-running stage musicals by the likes of Andrew Lloyd Webber. Rush, who had hitherto avoided commercial musical theatre, decided to audition for the lead role of the Vietnamese engineer in Cameron Mackintosh's Sydney production of *Miss Saigon*. The job offered employment stability (a 12-month contract) and a weekly wage of $4000–5000. He took singing lessons and almost won the role. Then *Shine* was suddenly financed, he swapped singing for piano tuition and his life shot off in another direction. *Miss Saigon* was warmly received by critics and played for 17 months but *Shine* became a worldwide arthouse hit, earned $10 million in Australia and US$36 million at the US box office, garnered Rush an Academy Award for Best Actor and changed the course of his career, spectacularly.

The $6 million movie was shot in South Australia, Sydney and London during 1995. In January 1996 it received its world premiere at America's peak independent film festival, Sundance. Australian audiences finally saw it the following August before it released in the US in November, timed to be eligible for Oscar voting and at the forefront of voters' minds when making their selections in January 1997.

Reviews of Rush's performance in *Shine* varied from dazzling to disregarding. Hollywood trade newspaper *Variety* and the *New York Times* both dubbed Rush's performance 'remarkable' while others, such as influential Chicago reviewer Roger Ebert, completely ignored him. Ebert's review was preoccupied with Helfgott's story and made no mention of the actors portraying him, possibly because Rush and Taylor were unknown in the US. Or was it because the actors, under Hicks's direction, delivered such plausible performances? Rush, it must be said, benefited from playing the pianist when his nervous condition was at its most pronounced and, therefore, most expressive.

Shine's premiere at Sundance, in Park City, Utah, was orchestrated to attract a buyer who would release it in America. It was a risk because launching *Shine* there made it ineligible for competition at the Cannes Film Festival in France the following May. Cannes is the traditional platform for 'arty' Australian films (read: not broad comedies) seeking an international profile. Had the Americans hated *Shine* it would not get a second chance to wow European buyers in competition at Cannes.

America is the toughest market for any foreign movie to penetrate but if one breaks through and becomes popular, the size of the American population guarantees a multi-million dollar return. Distribution into Europe will usually follow, as European audiences have always had a bigger appetite for arthouse fare than an American population suckled on Hollywood movies from birth.

The Sundance strategy worked handsomely. The premiere audience gave Hicks a standing ovation. The screening generated such strong word of mouth – or 'buzz' – that the queue for tickets to the following day's screening became frenzied. Within hours of the lights coming up Steven Spielberg was on the phone requesting a copy of the film. Fine Line fought off overtures by the intimidating boss of Miramax, Harvey Weinstein, and bought the rights to distribute the film in America for US$2 million – almost half its $6 million budget. Another sale, of almost US$3.5 million to Disney subsidiary Buena Vista International, for a handful of other international territories, saw *Shine*'s full production budget recouped before a single (non-festival) ticket was sold. Hicks phoned Rush from the festival to tell him, 'Middle aged men are leaving the cinema weeping.' Momentarily confused, Rush asked, 'Why, what's the matter with them?'

Shine was the toast of Sundance. Subsequently, Hollywood was intrigued with Rush without him ever having set foot in the United States. His Australian agent, Ann Churchill-Brown, confirms, 'They were very excited but they do get very excited.' She fielded calls from several US agents interested in representing Rush, including CAA's Fred Specktor, who combined a trip to visit Glenn Close (his client) on the Port Douglas set of Bruce Beresford's *Paradise Road,* with meeting Rush. The pair forged an enduring relationship. Rush recalls, 'I had an amazing entree into America.'

His first trip there? 'While I was rehearsing a play at Belvoir [Street Theatre in Sydney]. I was flown first class and picked up by a limo,' he marvels. The star treatment was required so he could audition for the gay guy role in *As Good As It Gets* (ultimately played by Greg Kinnear). Rush flew out of Sydney on Friday and was 'back to my $500 a week Belvoir job on Monday morning'. While in LA, he performed six hours' improvisation; they wanted him to return the following weekend but he said, 'Guys, I'm in a play, I can't do this, it affects too many people's livelihoods.'

Shine's Australian premiere was in Adelaide on 15 August 1996. Then Rush travelled to the US for what turned out to be a six-month campaign – initially he promoted *Shine* but as the film's popularity solidified, Rush's star brightened. The quintessential actor's actor became a Tinseltown luminary. During that period he collected thirteen 'Best Actor' awards from voters in Australia, the UK and the US, from critics' organisations, industry peer groups and eventually the esteemed Academy of

Motion Picture Arts and Sciences. In March 1997, Geoffrey Rush became the first Australian to collect a Best Actor Oscar (with the exception of 1976 honoree and sometime Australian, Peter Finch, who was born in the UK).

'I must have flown to LA eight times in two months,' he recalls. 'The film would open in eight cinemas, then [another] 20 cinemas. At the airport [during one of these trips] some college-type guy said, "Excuse me, are you Geoffrey Rush? I've seen that film where you play the piano".' He was floored by the recognition. About three weeks later, a cleaner at a US airport called 'Hey, piano man!' as Rush walked by. On one of the very first tours, 'We went to a restaurant in downtown New York – in a limo. I went outside for a cigarette and this guy did a double-take and said, "Hey, I loved your movie". And I just went: "I'm a Sydney stage actor", because at that stage I was doing *The Alchemist* in Sydney. Wow, someone in New York went, "I loved your movie". At that time the film was on in maybe three cinemas in New York, four cinemas in LA.'

Back in Melbourne, after winning a Golden Globe Award but before the Oscars, Rush was walking along a median strip in Flemington Road after a horse-riding training session at the showgrounds for his upcoming role in *Les Misérables*. 'I saw this truck belting down the road and there was this look of recognition from the driver who yelled out, "Hey, Geoff, good luck with the Logies!" I treasure it as a divine moment,' he laughs.

Even Rush's parents found the attention a little absurd. His father, Roy, was at that time a retired accountant living in Caloundra. Roy had separated from Geoffrey's mother, Merle, when he was a child. 'When I phoned my mother and told her I'd won an Oscar I could hear her thinking, "People like Spencer Tracy win Oscars". To her it didn't seem to make sense.'

The Australian media devoted huge amounts of space to 'discovering' Rush, who became 'an overnight sensation'.

Much was made of the fact that he once shared a house with Mel Gibson in the Sydney suburb of Randwick. The pair appeared on stage together in what is retrospectively considered a seminal 1980 NIDA production of Samuel Beckett's comedy, *Waiting for Godot,* and in the original Dad 'n' Dave production, *On Our Selection*. Gibson famously pursued movies. The media's common inference in Geoffrey Rush's 'discovery' was that he had finally 'caught up' with the Hollywood icon's career. Rush is disheartened by the notion that his decision to pursue theatre was in any way inferior to Gibson's choice, particularly given the acclaim afforded his own theatre career.

'When I was nominated for an Oscar, *60 Minutes* did a profile on me and the only angle they could take was: "Obscure impoverished actor comes out of a rather ratty, indifferent theatrical background to overnight success". I thought, you jackasses. I have had the most fantastic artistic collaboration with Neil [Armfield] at [Company B] for over 15 years [and] the feeling from them was I'd now moved on from playing half-empty houses in the theatre.'

His theatrical achievements are impressive. *The Diary of a Madman,* starring Rush, who was on stage for two hours, was revived twice for international and national tours. In 1991 it even toured to the former Soviet Union, its country of origin. Rush was also a staple of the Melbourne Theatre Company's hit 1990 production, *The Importance of Being Earnest*, headlined by Ruth Cracknell. From his first job in 1971 with the Queensland Theatre Company ensemble until *Shine* was released in 1996, Rush worked consistently. His curriculum vitae dwarfs many of his contemporaries. Adding insult to injury, the *60 Minutes* crew filmed the interview with Rush at Company B's Belvoir Street Theatre.

'People used to sleep overnight to get tickets to *Hamlet*! I thought, in [*60 Minutes*'] paltry imagination, this must be some kind of inner city ghetto theatre where strange misfits gather in moth-eaten groups for some kind of rarefied fix. I really loathed that mainstream perception – they [couldn't] define what I did in conventional terms. If I was muscly, hunky and good looking you go, "That's an entree to conventional Hollywood".'

Rush vowed never to do another interview with the program and has rejected invitations to be profiled on Channel Nine stablemates *Burke's Backyard* and *This Is Your Life*. He also eschews 'lifestyle programs'. 'I got burnt [by] the *60 Minutes* thing. I can't enter into that notion of what is perceived to be a popular actor. I loathe the idea that because of my acquired level of recognition I then would have the pomposity to display my garden. To me it is a completely meaningless human experience. And when I see people do it, I go, "Is there something lacking in your life?" It gets to a point where you see people holding up undernourished African children and you go, "Someone really has to call a halt to this now".'

Once *Shine* was completed, Rush began receiving offers for Australian film roles. He chose two Peter Duncan movies, *Children of the Revolution* (opposite Judy Davis and Sam Neill) and *A Little Bit of Soul*, but neither set the box office alight. He narrated Gillian Armstrong's epic *Oscar and Lucinda*.

His first US role was as Inspector Javert in *Les Misérables* for director Bille August. The seventh film adaptation of Victor Hugo's classic also starred Liam Neeson and Uma Thurman. Excellent performances distinguished a film that didn't connect with the audience. Next Rush appeared opposite Cate Blanchett in Shekhar Kapur's production, *Elizabeth*. The biopic of England's virgin queen earned tremendous reviews, Academy Award nominations as Best Picture and Best Actress (for Blanchett) and a respectable, considering its US$24 million budget, box office take of US$30 million in America.

The following year he co-starred in *Shakespeare in Love* with Gwyneth Paltrow and Joseph Fiennes. The Miramax movie proved to be another darling during awards season with Rush receiving an Oscar nomination as Best Supporting Actor, cementing his place in the Hollywood establishment. Or did it? He swears that's not how it works.

'In the bigger, broader Hollywood machine you're perceived as an arthouse actor and I can totally understand that. That's what I like to do; I'm not a "weekend [box office] opener". They'll have to find something rather extraordinary for me to become that sort of performer. Like a *Silence of the Lambs* ... There aren't that many character actors who "open" movies, except for maybe Jim Carrey, but no-one thinks of him as a character actor. That said, good comedies are the exception that break rules,' Rush adds.

Like all actors Geoffrey Rush's journey has been, to some degree, dictated by his looks; he's not conventionally handsome, as defined by Hollywood's limited criteria. 'You're either a good looking guy or a crumple head,' he observes. Most of his films, including *Frida, Shakespeare in Love* and *Quills,* loom large on the awards circuit; few have been traditional blockbusters with sizable budgets and equivalent ambitions. Rush identifies three in this category – *Mystery Men, Finding Nemo* and *Pirates of the Caribbean: The Curse of the Black Pearl*. He says, essentially, 'I'm a platform release actor who sneaks up on you later on DVD.'

'I'm a platform release actor who sneaks up on you later on DVD'

'After *Elizabeth* and *Shakespeare in Love* I got a lot of scripts to play historical figures.' They were all artists: English novelist Charles Dickens; the nineteenth century photographer Eadweard Muybridge; Bohemian composer Gustav

Mahler; and theatre director Vsevolod Meyerhold in a film about Russian film director Sergei Eisenstein. Producers seek to minimise their risks by casting actors in familiar roles. 'It's a very narrow range of experience I get offered out of mainstream Hollywood. Sick fucks or historical figures. They want you to do what you've just done. They go, "He can handle language, he's the right age and he's classical", but I go, "I've done that so I want to do [something else]".'

The nadir of his 'classical' period was being offered a script about two Shakespearean actors in nineteenth century New York who levelled up against each other, not unlike a Shakespearean *League of Extraordinary Gentlemen*. Rush shakes his head, appalled by the idea. 'I come from a school [where] diversity is key. The people I admire are the Alec Guinnesses or the Daniel Day Lewises. They're peddling their imagination, not their personalities,' he observes. Rush describes his range as 'somewhere between misfit-loser-lost characters or nasty-snide-happy characters'. How does he feel about that? 'I don't know,' he responds. If he was peddling his personality he might care; because he's acting, he doesn't.

Rush adored playing the Marquis de Sade (one of the 'sick fucks') in Fox Searchlight's *Quills*, opposite Kate Winslet and alongside his wife, Jane Menelaus. He knew it didn't have huge commercial potential but he was nevertheless disappointed by its low box office yield. 'It made US$7 million in America. They blew it. That film should have gone to US$40 million at least. It was dubbed best film of 2000 by American film buffs at the National Board of Review.' That said, Rush freely concedes middle America was never likely to flock to see a film about sadism. He tasted the mainstream reaction during some promotional interviews. 'I'd be on morning chat shows where they'd go, "Wow, the Marquis de Sade. What a guy. Any overlap with your life?"' Demoralising stuff.

As Rush sees it, *Mystery Men* was his first genuine Hollywood movie. An overblown, misguided melange about a posse of specious superheroes, it was directed by Kinka Usher and co-starred William H. Macy, Janeane Garofalo and Ben Stiller. It cost US$68 million (estimated), collected tepid to horrible reviews – 'Moments of brilliance in a sea of dreck', wrote Roger Ebert – and returned US$30 million at the US box office. Luckily for the actors, they didn't carry the blame.

'Wow, the Marquis de Sade. What a guy. Any overlap with your life?'

'When I read *Mystery Men* I said, "This is just fantastic". [The producers] said, "We're doing this off-centre film with a US$80 million dollar budget". I was the first on board, they used me as a kind of casting leverage but they said, "We wanna get a real eclectic actors' group". The big summer films at that time were *Independence Day, Armageddon*, that's what people were going to see and I suddenly went, "Here's a really good subversive film about backyard klutzes who wanna be superheroes".' It went off the rails, the final cut filleting a three-hour film into two and cutting a romantic subplot for Rush's character, Casanova Frankenstein. Test audiences questioned why the villain had a girlfriend. 'Then in cinemas it lasted two weeks,' Rush adds.

With '*Mystery Men* and *Pirates of the Caribbean* I knew I was on high-powered, big money films; there's a different smell in the air, not less creative. [On *Pirates of the Caribbean* famed Hollywood producer] Jerry Bruckheimer was very hands-on. Bruckheimer is a CEO, maverick, dangerous. He coerced Johnny Depp into doing it. US$135 million was a lot to play with and possibly lose – it could close a studio.'

Bruckheimer famously negotiated lower cast wages in return for giving them a greater share of any profits. Everyone was happy when the movie rocketed on to become the second most popular movie of 2003. *Finding Nemo*, Rush's third truly 'Hollywood' movie, opened not long after. The animated comedy from the famed Pixar studio (creators of *Toy Story* and *Monsters Inc.*) about a Great Barrier Reef tropical fish's quest to find his son became 2003's highest grossing movie worldwide. The American production also starred Aussies Barry Humphries, Eric Bana, Bill Hunter and Bruce Spence.

Rush is ecstatic about the results. And in *Nemo* he plays an Australian, albeit a kindly pelican. In 2003 he also played an Australian in the well-received Coen Brothers' movie *Intolerable Cruelty*. That character was English as written, 'but I asked if he could be Australian, they said "Sure". That's a new thing, to be able to do an American film in my own dialect.' It signifies two things: Australians are now so prolific in Hollywood, nobody bats an eyelid when Rush's character, a slimy, award-winning daytime TV soap producer, hails from Down Under. Also Rush has a degree of clout, derived from making some tough calls.

Rush's decision to work on *Pirates of the Caribbean* during the 2002–03 Australian summer marked a significant and contentious turning point in his career. He had committed to star in *Waiting for Godot* for his old mate, director Neil Armfield, at Company B in January 2003. In what would have been a twenty-first anniversary celebration of their collaborative careers, this production also commemorated the fiftieth anniversary of *Godot*'s premiere, underpinned the subscription season at Company B, where Armfield was artistic director, and was to be a highlight of the 2002 Sydney Festival.

Five months before the premiere, Rush reneged. Company B staffers were crestfallen, especially when they learned why. A news story in the *Sydney Morning Herald* articulated the mood: 'Actor Geoffrey Rush has pulled out of one of the biggest theatrical collaborations at the Sydney Festival for a part in a Hollywood film based on a Disney theme-park ride.' The Disney studio has never been a favourite among actors. Nor does *Pirates'* producer Jerry Bruckheimer have a reputation for being an actor's producer. Bruckheimer, at his best, produced *Flashdance* and *Veronica Guerin* but at his worst rolled out *Kangaroo Jack, Gone in 60 Seconds* and *Dangerous Minds* – commercial successes (of varying degrees) but hardly artistic triumphs. In *Pirates*, Rush would play an evil pirate, Barbossa, alongside Depp and Orlando Bloom, one a heart-throb for older women, the other a heart-throb for little girls. Gore Verbinski, whose direction of thriller *The Ring* was undistinguished, would direct. Disney's motives appeared to be purely commercial. Arguably Rush's theatre fans had every reason to be dismayed.

The actor saw his options differently. 'At the time I was making the decision I went, "I've worked in theatre 31 years, I've worked in movies for six. I've achieved a hell of a lot of what I wanted to achieve in theatre. I want to invest in my film possibilities" and I knew somewhere in that game plan, *Pirates of the Caribbean*, for what it's worth, was going to be useful. I knew unashamedly it was commercial [but] it was also a great role,' he adds. He wanted to work with Depp, 'who's an actor's actor', and Bloom, who he'd recently enjoyed working with on *Ned Kelly*. Producer Laura Ziskin's involvement was another attraction: 'She made *Mouse Hunt* which happens to be one of my favourite films.' Plus *Pirates* was written by the scribes behind the animated hit *Shrek*. 'If I had been up against some big well-known action star, such as Steven Seagal and the current best rap artist, I would have said no,' Rush says.

With his LA agent urging him to take *Pirates,* if only to raise his profile, Rush carefully weighed his options. His choice was vindicated when *Pirates* surprised the critics and dominated the box office. 'That's the hunch you've got to take. If I'm going to sleep with the devil, it's going to be a quality devil. *Pirates* was a chance to buy some cred [and] to a degree it's worked.' On the strength of being in a film that made US$650 million worldwide, Rush says he's now being considered for more significant roles.

His opportunities have mushroomed compared with just a decade earlier. A recent title role in *The Life and Death of Peter Sellers* for reputable American cable channel HBO (*The Sopranos*) saw him *supported* by a stream of top grade acting talent – Emily Watson, Miriam Margolyes, Stephen Fry, John Lithgow, Stanley Tucci and Charlize Theron. It premiered at the Cannes Film Festival in its Official Selection in 2004. But for the tenacity of *Shine* director Scott Hicks, Rush may not have had the opportunity to strut his stuff before millions of people globally – which, despite his references to 'quality' projects, is exactly where he wants to be. Geoffrey Rush doesn't believe quality and commercialism are contradictory.

'If I'm going to sleep with the devil, it's going to be a quality devil'

'I don't see entertainment as a dirty word. It means being titillated, thrilled, excited, and that can be on an intelligent level or just on a stupid level,' he says. That's why Shakespeare is his guy. Shakespeare, like the writers of *Finding Nemo*, wrote for the rabble down on the theatre floor and the toffs in the balconies. He reached out to all of them. That's what Rush wants too. 'Totally,' he enthuses.

Rush has often doffed his hat to Hicks for casting him, most notoriously when he collected his Golden Globe trophy. 'I couldn't believe the laugh when I said, "For all those people who were happy to back this film so long as I wasn't in it". I was genuinely saying, "Back Toni Collette with *Muriel's*

Wedding, back Baz Luhrmann with *Strictly Ballroom*. Let them play out their vision because we will get new and interesting work".'

He knows how close he came to not playing David Helfgott. During the to-ing and fro-ing before *Shine* went into production, producer Jane Scott urged Hicks to consider other actors for the lead. Rush wasn't famous enough for financiers eager for certainty in their investment. Harvey Weinstein said Miramax would be involved only if David Thewlis played Helfgott; Thewlis broke through in Mike Leigh's *Naked* that year. Rush recalls Hicks telling Jane Scott, 'If I don't make this movie with me as director, you as producer, Geoffrey as star and Jan Sardi as writer, it will end up being about a blind, black jazz saxophonist in New York.'

With dozens of roles and two further Oscar nominations under his belt, Rush says, 'I'm very pleased and unashamedly proud that I won [the Oscar] in an Australian film. It has happened subsequently to Australian actors but in a generalised international scene [not in Australian films], people winning Oscars for acting. I quite like the fact that it was about a Jewish pianist from Perth. A specific story that actually defines something.'

03

paul
hogan

Pivotal Projects

Strange Bedfellows (2004), Crocodile Dundee in Los Angeles (2001)

Flipper (1996), Lightning Jack (1994)

Almost an Angel (1990), Crocodile Dundee II (1988)

Crocodile Dundee (1986), The Paul Hogan Show (TV) (from 1973)

paul

When *Crocodile Dundee* was being filmed on the streets of Manhattan in 1985, an executive from Paramount Pictures turned up at the set, uninvited, and, as Paul Hogan recalls, 'followed us around the streets'. The Hollywood studio had been tracking *Crocodile Dundee*'s progress through sources in Australia and was eager to snap up the rights to distribute it in North America. To say Hogan's debut movie, in which he co-starred with an unknown American actress called Linda Kozlowski, was generating excitement sight-unseen, a year out from release, is understatement.

The movie's star and co-creator shrugs that the early interest came about because of 'luck' and 'someone had seen the dailies'. But seasoned industry-ites warn it is impossible to tell how a movie will play by watching the footage at the end of each day. Comedies are even trickier: timing is everything and, until final cut, it could go any which way. The film's producer and co-writer, John Cornell, also Hogan's then manager and the guy Hogan freely credits as the 'brains of the operation', conceded in some press interviews at the time that the groundwork for *Croc*'s success had been carefully laid. Years after the event, *Crocodile Dundee*'s worldwide roll-out and the making of Paul Hogan, international star, looks like a genius campaign, blessed by good fortune and stoked by careful management over many years.

When the $8.8 million movie, backed by a $9 million print and advertising campaign, was finally released in the United States on 26 September 1986, it rocketed to number one and stayed there for five weeks before steaming to a US$175 million box office gross – the second biggest film of the year. In Australia it still holds the record for the highest grossing Australian film ever – $48 million – and that's not adjusted for inflation.

The movie catapulted the 47-year-old Aussie larrikin into worldwide superstardom. It's an experience he still likens to going to the Olympics, lining up for the 100 metre sprint in jeans and bare feet and taking home gold. During those heady days Hollywood's elite even bestowed their highest honour upon Hogan – an invitation to co-host the Academy Awards. His Hollywood journey, which started before he'd even made a movie, remains unique in so many ways. And the movie? The fish-out-of-water story wherein he stars as Mick Dundee, a Northern Territory crocodile poacher who becomes wide-eyed at big city life? Well, Hogan is keen to point out art imitated life.

The Paul Hogan Show, written and anchored by 'Hoges' with Delvene Delaney and 'Strop' (Cornell) as sidekicks, was just about the biggest thing on Australian television in the 1970s. And Hoges's own journey, from Sydney Harbour Bridge rigger to TV star, is television industry lore. The larrikin father of five was spotted by Cornell when he appeared on the Nine Network's talent quest show, *New Faces*, as a dare. Cornell, then producing Nine's Mike Willesee current affairs show, had suggested to Willesee that the program could bene-fit from a weekly comic segment. Then Cornell suggested Hoges was their man. Willesee agreed and the working class hero was elevated from amateur to professional comedian, though he refused to quit his job on the Bridge for some time yet. Next came his own skit show – produced by Cornell – also on Nine.

'I had a handshake contract with Kerry Packer', Hogan recalls, '[in which] I said, "I can't find writers and I can't churn these things out". He said: "Well, when you think of enough funny ideas we'll put a show together".' As Hogan tells it, 'We did seven one year, three the next, nine the next, four the next,' and when there were no new shows, the network merely programmed repeats. During these years Hogan also fronted advertising campaigns for Winfield cigarettes (he still smokes Winfield Blue), Foster's Lager and the Australian Tourism Commission.

Through producing *The Paul Hogan Show*, Hogan got to know his audience and learned how to make television. He became familiar with American and British audiences by fronting ads for Foster's there. The UK ads came first. He co-wrote and starred; 'I did a pile of them, they were very funny and they got huge exposure."

Fosters' sagely overhauled the British campaign for North America where, Hogan declares, 'there's a lot of taboos', especially when compared with Britain. 'The Canadian and American ads were never as funny as the English ads,' he says. 'The English ones were half sending me up but sending them up too, so they always had a question mark over them.' In the US, 'rather than taking the mickey out of their sacred institutions, it had to be more about this backwards sort of guy in contemporary society. It was more in that fish outta water vein. It wasn't quite what I wanted to do.' But Hogan correctly judged that it was right for the market (Foster's had made him the client and allowed him to fire two advertising agencies before he settled on one he liked). The experience grounded his understanding of American humour and seeded the beginning of *Crocodile Dundee*.

He agrees. 'I was in New York for a while and we went back to Australia and directed tourist ads in the Northern Territory, Ayers Rock. When I went back to America to launch them at the New York Yacht Club everyone treated me like I was a Martian. I thought, I've got to do this.'

At the time there were no high profile Australians in America. '[It's] not like there were some. There were none. Chips Rafferty got in a movie or two but people thought he was English and had a funny accent. Australians to them were tennis players, they knew John Newcombe ... ' The Bee Gees were British and Olivia Newton-John still famously travelled on a British passport. There was no Australian voice in America – 'I was an exotic novelty and I thought, that's an angle.'

In the ad campaign for the Australian Tourism Commission (ATC) Hoges assured potential American tourists he'd throw another shrimp on the barbie for them if they made the trek Down Under. The idea was seeded when Hogan was in the US making the ads for Foster's and saw a previous ATC campaign. 'In America, not only every country in the world but every state has a tourism campaign, it's fiercely competitive,' he says. 'We [Hoges and Cornell] were friends with Alan Morris and Allan Johnston (founders of ad agency MOJO Partners). One of them [knew] John Brown, the tourism minister. He set up a meeting [where Brown] said, "Can you guys fix it?" We said we'd love to have a go.' Hoges then made a demo tape with which Brown sold the idea to his colleagues.

Hogan recalls his pitch: 'People won't travel 13 000 miles in a plane flown by a koala bear to see kangaroos in the street. If I go to your home and I want to come back, it was because I enjoy the company, not the furniture. Yugoslavia's got nice waterfalls and the Black Sea's got nice beaches (we were showing some beaches and stuff). You've gotta invite them, say,

"Come out here, we'd like to see you". The shrimp on the barbie ad came out of that.' That landmark shrimp on the barbie ad, the first of a Hogan series, screened only in New York and Los Angeles. 'If they had the budget [to] show them throughout America, you couldn't have got [the tourists] on the planes anyway. They filled the hotels and planes just out of New York and LA,' he says.

So, tourism was booming, Australia's profile in the US mushroomed and Hogan developed a cult following in Los Angeles (the world's movie capital) and New York (America's influential cultural capital). In retrospect, it looks like Cornell devised the tourism campaign as a platform for Hoges's US assault. Hogan refutes that as a 'stupid plan'. 'I did the movie because I'd reached the stage with television [where] I'd done 600 sketches and sent up everything,' he says. 'I wanted to do a sketch that lasts more than four minutes so I did *Crocodile Dundee*.'

'I wanted to do a sketch that lasts more than four minutes so I did Crocodile Dundee'

The script was written by Hogan, Cornell and Ken Shadie. Peter Faiman, who directed Hogan's television series, was signed to direct. (According to news reports from the time Hoges clashed with him during the shoot. He didn't return for the sequel.) Meanwhile, Cornell, as producer, put together an investment package which saw 609 high tax payers invest between $5000 and $500 000 for a 133 per cent tax deduction and a tax exemption on the first 33 per cent of net earnings through clause 10BA of the tax act. The fund was oversubscribed: 'We sent back a couple of million,' Cornell told the *National Times* in 1986. Also, a cinema distribution deal with Hoyts for Australia was back-loaded – meaning Hoyts took minimum risk and the filmmakers and investors stood to make maximum returns if the film found an audience.

Cornell fought pressure from investors to commit to a pre-sale deal with a distributor in the US or any other foreign territory – it turned out to be his masterstroke. A deal might have guaranteed them a return on investment but not nearly as much as eventuated. Hogan says of Cornell, 'He's got foresight, he's an optimist and a gambler.' He also had enormous faith in the movie's ability to strike a chord with audiences.

With *Crocodile Dundee* being readied for its Australian release, Hogan was free to do some publicity. In late November, on the strength of his cult status in New York and Los Angeles, the shrimp on the barbie guy recorded an interview with Diane Sawyer from US *60 Minutes*. In it she sought a little publicity by accusing him of ridiculing religious minorities. She'd seen *The Paul Hogan Show*, which at that time was screening in America, according to Hogan, 'at about midnight, after *Benny Hill*, on syndicated television'. Hoges told Sawyer he picked on some religions because of the way they dressed. 'If the gear they are wearing is what God wants, don't tell me He hasn't got a sense of humour. He's already sent them up.' Sydney's *Daily Mirror* reported his protestation. He also told Sawyer Americans were too tightly wound up, efficient but too intense. Remarkably his style fed, rather than detracted from, his growing popularity.

Back home in January 1986, he was made Australian of the Year. Three months later *Crocodile Dundee* opened across the country on the 25 April Anzac Day weekend. Its cultural influence was so pervasive that the then Prime Minister, Bob Hawke, lied when asked if he'd seen it, Hogan laughs. The PM blandly told a television interviewer he 'loved the scenery'. 'He never saw it,' Hogan smiles. 'He just felt it was unpatriotic not to have seen it!'

Meanwhile in LA, 30 April had been declared Paul Hogan Day. The LA mayor welcomed Hogan amidst celebrations and the launch of a new Foster's advertising campaign.

And Cornell? He'd told the *National Times* in March: 'I want to be in America negotiating for *Crocodile Dundee* when the Australian figures are coming in. Those people are influenced by how much it's taking at the gate,' he said. And he was right there. With the box office back home multiplying each week, Cornell swung into action and arranged two test screenings of *Crocodile Dundee* in LA. The resultant surveys showed audiences loved the film but they *adored* Mick Dundee. Armed with these results, Cornell made representations to the top five studios, then settled into a deckchair at the plush Bel Air Hotel and waited ... for what must have seemed like only moments, before the phones started ringing.

Crocodile Dundee was sold to Twentieth Century Fox for distribution worldwide (that is, everywhere but the US and Australia). England, where Hoges had a huge following from the Foster's campaign, was the jewel in the crown. Paramount acquired the US rights, but negotiations dragged on for months, finally concluding in July. The Paramount deal included rights to a potential sequel, an idea that didn't interest Hoges at the time. He changed his mind later: 'I wanted to round the movie out. It started [in Australia] and went to New York, I wanted it to come back to [Australia].'

Cornell's international distribution deals mirrored the Australian one. Hogan says, 'We worked on the principle that if it works, it's gonna be ours.' They negotiated a small fee for a larger share of the profits. 'We had to take enough to keep investors happy, we couldn't make them punt with us [but] if we hadn't had investors at home we'd have taken nothing up front. We [thought if it does] US$50 million in the States we'll be laughing.'

Croc's box office success in Australia fuelled bravado in their US negotiations. Hogan recalls if a studio deal was con-

tingent on getting the movie dubbed into the American lexi-
con, they were in the position where they would respond
'Thank you very much' and leave. 'We went there with that
attitude, particularly John,' Hogan recalls. 'He went over there
like an arrogant farmer, sort of like, "I'll call you back", and
he didn't.'

In July, after just three months release in Australia,
investors received their first cheque and broke even. Then the
serious profits began rolling in.

In the US, Paramount committed to a promotional campaign that cost more than the original film. The studio projected the autumn release would generate about US$90 million at
the box office. It took US$175 million, another US$20 million
in the UK, and many more millions worldwide. Its investors,
which included Cornell, Hogan and 'half the Australian crick-
et team, who were our mates', banked personal profits in the
tens of millions, depending on the size of their investment.

With the Paramount deal done, the American publicity
campaign cranked into action ahead of its 26 September
release in 875 cinemas. The studio had two months to make
Paul Hogan a household name. An 18-city tour, in which
Hogan estimates he gave hundreds of television, press and
radio interviews, took three weeks. It was most likely during
this heady period Hogan turned down an invitation to go on
The Tonight Show with Johnny Carson because he refused to
work scripted or even give the producer an idea of what he
might talk about.

During the film's roll-out, Foster's maintained its campaign featuring Hogan on billboards and television commercials. The Queensland and Northern Territory tourism commissions, with Qantas, mounted a $1 million, 60-market cam-
paign in which they gave away 120 return airline tickets from
the US to Cairns in a promotion for Australia's Top End. And

when the film finally opened, 'It stayed number one [at the box office] for five weeks; in fact it did more in the fifth week than it did in the opening week,' Hogan says. A rare event.

So, how did the Americans treat him? 'Wonderfully,' Hogan smiles. 'Like I *was* Crocodile Dundee. Talk about type-casting, they'd call me "Mr Dundee" in hotels. Particularly New Yorkers treated me like I was their favourite outta town son,' he adds without a hint of having been bothered by it.

'I was forty-seven and I didn't care about becoming type-cast because I wasn't like Heath Ledger or some young actor' trying to build a career. This is the key to Hogan's story. His rise was fast and extraordinarily high but it was one-dimensional and he was reconciled to that fact. But then he created Mick Dundee and had a big enough share of the profits to never have to work again. Still, Hollywood began courting him for other movie roles.

'[Americans] would call me "Mr Dundee" in hotels'

'I was getting buckets of scripts sent to me for the kind of movies Van Damme, Steven Seagal and those kind of guys [would do]. I got sent every script, no matter how inappropriate, because at the moment you're "hot". I was the new adventurer in the town, the new Indiana Jones ... I was always stabbing people, that was the kind of stuff.' Well, he had stabbed a few crocodiles.

'You're real hot for about six months, then you're hot for another year [or so],' he muses. And during his 'six months' Hogan was invited to co-host the Oscars. 'That was fun, when I was the new freak in town.' Hogan remains the only non-American ever invited to host the movie industry's annual kudos-fest and he claims, 'I was also the only one [ever] allowed on without a script.' Legendary Hollywood producer Sam Goldwyn produced the telecast that year and he was a fan of old

Hogan shows, so he permitted Hoges to work unscripted.

'They thought I was a freak because I didn't use an autocue. Goldwyn asked: "How long do you want?" That's another great insight into the place,' he adds. 'The fact so many people can't open their mouth unless it's on autocue. [For example] "Sam has always been a great personal friend of mine ..." and they're reading it!...The Oscars was sacred, which I didn't find very sacred. I was never invited back.' What did he do? 'I just took the mickey out of them,' Hogan replies. He even ad-libbed from the stage to his fellow presenters: 'This program is live. There's about one thousand million people watching. So, one wrong word, one foolish gesture and your whole career could go down in flames. Hold that thought and have a nice night.' And, no doubt, his six months were up. 'I thought the awards were, and still are, just harmless fun. People start crying about them. They put your price up, maybe [but] they're not something to slobber about.'

Hindsight has a tendency to rewrite history but Hogan maintains he was confident *Crocodile Dundee* would at least work in Australia. *The Man from Snowy River* was the only Australian movie to break out of the arthouse market, earning $17 million in 1982. 'That wasn't a film, that was a movie,' Hogan says. The Australian box office, plus earnings of US$21 million in America, 'doesn't make it a blockbuster but certainly makes it a commercial hit as opposed to an art film', he says. Two other Australian films with notable box office in Australia during the first part of the 80s were *Gallipoli* and *Mad Max II*, which returned $12 and $11 million respectively. Hogan didn't want to make a 'film'. '*Crocodile Dundee* became the biggest not because it was brilliant but because it was a "movie",' he says. 'There was no reason it wouldn't work in Italy.'

Hogan was now more famous than the country he hailed from. Yet he decided to turn down all the 'stabbing' scripts and make the sequel, to take the story home. *Crocodile Dundee II*, released in 1988, was successful but not the goldmine of the first. It earned $24.9 million locally (the third highest grossing Australian film ever) and US$109 million there. And, of course, the critics didn't like it much. Hogan didn't care, he prefers to give Australian awards and critics a wide berth because he believes what he does is 'entertainment'. He wouldn't submit *Crocodile Dundee* for AFI Awards 'because I remembered how they'd pooh-poohed *Snowy River*, [saying] it was too commercial and too American.'

Crocodile Dundee II again starred Hogan and Kozlowski, who he eventually married. But before then, he divorced Noelene, the mother of his five children, and decamped to the US to escape the Australian press, which had a voracious appetite for the story.

Hoges says those early years in Los Angeles were 'interesting'. 'Being part of the business and seeing how it works, I met a lot [of] people. The first years it was all fun and then it got boring. I moved around a bit and still got bored.'

Hollywood didn't have much to offer. 'I'm a comedy writer and producer,' he says. 'John Cornell has always been the brains of the business; we'd been self-employed packages since 1972 for a channel or for anyone else.' Cornell stepped up to direct *Crocodile Dundee II*, and earned sound critiques. That same team, including Kozlowski and cinematographer Russell Boyd, reunited for *Almost An Angel* in 1990. But the almost unqualified turkey, wherein Hogan dusted off his innocent abroad schtick, again, spelt the end of their collaboration.

Around this time Cornell hung up his clapper board, while Hogan went on to make *Lightning Jack* – with funds raised from a public float on the stock exchange. Simon Wincer directed the western about a stupid white guy (Hogan) who thinks he's smart and his apprentice, a clever black guy (Cuba Gooding Jr) who can't speak. The critics again howled with derision but, as Hogan points out, *Lightning Jack*'s US$17 million US box office exceeds other Australian movies – including apparent 'hits' such as *Muriel's Wedding* (US$15 million), *Strictly Ballroom* (US$12 million) and *Young Einstein* (US$11.5 million).

And what of the investors? Hogan says the clever ones saw a profit from their investment. And those who might have been expecting *Crocodile Dundee*-like returns? Well, he 'was disappointed on their behalf too but I never, ever said this is going to be another *Crocodile Dundee*.' How could it?

By this time Hogan had developed a thick skin for criticism. He notes matter of factly, it's part of the Australian character. 'It's an English thing too. You just accept it.' So, aged fifty-three, with more money (from *Crocodile Dundee*) than he could ever spend, Hogan resolved to enjoy life.

'And I did *Flipper* because it was ten weeks in the Bahamas swimming with dolphins and they let me rewrite my part,' he says. 'The dolphin was the star and then Elijah Wood. I worked one day in three and I've got my wife and my dog in the Bahamas. It wasn't an artistic decision, to stretch the envelope or polish my craft. That was a holiday. I made some friends and actually wrote another movie [during] those hours [waiting] in the trailer until you come out all dressed up and go, "Don't do that, Flipper".'

During this period Los Angeles began to irritate Hogan, so the couple bought a home in Santa Barbara ('I'm a terrible mover,' Hoges volunteers, a comment that any psychiatrist would have a field day unpacking). In LA, 'You're living in a factory town and that's all anyone ever talked about: the work. And 85 per cent of the people are unemployed. It's weird and slightly depressing,' he says. 'It wouldn't happen in any other industry. If there was a mine in Broken Hill and half the mine shut down and only 15 per cent of the miners were working, the other 85 per cent wouldn't hang around on top of the hole all day [going] "What was it like down there today, mate? Maybe I'll get a go next week". But that's the way Hollywood is.'

Hogan was by now a long way from his creative roots and he always believed no future experience could surpass that of *Crocodile Dundee*. 'If you've got a comedy gut you don't get it out of movies. It comes right back

'I never wake up in the morning shattered because someone said on television or wrote in the paper that I sucked'

down to stand-up or television, in that order. Movies come after that because you're doing gags here and no-one's going to laugh at them until May next year. It's not funny when you're doing it eleven times and there's no audience.'

In 2003 and again living in Australia, Hoges took a co-starring role in *Strange Bedfellows*, a little Aussie comedy written by a 32-year-old Melbourne director. It's his first Australian film since *Crocodile Dundee in Los Angeles,* the third in the series, which he confesses was spawned from 'boredom and the thought it might be fun to do another one'. The movie performed adequately in 2001 but foreign pre-sales ensured it returned a profit. 'And it was fun to do.'

Hogan's enthusiasm was renewed by *Strange Bedfellows*, a rural comedy promising a 'movie' not 'film' experience. During the shoot he displayed his usual passion for input by rewriting his lines, watching the dailies and giving the director a few tips. He has a young son and life is sweet. Ask him what it's been about since *Crocodile Dundee* and he replies: 'Life, it's more about life than art. It did occur to me if I don't do anything else it doesn't matter,' he adds. 'I can go and do the clubs if I've really got the urge to entertain people.'

He's tasted outrageous success and lived it without any qualms. When he was in his thirties, married with a family and labouring, that was his world. 'Your lifestyle changes completely, unless you're stupid,' he contends. 'The great part is you get to travel round the world and see other countries, I'm eternally grateful for that.' Subsequently, the slings and arrows don't hurt. 'I never wake up in the morning shattered because someone said on television or wrote in the paper that I sucked.'

Back in LA, in the streets just below the famous 'Hollywood' sign, near the Kodak Theatre (home of the Oscars), a guy dressed like Crocodile Dundee poses for photos with tourists every day. 'There's a Marilyn Monroe, an Elvis impersonator and Crocodile Dundee,' Hoges nods. 'He came out 18 years ago.'

Has he ever said g'day?

'No, I've never felt the urge.'

04

eric bana

Pivotal Projects

Troy (2004), The Hulk (2003)

The Nugget (2002), Black Hawk Down (2001)

Chopper (2000), The Castle (1997), Full Frontal (TV) (1993)

eric

It's 1991 in Richmond, the inner city Melbourne suburb once known colloquially as Struggle Town, and 22-year-old Eric Bana is midway through his own struggle – to forge a career in stand-up comedy. In those early days, he showed scant promise. The son of a Croatian logistics engineer and a German hairdresser had neither the ego nor the tortured upbringing that fires the best comedians. His early comic routines consisted of amiable observations about girlfriends and the 'footy'. That was his world.

Nobody at the Church Street pub that night would have wagered that Bana would forge a spectacular path through his chosen field – the talent that propelled him to become a Hollywood star was then well hidden. But it took just a few years for Bana to emerge on Australian television as a mimic of rare skill. 'I've never seen a quicker ascent to Hollywood lead roles than his,' says Bill Bennett, Bana's director in the warm 2002 Australian comedy, *The Nugget*. Bana laughs. 'I don't have a problem with it. It's always the final jump in the J curve that gets noticed. I guess what he's saying is, I didn't have to do 15 films as a co-star before I got a lead and that's right.' But that night, and a few others in 1991, he was introduced merely as the comedian who worked behind the bar.

The young Eric Banadinovich was a child mimic, emboldened by his first impression of his grandfather, but that's as far as it went. After school, Banadinovich got a job as a clerk with a sea freight company, which meant 'just hooning around the docks and [Melbourne's] World Trade Centre in the company car. Fun, but by no means my end goal.'

Some time later, when he was working in a pub and the manager suggested he get up on stage to do some jokes, the new Eric 'Bana' thought, why not? Deep down, he harboured a secret desire to be an actor; more importantly, he believed he could do it – he just had no clue how. Standing up on stage in front of a group of strangers seemed a surer means of realising his goal than doing paperwork, washing cars, selling clothes or stacking supermarket shelves, as he had done up to this point.

'Comedy provided the initial taste that [acting] was a possibility,' he readily admits. 'I really wanted to do this but didn't have much of an idea about how one goes about it other than through NIDA [the National Institute of Dramatic Arts, Australia's premier acting college] and I did know NIDA wasn't going to be for me.'

Bana shunned teaching institutions because 'I've always been one to come to his own conclusions through experience. I felt I could act; there was a reason why I was able to do impersonations, characters, voices and accents, and for me there had to be a parallel between that and acting,' he says. When the pub manager suggested he try stand-up comedy, he quickly saw its potential for helping him realise his acting ambition. Even better, he enjoyed it. So in 1991 he decided to have a serious tilt at a career in comedy. After two years of honing his act on the live circuit, fellow comedian Glenn Robbins told Bana of a new sketch comedy TV show, *Full Frontal*, requiring a cast. Bana sent a tape and was accepted.

While some of his cast mates, such as Irish comedian Jimeoin, were more polished performers, Bana had great appeal with suburban audiences. He even sacrificed some of the spotlight to write sketches for his co-stars, a magnanimous act which paved the way for him to take the straight role. That way he could 'act'. 'And from there it all seemed relatively obvious,' he says. 'I figured, if I got enough experience on camera and paid attention, *Full Frontal* was going to be my NIDA [and] somewhere down the track I was going to be able to make the jump to drama.' He admits it was more a hope than a 'solid plan'.

With his deft skewering of Australian personalities and the creativity to manufacture his own characters, Bana became one of the few enduring cast members of *Full Frontal*, which ran for three years. After a while Bana considered leaving to pursue straight acting but when he confided this plan to co-star Kym Gyngell, Gyngell advised him to stay: 'Just as you think everyone's sick of you, they're just starting to get to know you.'

'It was really good advice,' Bana concedes. 'I did see people come and go with a level of paranoia. They'd come in and do a year and then think they're a bit of a household name. You think just because your face has been in the paper twice everyone knows who you are when in fact no-one knows who you are. It was really worth hanging around.' It proved prescient on a number of levels. Channel Seven soon gambled on Bana's own specials, which led to his own variety show. It was dumped after its first season. But also at Seven, Bana met his future wife, Rebecca, a network publicist.

In 1996 Bana scored his first film role, in the amiable comedy *The Castle*, after its creators wrote the small role of Con Petropoulous, the kung-fu loving son-in-law of the embattled Kerrigan family, with Bana in mind. Despite its low budget and rough technique, *The Castle* became a smash hit in Australia, thanks in part to the pedigree of its creators, a close-knit troupe of four comedians led by director Rob Sitch. Bana was merely one of several comedians in the film and as such didn't see it as a big break. Nevertheless, he was 'extremely excited': 'I thought, hey, one film credit was going to be better than nothing.'

Despite it being shot quickly and 'extremely cheaply', like television, Bana sensed a subtle difference in friends' and fans' perceptions of him. 'It's like when you're a kid and you find out someone in your street's a footballer, that kind of celebrity,' he says. 'It had that difference. Even though I'd done lots of television, I'd now done a film and in some small way that counted for something.' He still doesn't know if that change was merely 'psychological' but he sensed one film might lead to another.

So it was. Producer Michele Bennett and director Andrew Dominik were adapting for cinema the life story of Mark 'Chopper' Read, a criminal who'd become a dubious cult hero through his series of best-selling crime diaries. A year's search for the lead actor proved fruitless until Read suggested Bana.

The comedian was on the second day of his four-day Hawaiian honeymoon when his agent, Lauren Bergman, rang to tell him about the film and Dominik's interest due to Chopper's recommendation. 'Straight away I kind of pictured myself as Chopper Read,' Bana confesses. 'I'd seen enough of him to [know] whether or not I could become that character and I immediately felt I could.' But not during his honeymoon. On returning to Melbourne, Bana sent a test tape and within a week Dominik flew down from Sydney. At this stage, Bana was filming the *Eric* series of six one-hour television comedy specials. Hence the four-day honeymoon.

The following Saturday, Bana, Dominik and a casting agent assembled at a Melbourne casting agency and spent 'eight or ten hours' workshopping scenes. After a gruelling day Bana held little hope of nabbing the part but he believed Dominik appreciated his abilities. A month later, he had the role.

Bana admits he was 'extremely obsessed' with it. 'As cool as it sounds initially – that I wasn't going to audition during my honeymoon – I was very keen on the idea.' And this time it *felt* like a film shoot. 'No matter how much you're told film is slower, it really takes some getting used to, particularly the rehearsal process,' Bana says. He contends some scenes 'Andrew was obsessed with' were rehearsed 100 times. In fact, the entire *Chopper* shoot 'called into question a lot of things that I rely on,' Bana confesses. 'Up to that point I'd relied totally on instinct and gut feeling and suddenly, you're dissecting a scene, talking about it for hours and doing it 100 times; it almost gets to the point where you don't understand why it needs to be delved into to such a degree.'

'I'd relied totally on instinct and gut feeling'

This was Bana's, admittedly confusing, first taste of 'the luxury of filmmaking' and his instinct for speed and intuition clashed with cinema's painstaking tedium. 'I've since learned a combination of the two is probably the ideal,' he notes.

This wouldn't be the first time Bana realised he was different from the 'actors'. He recalls the director and actors confusing him while discussing 'beats' within the script, the points when one thought finishes and another one starts. 'I didn't know there was a name for it,' he admits. 'And why does everyone have so many notes on their script, what's that about? So I very much felt like an outsider, although I felt they had a lot of faith in me and made me feel confident I was doing the right thing.'

It wouldn't be the last time he felt like a film set outsider. 'I don't know whether it's through my own paranoia but you do feel some level of there's something going on in the room that you're not a part of. I never let it bother me because I figure once the cameras start rolling everything will be sorted out and it usually is.'

Chopper was released in Australia in August 2000 to critical and audience acclaim. While it earned $5.7 million at the Australian box office in 2000, its cultural and media impact was arguably greater than for the other successful, and non R-rated, local films of the year, *The Dish*, *The Wog Boy* and *Looking For Alibrandi*.

Despite Dominik's acuity, *Chopper* is Bana's film. His performance is wondrous; the role of a lifetime in his first lead. Spanning 13 years of Read's life, the characterisation showed Read at his charismatic best and his punishing worst. Bana even gained ten kilos in four weeks for the role.

In November, Bana won the 2000 Australian Film Institute best actor award. It would only be a matter of time before Hollywood discovered *Chopper*. But just to make sure, two months earlier, Dominik and Bana took the film to the Telluride and Toronto film festivals in North America. While Bana describes the boutique

'I figure once the cameras start rolling everything will be sorted out and it usually is'

Telluride Film Festival as 'one of the best three or four days of my life', he laughs, he 'nearly died' in Toronto. 'It was like a slug-fest.'

Hollywood's voracious talent agencies had heard about Bana before he'd even left Australia and he agreed to meet them while at the festivals with his manager, Bergman, to 'kill two birds with one stone'. It was more a fact-finding than job-hunting mission. Bana wanted to learn as much as possible about the still mysterious American film industry. He'd heard of other Aussies who'd cracked Hollywood with their required entourages of agent, manager, business manager, publicist, lawyer and so on. Bana believed he had no choice but to hire them all. 'But then I was like, hang on, who actually gets you the work?' he notes. 'And once I identified who it is, as far as I was concerned that was all I needed.'

The quest for representation in America was predicated on the chance that *Chopper* would do well there, as Bana tells it. It wasn't a box office hit but he need not have worried. 'He came to America with a very small film that nobody in the country saw but everybody in the industry saw,' says US resident Anthony LaPaglia. 'Every important person in the Hollywood industry saw *Chopper* and just loved him.'

Bana met with talent agencies while in Toronto and set aside a week and a half for interviews in Los Angeles. By then, he was under siege: 'Actually they get quite rabid about it; they see you as potentially the next big thing that's coming out of Australia,' he says. 'I think some of them realistically have the skill to fully realise your potential and some of them are just shit-scared that if they don't sign you up they're going to get fired.'

Within that 'frenzy', as Bana calls it, he had to determine who appreciated his potential and, more importantly, who was capable of capitalising on it. 'I found about a third of them were fully on the same page as me in terms of what I wanted to achieve but there was only maybe two or three that could have possibly been able to do what my agent has done,' Bana contends. And only one could have delivered so spectacularly, he adds: the William Morris Agency's John Fogelman.

As with other Australians who have 'succeeded' in Hollywood, Bana refused to be seduced. He was pragmatic. 'I had all the heads of the agencies calling me up at my hotel saying fantastic things, making me feel amazing, but as an Australian who's got 37 bucks in the bank, all you really want to know is "How? How are you going to fucking make this happen as opposed to telling me that this could happen?'" Bana concedes 'to a certain degree' he thought 'it' might happen as well, but he wasn't there to hear that. He wanted facilitation. Bana and Dominik compared notes on their courtships, 'pissing ourselves laughing' about how many people attended their meetings. 'Why are there ten people in this room?' Bana asks. 'I don't need ten people in the room with me because I'm thinking, shit, is this what you guys do every day?'

Fogelman didn't attempt the hard sell – WMA is big enough to make that unnecessary – so he was calmer than others. 'They tell you "you're AWESOME!"' Bana exclaims. 'Right, but my mum thinks I'm awesome too and she's not about to become my agent.' Instead, Fogelman behaved as Bana's agent by setting up meetings with directors and studios. 'It was almost like taking the car for a test drive as opposed to telling you how powerful it is,' Bana says. 'And that really was a point of difference.'

Despite Hollywood's bizarre seduction techniques, Bana felt this was the first 'concrete evidence' something would result from *Chopper*. While waiting for that result, he moved to television drama, with a regular role on ABC's rural soap, *Something in the Air*. It wasn't quite the place for 'the next big thing'. But a batch of US jobs was on the table, including a support role in Ridley Scott's contemporary military drama, *Black Hawk Down*. Fogelman advised Bana to return immediately to LA 'to do this properly'.

Bana was paranoid that that was code for 'move to the US', a notion he made 'really clear right up front to all of them' wasn't going to occur. Ultimately, his agent 'absolutely loves the fact' Bana remains in Australia because it becomes a powerful bargaining tool. Studios can't take his presence for granted. Still, Bana flew to LA at his own expense to meet with

Scott: 'Rebecca, myself and the little fella sat in row 115 and flew to LA for a fortnight.' He describes the trip with his 13-month-old son as 'the flight from hell'.

Upon arrival Bana went straight into a series of meetings and read a 'shitload' of scripts. Now, six roles were on offer, a few with meaty parts. Both Bana and Fogelman considered *Black Hawk Down* the quality project due to its book, script and director, whose movie *Gladiator* had just won the Best Picture Academy Award. A week later, Scott called Bana in Australia but with no firm promise of a major part, let alone a speaking role.

Bana doesn't regret ignoring the other films. 'It was a good decision because they weren't that flash. They only sounded good because of who you were going to be in the movie with,' he says. 'You want to tread carefully and choose the best possible project but you can get seduced by a big co-star. There's no guarantee; who's to say they've got good taste?'

When Scott finally gave him the green light, Australia celebrated another actor cracking Hollywood but Bana knew he still had the job ahead of him. 'I could feel the vibes of "He's got to prove himself [in America] yet; can he do an American accent? Can he fit into our system? Can he work on a big film without cracking under the pressure?"'

Scott didn't submit Bana to an audition: 'No-one ever has [since *Chopper*]. I'm dying for the day I get to audition again.' Strangely, having earned the right not to audition, Bana wants to so he can counter his paranoia that he's not right for the role. 'The only way of really knowing if you're the right person is if they're able to test you with other people,' Bana concedes. 'As much as I hate auditioning, at least through the process you do feel as though you're there for all the right reasons as opposed to [being] a name that's going to make the financiers a little more comfortable ... There were times in pre-production on *The Hulk* I wanted to grab Ang Lee and say, "Why the hell have you cast me in this? There seems to be so much wrong, I don't know why I'm here",' Bana confesses. 'Whereas if I had auditioned, I perhaps wouldn't have felt that.'

Bana negotiated his way out of *Something in the Air*, much to the ABC's chagrin, and moved to Morocco with his family to film *Black Hawk Down* in 2001. By all accounts, including Bana's, there was a terrific camaraderie among the male cast, particularly between Bana, William Fichtner and Nikolaj Coster-Waldau, who'd bonded during a boot camp in North Carolina. 'It really felt like a big footy team,' Bana admits. 'We treated each other well. I guess you feel like an outsider initially but everyone made each other feel comfortable pretty quickly.' Bana's role as Hoot expanded as the script developed. While filming in Rabat, Scott used the Delta Force commando more and more as an action figure. Bana's Hoot eventually became one of the most resonant figures in the visceral war drama.

While in Morocco, Bana heard of the upcoming *The Hulk* project. 'My agent said, "I want to tell you about a project but before you say anything let me get out all the facts" ... Initially I wasn't crazy about it and then he told me Ang Lee was going to be directing it and I got extremely interested,' Bana admits.

While it was a long shot, particularly as *Black Hawk Down* was still months away from release, his agent asked if it was worth campaigning for the role. Of course. How could one shun the opportunity to play an iconic Marvel Comics character? But time went by and Bana was told Lee knew who he wanted already. Nevertheless, Lee wanted to meet Bana if he ever came to New York. 'That doesn't sound overly positive but it's another opportunity to meet a great director and I shouldn't pass it up,' Bana thought.

In June 2001, Bana returned home from Morocco with his family and took a couple of weeks off before flying to New York for lunch with Ang Lee and his writing-producing partner James Schamus. It was 'a very loose discussion' in which Bana expressed his interest in *The Hulk* before they told him there was no script available. It didn't seem like a business lunch and Bana left thinking he'd had fun but nothing was said that made him think he might get the part. In fact, he thought it was already cast.

Lee laughs. 'It wasn't a set deal, I was still casting,' he says. Lee was given a copy of *Chopper* by his casting director and immediately put Bana on his short list. 'He's the Hulk right there,' the director says. 'You can tell a good performance in that film. The look on his face told me.' Then, at the lunch, Lee says he saw a man who 'looked handsome, looked vulnerable. I got good vibes about his look, his aura.' Suddenly he had an actor who could play the meek Bruce Banner role while suggesting the 'rage, rage, rage' within. 'That's my job,' Lee chuckles. 'I have to pay very close attention to the hidden things despite appearances.'

Bana returned home to prepare for Bill Bennett's comedy, *The Nugget*, the film he chose, parochially, instead of taking the lead role in the big-budget action thriller, *XXX*. Bana played a council worker who lucks upon Australia's largest gold nugget. The shoot in Mudgee, a small town three hours west of Sydney, was uneventful enough until Bana's popular co-star, Belinda Emmett, was re-diagnosed with cancer. It cast a pall over the set.

Then Bana's US agent phoned to say he was still in with a chance. 'And I said "With what?" There were a couple of other things floating around. He said *"The Hulk"*.' Bana was shocked; he'd consigned *The Hulk* to the not-a-chance file. A week later, four days after terrorists struck America on

September 11, 2001, Bana was half a world away in Mudgee when he received another call from the US. 'It was a beautiful spring day, the birds were chirping, kangaroos were jumping in the back paddock, quite literally, and I was by myself – my wife had gone out with my son to the shops – and I just remember being stunned and frozen stiff, I just couldn't believe it.' He'd been offered the part of Bruce Banner in *The Hulk*. Yet nobody knew if any films would even be made after September 11. 'It all seemed so surreal and part of you thinks, should I even be excited about this because who knows what's going to happen?'

And Emmett's diagnosis weighed heavily: 'It was just a really bizarre moment because you didn't feel like you could celebrate, it wasn't appropriate to, whilst at the same time you're excited. It felt highly inappropriate to be happy about something. It was a very humbling time.'

Then came apprehension. Bana barely knew Lee, let alone what working with him would be like. Nor did he know how serious the film would be, only how he hoped it might be, given Lee's pedigree. 'It was probably the first and only time in my career I'd say yes to a project without having read a script simply because of who it was,' Bana concedes. He was whirling in a tumult of 'fear, excitement and trepidation. It's like, shit, what did I do to deserve this?' he admits. 'Guilt was a big part of it.'

Given the litany of comic book film adaptations that stall in a creative and financial bog, *The Hulk* progressed with little trouble. Bana counts his blessings. He says, 'I base my whole life around the film I'm doing that year, so if one of them does fall over it is a big deal because I have to spend months trying to find something else.'

Being cast as the lead in Lee's *The Hulk* was a huge leap from *Black Hawk Down* and Bana noticed changes in Hollywood's perception of him before, during and after production. Initially, it was doubts about whether he would hold up. Then came the mystery during production, when outsiders didn't know how it was progressing. Finally, when the film wrapped, Bana noticed 'a big change in the environment in terms of your status within the system because suddenly you've finished the film, didn't get hit by a car, you've gotten through the shoot and you are going to be *The Hulk* now.'

The Hulk had not only the power of Universal Studios behind it but the now influential Marvel Comics. Yet Bana didn't feel burdened by expectations: 'I felt between the Hulk itself, the CGI [computer-generated imagery] Hulk, Ang Lee, Jennifer Connelly and Nick Nolte, there were so many other tent poles to hold up the canvas I never felt they were pinning everything on me,' Bana contends. Lee agrees, noting his freshness was a plus for him and the studio. 'It's a franchise project. The Hulk would be the centre of attention, we gave the most budget to the green guy. We didn't need a big movie star to carry it; a fresh face is better than a known actor.'

As it was with Bana's next film, the Greek epic *Troy*, directed by *The Perfect Storm*'s Wolfgang Petersen. 'The story and the script [are] so bloody enormous and next in line come Brad Pitt and Wolfgang Petersen ... So even though I get the benefit of this amazing part and this amazing film, I'm still yet to be in that place where I'm sticking my neck that far out.' Besides, *Troy* was a perfect fit for someone sifting through leading male or second lead male roles which he says tend to be 'heroic or semi-heroic or violent or semi-violent'. No romantic comedies just yet.

Lee still enthuses about working with Bana on *The Hulk*. He met all expectations despite his relative inexperience. 'He needed to be taken care of on set, he didn't know much about photography,' Lee says, despite noting Bana's face is 'very camera friendly'. 'That freshness can take you more time [helping him] but you don't have all the movie star schtick or need to redo the audience's perception of the actor.'

The Hulk opened in the United States in July 2003. The critics questioned Lee's ponderous style and overbearing themes but Bana and co-star Jennifer Connelly earned encouraging comments. The *Bangkok Post* even went so far as to comment 'Bana is so good you forget he's Australian.'

The US$137 million-budgeted *The Hulk* earned more than US$240 million globally. Somehow, that is considered a disappointment. There is little chance of the franchise spawning a sequel, although Bana had to commit to at least another film if required. Lee has not.

Bana has the great Australian back-up plan ready. People ask what he'll do in two years' time when both his children are in school; there'll be no opportunity for more six-month long blockbuster shoots: 'I'll either find movies that don't take six months or I just won't do them at all,' Bana says. 'That's kind of like a totally believable option in my head; it's not like I'm obsessed with the idea of keeping my place in the tree – wherever it is – and not letting anyone get above me.' And Bana is keen to avoid some of the extraneous pressures of the business, living in Melbourne being an obvious solution. 'It's very easy to not be overawed when you kind of live like everybody else,' he argues. 'If I was twenty-one and single and living in LA it'd be completely different.'

His agent tells Bana his voice isn't the same when he's home in Australia. And Bana likes that. The world is where he works, Australia is where he lives. 'I know what that energy feels like over there and to an extent, it's fantastic and fun. I love it when I'm caught up in it but I really enjoy the position of the two,' he says. '[Americans] don't get that. Unless they live in Montana or somewhere they don't ever get to feel that richness of life we all feel by coming home.'

Also, home allows perspective on an intense three-year
progression in Hollywood, which continued with his well-
received turn in 2004's historical blockbuster *Troy*, and his
being cast in Steven Spielberg's next film.

*'I would have
thought you'd be on
some sort of wonder
drug that would
make you feel better
if you've achieved
what I achieved but
you feel the same'*

Looking back, Bana recalls 'four or five
beats, as you call it', events that fell in a
particular way ensuring his career progressed. First, realising he could do stand-
up comedy 'suddenly gave me some sort of
self-worth and feeling there was some cur-
rency in that talent'. The second was scoring a role on *Full Frontal*, which Bana contends was 'probably as major as anything
that's happened since because that was the point where the
outside world realises you have something to offer'.

Then came *Chopper* and appreciating he could win an
audition – and subsequently, choosing his American agent.
Those four moments are enough, as Bana concedes: 'What I've
got to fall back on is just absolutely fucking brilliant.' The
upside of international failure would be returning home to his
family and 'leading a kind of – I'm sure there would be a major
adjustment period – normal, healthy, fulfilled life ... If that's
the worst it gets, why shouldn't I feel as though I can jump off
a building career-wise? The mat at the bottom is so thick and
spongy that I can't get hurt. I might get bruised and like anyone who has an ego, I'd take a few hits along the way, but
essentially, that mat is just so inviting, failure doesn't play on
my mind.'

Unbelievably, at least to anyone looking at a financially
secure cover-boy, Bana adds he's just as happy today as he was
eight years ago doing stand-up. 'I have moments of elation and
can't believe my luck that I can afford to go out for dinner or
drive a nice car or whatever but essentially how you feel in a

day-to-day sense is pretty much the same,' he says. 'I would have thought you'd be on some sort of wonder drug that would make you feel better if you've achieved what I achieved but you feel the same.'

There's no regrets. In fact, Bana concedes he's felt lucky his film career has happened so young. 'What's weird is I always thought it was more likely for someone else to get to this level than myself, so while I thought it was doable and believable I was also quite pessimistic and didn't want to get too excited ahead of time.'

Bana didn't want to believe the hype and warnings, if only to protect himself. 'Did I think it was remotely possible? Yes. Did I really, really think it was actually going to happen? In the back of my mind, probably no.'

05

gillian armstrong

Pivotal Projects

Charlotte Gray (2001), Oscar and Lucinda (1997)

Little Women (1994), The Last Days of Chez Nous (1992)

Hightide (1987), Mrs. Soffel (1984), Starstruck (1982)

My Brilliant Career (1979)

armstrong

Gillian Armstrong's entree to Hollywood was very gradual and, initially, blessed. In 1979 her seventh film and debut feature, *My Brilliant Career*, starring an ebullient Judy Davis as a determined budding novelist, was a hit with audiences at home and abroad. Its world premiere was at the Cannes Film Festival, then in the United States it opened America's eyes to Australia, the climate, the characters and landscape.

At the end of the 70s, the Cannes Festival du Film, a film market and festival held each May in the south of France, was a gateway for Australian films to international markets. The only gateway. *My Brilliant Career* was just the second film of the Australian New Wave afforded the privilege of screening there in competition. The first was Fred Schepisi's *The Chant of Jimmie Blacksmith* the year before. In 1975 Ken Hannam's *Sunday Too Far Away* screened in Cannes's Directors' Fortnight sidebar and in 1976 Peter Weir's *Picnic at Hanging Rock* generated fevered responses at its marketplace screenings.

Armstrong recalls her entree to Cannes with ingenuousness, saying she didn't realise the event was a big deal and before arriving in the French resort town, she'd not even watched her film with an audience. It hadn't yet opened in Australia. 'It was very scary,' she recalls. 'They went bananas about it and loved Judy as well.'

She was invited to screen the film at the New York Film Festival the following October. 'If you're a success at Cannes you get invited to those major festivals,' she explains. The screening in New York marked the start of Armstrong's American Odyssey – a five-year journey leading to the release of her first Hollywood movie, *Mrs. Soffel*.

After the screening of *My Brilliant Career* she was pounced upon, literally. 'I remember a fantastic reaction, huge applause, then these people started coming at me,' Armstrong recalls. Boaty Boatwright, an agent with the William Morris Agency (WMA), clambered onto the stage where Armstrong was standing after being introduced to the audience. Boatwright gushed about the film before asking Armstrong how her previous meeting went with representatives from the WMA in London, soon after Cannes.

Armstrong recalled the agency had tracked her down while she was staying with friends in London. Initially she thought WMA was an advertising agency but once she understood they represented filmmakers worldwide, her next question had been: 'Why would I need someone to represent me around the world?' 'I had no expectation I would work anywhere but Australia,' she remembers.

'I had no expectation I would work anywhere but Australia'

Boatwright nevertheless urged Armstrong to meet with her Los Angeles-based colleague, Judy Scott-Fox.

The agency thought filmmakers' interests were best served by having representatives based where the decisions were made and in those days the film industry was particularly LA-centric. Armstrong visited LA on her way home and met Scott-Fox. 'She was careful,' Armstrong says. 'Didn't want to freak me out and said, "Oh there could be opportunities where you could work outside the country".' At first the young Australian wasn't convinced but her ears pricked up when Scott-Fox informed her the agency represented many writers whose scripts they would happily push her way. That was the clincher. Armstrong agreed to let Scott-Fox represent her in what marked the start of a relationship that spanned 15 years and only ended with Scott-Fox's premature death, aged fifty-four, in 1994.

Within weeks of Armstrong's return to Sydney, 'American scripts began to arrive and then [came] the phone calls,' she says. Dustin Hoffman and Jane Fonda, two actors at the peak of their power, were on the line at different times saying they loved *My Brilliant Career* and would she direct their next movies? Armstrong admits to being flattered but resolute. 'I didn't have a [false] idea about how easy it was to make a film, I knew it was hard. Not the financing – these were all fully financed films with stars – but I knew that directors don't make films on their own. I made [*My Brilliant Career*] with an incredible team of Australians and I felt it would be foolish to rush off into a foreign country when I had been so well supported.' Instead she made a handful of documentaries while searching for a project to make with people she knew and trusted.

In early 1980, she returned to LA and New York to publicise the theatrical release of *My Brilliant Career*. During that visit, Scott-Fox did what agents do and set up meetings for her with studio representatives. The most unforgettable of these was with two older male studio executives from 'one of the more conservative studios at the time, probably Columbia or Warners'. They were due to meet at the Beverly Hills Hotel's legendary Polo Lounge. Armstrong had been accompanied on the tour by her partner, John, a documentary editor whose surname she prefers not to publicise so as to protect the identity of her daughters. John was keen to scope the Polo Lounge, so he accompanied her to the meeting.

Gillian and John sat opposite the duo, who were bedecked in crimplene trousers, old fashioned even by the early 80s. Studio executives met such hot new directors in order to try and entice the director to work for them. It soon became clear this doddery pair had never attempted to woo a female director before. Armstrong recalls neither of them could even look at her, spending the entire meeting talking about her while looking at John. He was flummoxed – he was only there to check out the venue. Unsurprisingly, she didn't work with that studio.

While meeting with Sandy Lieberson, who was running Twentieth Century Fox, she caught another glimpse of the real, brutal Hollywood. '[Lieberson] said, "This is quite a day for you, you meet a studio head and I won't be one in five minutes".' He'd just resigned to take a position with Alan Ladd Jr's The Ladd Company. Armstrong spent the rest of her visit walking around Hollywood ogling. 'I was like a tourist going, oh there's the lions on MGM, there's the Paramount gates.'

'I suppose I spent a year running around with *My Brilliant Career*', attending film festivals and assisting with publicity as it launched in each territory, she recalls. 'I started to notice these scripts I was being sent from America; I was already being put in a box. Every film was about women achieving and they were all set in the past' – themes she felt she had thoroughly explored in *My Brilliant Career.* 'I thought, I don't want to make the same story again.'

She made three documentaries instead: 'I did the documentaries between features because they pay. Australian features [paid] so little I had to actually get a job when I was finished. The documentaries I got on the artists (*Touch Wood* and *A Busy Kind of Bloke*) were great fun to do and I thought, this gives me the chance to not rush into another feature, actually take my time to choose something I'm really passionate about. I realised then those features, they're part of you forever. You make a rash decision and they take a year, two years of your life. So I thought, I can make a bit of a living making the documentaries.'

Then she rolled into production on a natty pop musical starring newcomer Jo Kennedy and an unknown Geoffrey Rush in his second movie role. 'I'd heard through some film crew friends about this fantastic script [producer] David Elfick had called *Star Struck*,' she recalls. It was written by Stephen MacLean, a rock journalist who'd been living in London and New York. 'I got my Australian agent to approach David and I think he initially went, oh no, she's that girl that does lace and period films.'

Elfick agrees: 'I was a little worried because it was a radical departure from *My Brilliant Career* [and Armstrong's short films] *One Hundred A Day* and *The Singer and The Dancer*. None of those films would give any indication she could make a fast-paced musical.' Then Armstrong happened to meet MacLean at a party, the pair hit it off and MacLean backed her as director. Elfick acquiesced.

The film about a wannabe pop star, set in a pub under the Sydney Harbour Bridge, returned a respectable $1.5 million in Australia but very little in the US. Distributors Cinecom 'couldn't get cinemas', Elfick recalls, 'but it played for years'. Specifically, according to Armstrong, in gay San Francisco, where her ocker fantasia became a cult hit.

Elfick is even inclined to believe the home-made punk rock look sported by Kennedy and designed by Luciana Arrighi and Terry Ryan was the inspiration for Cindi Lauper's signature look in her 'Girls Just Wanna Have Fun' era. Arrighi later worked with Armstrong in Hollywood.

With *Star Struck* in the can, Armstrong took up an offer from The Ladd Company, whose executives she had first met at the Cannes Film Festival, then again in New York. They invited her to visit when she was in LA. Armstrong was overjoyed to meet three women – Paula Weinstein, Allyn Stewart and Lucy Fischer – whose presence in the industry at that time was rare. Also, 'Sandy Lieberson, who was head of production, had a number of English directors [and an English wife]. He was smart enough to realise that [as] foreigners, we were different and it was very frightening to come in,' Armstrong says.

The Ladd Company offered her a four-month scholarship to visit the US. They gave her an office on the studio lot and a brief to 'meet writers, producers, go out on sets, get a sense of the scene. See if there's any American writers you'd like to develop something with. It was fantastic.' She was just 29 years old, a woman in an era when female directors were very rare. She was Australian and she was on the payroll of a Hollywood production company. In return for this largesse, 'I think they might have had first right of refusal to anything I found over the next couple of years, which was basically them saying if I found something I wanted to do they will fund it. I didn't really find anything I liked. I met a number of writers. I did learn a lot about the system.'

She attended marketing previews of *Blade Runner* and a Bette Midler concert film with executives. 'It was really interesting to [observe] discussions about recutting the film and I'm like, oh yeah? The director's cut has only just come out of *Blade Runner*; I saw the first cut, they changed the voice and everything.' Her study tour also included a visit to the set of Mel Brooks's *History of the World Part 1*: 'It was such a cliché to see everyone dressed as Romans and chatting on phones'; and *Tootsie*: 'That was good to see, even though film crews are the same all over the world.'

'Film crews are the same all over the world'

She travelled to Santa Fe, New Mexico, New Orleans. 'It was clever of Sandy because it meant later on when scripts came to me I had seen parts of America, I could understand the stories better.'

During this period, she also stumbled across some of the madder aspects of the business. 'I met some writers who had ten screenplays on their shelves, none had ever been made yet they lived in mansions with pools. That was a great education for an Australian. I learned finally getting a green light is tough [and] you [can] write a script that's hot and everyone wants it but in the end that script might not be made because the budget was too high, or they didn't get the right star.'

During this spell in LA, Armstrong hooked up with Fred Schepisi, who had many years earlier taught her at Melbourne's film school, Swinburne College, and had given her a tea-making job on his short film *Libido*. 'He had a house in the LA hills and said, "Come up anytime, there's always a barbie on". I learned a lot from Fred about living and working in Hollywood, how difficult it is working the studio system. He had fantastic parties [frequented by stars]. In LA everyone is so image conscious, it's such a career town, they're reading the [box office] grosses at breakfast in *Variety* and the *Hollywood Reporter*, it's an unhealthy life.

'I would go up to Fred's house and hear all the stories and dramas that were going on. The actors who were there would say, "Fred's amazing, his barbies [are] so relaxed". Very rarely was I invited to people's homes and if you are, it's completely catered, with chefs in the kitchen and staff.'

The heat from *My Brilliant Career* stayed on Armstrong for several years during which her reticence to move to Hollywood did not wane. 'LA in those days was such a white bread town. You couldn't even eat in a restaurant after 10 o'clock. No-one knew what a cappuccino was.'

Naomi Watts, Thandie Newton and Nicole Kidman in John Duigan's *Flirting*. Said Duigan of his invitation to Kidman to join the cast, 'I asked her if she wanted to play a schoolgirl for the last time.'

Kennedy Miller's Vietnam war mini-series, *Vietnam*, was a television event.

Geoffrey Rush collected an Oscar for his lead role in Scott Hicks's *Shine*. This shot was taken while the trio [Lynn Redgrave is in the middle] shot scenes in London. These scenes did not appear in the final film.

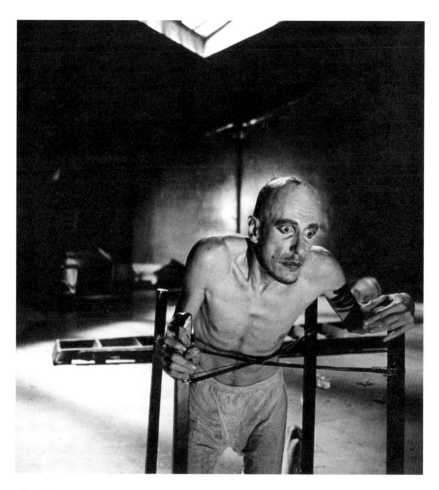

Geoffrey Rush, in his much-lauded lead role in *The Diary of a Madman*. This photo was taken long after midnight at a rehearsal before the production's debut season with director Neil Armfield at Company B, Belvoir St Theatre.

Paul Hogan, and his many guises, dominated Australian television before making his big-screen debut in *Crocodile Dundee*. 'I had a handshake contract with Kerry Packer [where] I said, "I can't find writers and I can't churn these things out". He said: "When you think of enough funny ideas we'll put a show together".' As Hogan tells it, 'We did seven one year, three the next, nine the next, four the next.'

Paul Hogan made his first movie because 'I'd reached the stage with television [where] I'd done 600 sketches and sent up everything. I wanted to do a sketch that lasts more than four minutes so I did *Crocodile Dundee*.' Released in 1986 it remains the highest-grossing Australian movie ever.

'Straightaway I kind of pictured myself as Chopper Read,' says Eric Bana, perhaps disturbingly.

Gillian Armstrong and cinematographer Geoffrey Simpson teamed up first on *The Last Days of Chez Nous* in Australia and again on Armstrong's breakout Hollywood hit, *Little Women*.

Bryan Brown said that whenever he was cast in films of iconic Australian stories, 'You pray you don't fuck 'em up'. *The Shiralee* [pictured here] and *A Town Like Alice* turned out OK. *'Eureka Stockade'* we got wrong and it wasn't good. Luckily two of the three [were] done incredibly well.'

Lewis Fitz-Gerald, Bryan Brown and Edward Woodward in *'Breaker' Morant*. Brown thought his Lieutenant Handcock was a one-barb phoney with the worst moustache in the war. Then he changed his mind: 'I quite like how I look in it now and everyone tells me what a great character it was so I have to go along with it.'

Phillip Noyce weathering a rainstorm on *Heatwave*, a decade before his exit to the US. 'Although we had great opportunities in Australia, no matter how much money was available, there still wasn't enough to go around for all the skilled filmmakers,' Noyce said of his decision to go to Hollywood.

Love and Other Catastrophes was big in Australia, not so big in Hollywood, recalls its star, Frances O'Connor.

So it was fitting that while on a publicity trip to promote *Star Struck* in New York, she finally attended the meeting that changed her mind. Scott Rudin was a budding producer in his early twenties already showing signs of a long prosperous career ahead. 'He came to have coffee in Central Park, he had a photograph of this jail in Pittsburgh and he told me the outline of a true story that was the first American thing I was intrigued by,' Armstrong recounts.

Mrs. Soffel, the tale of a prison warder's wife who falls in love with a charismatic death row prisoner before breaking him out, would star Diane Keaton and a young Mel Gibson. It was shot amid heavy snow in Toronto, where both the dollar and the snow season stretched further than in the US. The intimate drama holds up well but the experience of making it pushed Armstrong to the end of her powers, despite the set being a safe distance from the excessive scrutiny of executives at MGM, a studio then in turmoil. 'There were older executives [who seemed to have] weird mafia connections, wives who were ex-Miss Worlds. It was really old Hollywood,' Armstrong notes.

In a fine example of studio instability, from the beginning of production until the film was released, the director reported to three different bosses. 'Eileen Marzel, then Peter Bart [later editor and chief of *Variety*], then Freddie Fields [but] they had all gone by the time I got back to show the final cut,' Armstrong recalls.

The studio was in flux. The execs had pinned their hopes on the success of Peter Hyams's *2010*, which, it was becoming obvious, would not recoup its budget. Also, '*Heaven's Gate* had just happened so they were thinking we're all going to run wild,' Armstrong says, alluding to the 1981 movie that turned out to be the biggest Hollywood flop of its decade. Its title became synonymous with films that overran their budgets. The big budget western directed by recent Oscar-winner Michael

Cimino featured a star-studded cast and the studio, United Artists, had high hopes. After months of delays and shocking cost overruns Cimino delivered a five-hour extravaganza later cut by 90 minutes. That version premiered in New York City, then never appeared again. It surfaced six months later with another 70 minutes cut by the studio in a desperate attempt to recoup some of its losses but it was too late and it played to empty theatres. The disaster spelt the end of United Artists. MGM, which was having troubles of its own, subsequently acquired the studio.

At the very outset Armstrong managed to import two Australians, her cinematographer Russell Boyd and costume designer Luciana Arrighi. 'I really wanted to bring my first assistant [director]. I was very nervous about shooting with an American because there had only been five films in the [previous] 30 years directed by women. There was a sense about Australia at that time that our men were really sexist but I thought it was the absolute opposite,' Armstrong says.

'There had only been five films in the [previous] 30 years directed by women'

A director's primary on-set relationship is with their cinematographer, then their lead actors. The next most important role is the first assistant director (a.d.). 'I started meeting many, many American first a.d.s, then I was like, how do I know what they're going to be like on the day? Of course they're nice to me when we're in the office but how do I know what they're going to be like when things are going wrong?

'It was getting late and I finally met this guy in New York and we got on like a house on fire. Scott [Rudin] agreed he was the one and the production manager was getting nervous that we didn't have a schedule [the first a.d. does the schedule], so she thought she would sneak him up for a weekend in Toronto, drive around the locations, and then go back to New York and do the schedule.

'Once back in New York they would organise his papers but one of the Canadian crew dobbed him in to the immigration department, and he was arrested at immigration and carted off. There was a huge hoo-haa. They said I hadn't interviewed enough firsts in Canada; at that point the Canadian industry was really quite small and I had been told with a big film, action, two stars, their firsts weren't really up to it. So I had to go through this whole rigmarole, interview every out-of-work first in Canada. One of them said, "I feel really sorry you." He almost got the job.'

She ended up employing a first a.d. who had worked with Martin Scorsese. But was he any good? Working outside her own industry, Armstrong didn't have the contacts with whom she could compare notes. She knew soon enough. At the end of the first day's filming, Armstrong and Boyd realised the light was fading, so they wrapped the day's shoot. This was supposed to be the first a.d.'s job.

'I discovered it was a whole different thing that happened in America. [On] a really big film the director has complete power,' she says. So the first a.d. doesn't manage time as they do in Australia, where budgets are so tight every morsel has to be squeezed from the day. 'It is the best training in the world.' The first a.d. didn't have the skills Armstrong needed. 'He was an ex-stunt guy with a big voice who could yell. It turned into a disaster and we had to let him go. We went back to the studio, who went to immigration and asked for a first I'd worked with before.' She was joined shortly thereafter by her first from *My Brilliant Career*.

While scouting locations, the crew stayed in the same hotel and when the producer and director invited the location scout to join them for dinner, he said, 'I've never eaten at the same table as the director and producer.' Armstrong comments, 'Even [his] manner was very funny, the location guy was like

"Yes, ma'am, no ma'am". Wanting to pick up your bag all the time ... A good thing about Australian society is there's a greater sense of team spirit. The studios are another thing, I had no idea what was ahead.'

The biggest shock came when one of her producers, Rudin, was sacked by Peter Bart before shooting began. 'There were personal politics at work. Some of the executives were jealous that Scott was only twenty-four.' Yet Armstrong also admits his youth put them in some tricky situations, such as the time he advised her to point blank refuse to speak with execs visiting the set.

Officially Rudin was rolled because the budget had come in a million dollars over. '*Mrs. Soffel* was to be a US$12 million film. They had wanted me to cast an up and coming actor with Diane [because] they didn't want to pay for two stars. Mel Gibson was already a star [and wanted the role]. I met lots of young actors and had to come back and say, "I don't think anybody is better than Mel, he is perfect for the part".' But using him would have pushed the budget up another million, which Gillian asked for. The studio flew into a rage. 'I was surprised. What's a million to them when you've got another star?' Armstrong didn't know of MGM's financial troubles and assured herself that once they began seeing the rushes they would calm down.

'The other thing I realised [was] a studio point of view. I'd come from an independent industry in Australia where you have a finite budget [where] you can't go over [because] there's no more money. So I was being terribly honest but in their minds they add a couple of hundred thousand, a quarter of a million, whatever, assuming you were going over. That's why they're so paranoid. So it was a lot of lessons for me.'

With Rudin sidelined (despite finding the project he wasn't permitted to view the rushes or, later, attend the premiere), Armstrong worked with the other producer Edgar J. Scherick, who formerly ran America's ABC TV network. 'He fought for me and for the film all the way through it. He was really fantastic. It was such a male world, all those male studio executives there. It really was very good for me in the end that I had a heavy, a real player.'

It was decided the picture would open in December to be eligible for the forthcoming Academy Awards. It is a competitive time of year but everyone agreed Gibson and Keaton deserved a shot at an Oscar. Then they became their own worst enemies. It was fashionable for serious actors at that time to eschew media interviews – press or TV. 'That was considered beneath them,' Armstrong recalls. She was in Australia giving birth to her first child, the studio brass had been marched on and, 'Gibson and Keaton hardly did anything. They didn't go on any of the talk shows or breakfast shows. There was nobody there to baby it.' *Mrs. Soffel* flopped. 'That was an interesting life experience,' Armstrong deadpans.

But the reviews were good enough that Armstrong's career was unhurt. Her next two features were made in Australia with the cream of the local film industry, though it must be said they were mostly women. *The Last Days of Chez Nous*, an emotional relationship drama, was produced by Jan Chapman (*Lantana*) and written by Helen Garner (*Monkey Grip*), and *Hightide*, which reunited Armstrong with Judy Davis, was produced by Sandra Levy (later drama chief at the Australian Broadcasting Corporation) and penned by Laura Jones (*Angela's Ashes*).

It was a full decade before Armstrong returned to Hollywood at Winona Ryder's invitation to direct a film version of Louisa May Alcott's period novel *Little Women*. 'I actually said no to *Little Women* three times. It was too close to *My Brilliant Career* and I didn't want to do another young woman who wants to be a writer story but Denise Di Novi who had been

Tim Burton's producer (on *Heathers* and *Batman Returns*) was very persuasive. [She] said it's not *My Brilliant Career* and anyway there's a whole generation of people who have been born since that film was made and have never seen it, it's still a story worth telling. Anyway I flew over and met them.'

The US$19 million movie with an all-star cast of veterans and newcomers including Susan Sarandon, Claire Danes, Kirsten Dunst, Eric Stoltz, Gabriel Byrne and Christian Bale was a hit and grossed US$50 million in the US.

Then, back in Australia, Armstrong cast Cate Blanchett in her first mid-budget movie, *Oscar and Lucinda*, an adaptation of Peter Carey's book, which co-starred Ralph Fiennes. That movie, made for US$12.6 million, which stretched a considerable distance at that time, was one of the first made in Australia with Hollywood studio money. Fox Searchlight came to the party but left disappointed. The film was expected to gross more than its US$1.9 million in the US and $1.7 million in Australia. *Charlotte Gray*, made for US$20 million and released in 2001, fared worse. Again starring Blanchett, the adaptation of Sebastian Faulks's novel about a wartime resistance fighter recouped less than US$1 million in the US.

Armstrong says the budgets for serious dramas are shrinking in an era ever more obsessed with making movies for teenagers. 'There are fewer straight dramas being made, it's now split into very big budget special effects movies, whether cartoon remakes or action films, and then the dramas are very, very low budget, like *The Good Girl* or *Y tu mama tambien*. They [have] budgets as low as the Australian budgets.'

Just as well Armstrong is not afraid of a tight budget. 'I'm happy to make small films and American small films. In many ways you get more freedom because the less money [is] at stake the less they're on you.' Her memories of being bullied by MGM remain vivid.

06

bryan
brown

Pivotal Projects

Dirty Deeds (2002), Two Hands (1999)

Dead Heart (1996), The Shiralee (TV) (1988)

Gorillas in the Mist (1988), Cocktail (1988), F/X (1986)

The Thorn Birds (1983), A Town Like Alice (1981)

'Breaker' Morant (1980)

bryan

Bryan Brown is a chameleon: a smart, enthusiastic actor who has developed a laconic screen persona and is happy to play the larrikin. He has taken the stage with John Gielgud yet is considered limited, merely a stereotypical Aussie actor, and one who admits he has a Hollywood career 'despite himself'.

Raised by his single mother in Sydney's western suburbs, Brown turned down a scholarship in economics at Sydney University to study as an insurance actuary. That way, he could combine study with earning an income. He didn't like it much but 'had fuck-all else to do', he says. He moved to selling insurance, which was more fun and allowed him to pursue his interest in amateur theatre.

By age twenty-five, Brown was disillusioned with theatre in Australia but aware time was ticking if he wanted to pursue it as a career. He'd noticed original Australian works were rare in a domestic theatre scene awash with English and American plays featuring actors exercising foreign accents. 'What's the point of acting in Australia?' he asked himself. If he was going to perform English plays with an English accent he may as well do it in England. So in 1972, he flew to England.

Once there, his first role was as a 'coughing orderly' in a Peter Nichols's play set in a hospital, *The National Health*; he only won the job because the character didn't speak. He then worked at an infamous London obscenity trial reading tracts from *Oz*, the magazine published by several expat Australians who were charged with disseminating lewd material. Six months later, Brown secured a 12-month contract with an educational theatre troupe in Billingham. He recalls thinking, 'I have no idea what I'm doing but it's a really lovely way to be working, gypsy-ish, very exciting.'

It dawned upon him he might actually be able to pay his way through life doing what he loved. 'I thought, even if it is a hundredth of what I would have been paid, this is a lot better than sitting in that fucking boring office at AMP being an actuary. I didn't expect to earn any money from acting.'

He continued to write applications for more acting jobs. He had nothing to lose and he was enjoying himself. 'I worked hard, went and pushed scenery, I didn't care what I did as long as I was in the theatre.' He eventually secured an audition with Peter Hall, artistic director at Britain's esteemed National Theatre, and signed a 12-month contract for three plays.

Towards the end of 1974, his mother sent him a photograph from home. She was looking older. He resolved to return for a six-week holiday. He stayed for six years; the next time he visited England was as a star of Bruce Beresford's Boer War drama, *'Breaker' Morant*.

Brown experienced an epiphany upon arriving back in Australia, one that has underpinned his entire career. He saw Alex Buzo's *Rooted* at the Nimrod Theatre and heard contemporary Australian voices and characters on stage, seemingly for the first time. An Australian cultural renaissance was underway. In Melbourne, playwrights at the Pram Factory theatre, such as Jack Hibberd and David Williamson, seized the chance to tell their own stories. In Sydney, film directors Beresford and Peter Weir were fashioning unashamedly Australian characters. Not that this hadn't happened before, just not with such dynamism or frequency. 'I sat there and went, oh fuck, that's exciting! Massively exciting, far more exciting than thinking about going back and getting into the next year of the National.'

Brown wanted to be a part of it. His England experiment had served its purpose, giving him stage credits and training. He needed local credibility though, so he bought the rights to Robert Patrick's American play *Kennedy's Children* and produced it at the Melbourne Theatre Company and Nimrod. He also toured, performed in *The Rainmaker* and at the Black Theatre in Redfern 'desperately trying to get into this new Australian scene'. Budding film director Steven Wallace saw Brown in Redfern and cast him in a 50-minute feature, *Love Letters from Teralba Road*. Brown earned his first screen role as he was about to turn thirty.

With hindsight, Brown thinks his late entry to acting aided him 'enormously'. He was grounded by the everyday experiences of 'getting a job, hating your job, finding a better job, enjoying being a salesman, stumbling into something [and] playing around with it for a few years, travelling ... Once I got into this game and saw how it fucks people up, just fucks them up, I'd grown up and knew what was bullshit,' he says bluntly. 'Hollywood is full of bullshit.' In fact, 'The best bullshit you've ever seen is in Hollywood,' he adds. 'Nobody does a bad meeting in Hollywood, you come out thinking you're a star. You think, they told me I was sensational, the phone's going to ring in a minute.' It doesn't. Brown believes broad life experience teaches you not to read too much into a film executive's enthusiasms.

Brown's late start didn't hinder his career. He nabbed another five film roles within a year. Subsequently, he was booed at the AFI Awards 'because I was in every fucking movie! Everyone had their noses way out of joint,' he recalls.

'Understandably, [but] it wasn't my fault. It was just one of those things.'

Brown was prolific in 1978 and 1979 with roles in TV mini-series (*Against the Wind*) and popular local films including *Newsfront* and *The Odd Angry Shot*. The supporting roles kept coming until *'Breaker' Morant*, a film Brown didn't assign much significance to at the time. In fact, he watched Stanley Kubrick's *Paths of Glory* before filming and rang director Bruce Beresford to tell him: 'They've made the fucking movie already, mate, what are we doing this for?'

The shoot was enjoyable although Brown despised his performance and his character's look. He thought his Lieutenant Handcock was a one-barb phoney with the worst moustache in the war. 'I quite like how I look in it now and everyone tells me what a great character it was so I have to go along with it. But when I saw a cut of it I couldn't wait to get out of there, I felt lousy.'

'Breaker' Morant was not lousy. The true story of three soldiers court-martialled during the Boer War coupled fine performances and direction with a narrative that tapped into the Australian identity's anti-authoritarianism. It earned $4.7 million in Australia, US$7 million in America and won ten AFI Awards, including Brown's Best Supporting Actor prize.

'And that led to Hollywood,' Brown adds matter of factly. He hadn't banked on it being a life-changing experience, he says he doesn't think that way. 'I don't have any goals, I don't have any dreams, I don't have any ambitions ... I like working and being good at stuff and seeing where it goes,' Brown contends. 'I have a massive commitment to my family and that's where everything goes from – but then I grew up in a committed family so that's not unusual. I don't have

'I don't have any goals, I don't have any dreams, I don't have any ambitions'

dreams because quite truthfully, if I'd tried I couldn't have dreamt up my life in a million years.'

When Brown promoted 'Breaker' in New York in 1980, he began to appreciate the film's impact. He observes that Americans, at their best, enthusiastically embrace the new and accomplished. Initially, that threw him. 'That's why people get lost with all the raving, they forget that the next day they're raving at someone else.'

Brown's television mini-series *A Town Like Alice* hit the world's TV screens only months later, he recalls, 'a double whammy for Hollywood for me'. *Alice*'s commercial appeal consolidated the artistic achievement of '*Breaker*'. Suddenly Brown had two very appealing, very Australian characters gaining international attention, which was a blessing and a curse, he says. 'One, it made them want me because they're always looking for new characters but two, it made them go "What the fuck do we do with him because he's so Australian?"'

Creative Artists Agency (CAA) sought to represent him, 'and I said, "Fine," not really knowing what all that meant'. Brown didn't even meet them. When they eventually did meet, the wily CAA agent gushed about what a huge future awaited Brown in Hollywood. He was old enough to demur: 'I'll decide what my future is.'

The actor was expected to move to LA, learn the accent and meet and greet Hollywood executives. He told them he had to return to Australia and film *Far East*, which 'I'd promised to do with a mate of mine, John Duigan'. No-one appreciated Brown might be serious. After all, you don't turn down Hollywood.

Saturday Night Fever director John Badham offered Brown a part in *Blue Thunder*. He'd seen '*Breaker*' *Morant* and noticed an actor with 'a natural strength, charm and masculinity'.

Badham adds, 'It's a treat when you don't have to rely on the same old people.'

Blue Thunder's dates clashed with *Far East*. CAA's Fred Specktor implored Brown to ask Duigan to reschedule but *Far East* had to film before 30 June for tax purposes. Brown said he wouldn't budge. Specktor was apoplectic, telling him he'd be paid five times his Australian fee or more. 'Yeah, but I told you I promised him I'd do it,' Brown replied. 'They said, "You can't now".'

This was the point Brown realised he had to decide where his priorities lay – in Hollywood or Australia. Making big-budget studio movies or smaller Australian films. He turned down the US job. Badham says that after years working as a casting director he was 'used to people turning me down. He'd promised a friend and you've got to respect that.' In 2003, Badham and Brown finally collaborated on the telemovie *Footsteps*.

Brown quickly discovered Hollywood wouldn't be a pushover. There would be prices to pay 'and you better work out what part of the price you're happy to pay'. He heard later there was much consternation, if not incredulity, at CAA about his preference for an Australian film before an American one. But within a matter of months, he had the best of both worlds – a role in a US mini-series about an Australian story, *The Thorn Birds*. It was another international hit, particularly so in the US, even if it didn't raise his stocks as a 'film actor' as *'Breaker' Morant* had. He then took on the Australian TV mini-series, *Eureka Stockade*, in which he played rebel Peter Lalor.

It was the beginning of an intense period. Brown married English actor Rachel Ward in England in April 1983 and averaged three projects a year for the next four, one of the first of which was Paul McCartney's semi-autobiographical *Give My Regards to Broad Street*. The former Beatle woke Brown with a phone call while the Australian was in Hawaii filming *The Thorn Birds*. A sleepy Brown was wary but realised it actually was McCartney. 'I remember hanging up and saying to Rachel, "This has got to be such a bag of shit for me to say no but even then I'm not sure I can say no to a Beatle".' McCartney's idea for a humble one-hour video about his life attracted myriad backers and grew into an overblown, expensive movie. 'The idea couldn't sustain that,' Brown observes. Oh well, spending time with McCartney and Ringo Starr, 'the funniest bastard in the world', was 'delightful'.

Brown followed the mini-series *Eureka Stockade* (and his first call for an Australian republic) with *Kim* for American television (he played Mahbub Ali), while Ward filmed *Against All Odds*. It was decision time. Should they stay or go? Brown remembers bumping into Mel Gibson and his wife Robyn in a California hardware store and asking when they'd return to Australia. Robyn replied they had planned to but weren't so sure now. Brown realised Gibson had just made the decision to base himself in LA. 'I remember that because I couldn't wait to get back,' Brown says. 'Everyone's got a journey and Mel should be there as much as anybody but I remember him saying Sydney wasn't the centre of filmmaking for him and I remember thinking it is for me.

'I couldn't cope with sitting in Hollywood just doing American films,' he says. Brown needed more than that. 'Hollywood's enabled me to continue to do Australian films, if I couldn't do them I'd really feel lousy.' Nevertheless, Brown starred in an enviable array of US hits in the late 1980s. The first was *F/X*, a sprightly thriller about a movie special effects man hired to stage a Mafia hit. Initially, Brown turned down the role because he was looking after newborn daughter Rosie while Ward filmed *Fortress* in Melbourne. His agent told him he was the lead opposite Brian Dennehy. Brown liked the script, despite its 'guns and people killing each other', but said 'The fact is, Fred, I can't do it because I'm looking after the baby.'

Again, his agent was incredulous, repeating it would be Brown's first lead in a US studio movie. They devised a schedule where Brown was only out of Australia for five weeks. It wasn't a power play, Brown admits, he was 'just juggling stuff'. His agent deserves a lifetime achievement award, he adds. 'He laughs about having me as his client but we're very close. At least I did the right thing by him and pushed Geoffrey Rush his way, so that got him off my back,' Brown smiles.

Hollywood beckoned. *F/X* producer Jack Weiner told the *Sun* newspaper at the time, 'Bryan is one of very few good leading men in rugged roles who can act. He has the rawness of Steve McQueen, and those ice blue eyes. After Harrison Ford, Redford and Newman, there aren't many others around.'

F/X's reviews were far more positive than usual for a stock-standard thriller, the *New York Times's* Vincent Canby highlighting the 'attractive, offbeat leading man' and the *Chicago Sun-Times's* Roger Ebert writing 'Rollie Tyler [is] given a nice, laconic professionalism by Bryan Brown'. Brown deflects the plaudits: 'It was a massive sleeper that came out of nowhere because Robert Mandel, the director, made that movie more than it was.'

The good notices rolled in, and so did the work. In 1986, Brown's star was so bright he was approached to take the James Bond mantle from Roger Moore. '*F/X* put me into that area of movies.' He told Specktor he wasn't interested. 'The movies had fallen apart by then and I actually never saw myself as James Bond.' Nor did action movies appeal. He rarely does them. 'I've played in movies that have guns and stuff like *Two Hands* and *Dirty Deeds* but they're also culturally strong movies with themes as well.'

Brown also struggled to appreciate a system where participation in one $100 million-earning movie meant you could then choose as you pleased. 'There is a template [for stardom] I never saw or understood,' he admits. 'It meant you had to do something you don't like doing. I never saw it like that; I just saw acting as acting.'

Next was a US$30 million adaptation of James Clavell's best-seller, *Tai-Pan*, for which Brown beat former Bond, Sean Connery, to the lead role. A 1985 newspaper report noted *Tai-Pan* was 'the biggest budget film any Australian has ever starred in'. Unfortunately, upon release *Tai-Pan* was universally panned.

Then came *The Umbrella Woman* (aka *The Good Wife*) opposite Ward and Sam Neill in Australia. Expatriate Aussie director Roger Donaldson appreciated Brown's performance in it and offered him another role. Brown recalls Donaldson saying, 'Mate, I'm going to send you the best script you've ever read. We've got this young guy called Tom and I want you to play the other lead. It's a fucking great character.' The script was *Cocktail*.

Brown contends *Cocktail* 'was close to the best script I've ever read – very dark and about celebrity. Disney [via Touchstone Pictures] watered it down a great deal.' In one scene Brown's character, Doug Coughlin, 'beat the shit out of Tom Cruise's character'. No-one could beat up *Top Gun*'s rising star so the scene was cut. Then the producers implanted a love story. 'But when I read the initial script I went, fuck, is this gutsy.'

Brown wanted the role but, recalcitrant Hollywood player that he was, wouldn't audition for it. Donaldson implored him to come and meet Cruise in LA so they could show studio executives the two stars together. Upon arriving in LA, Donaldson said they had to fly to New York to put something on tape. Brown had been conned.

'Poor Roger's on the spot but the great thing is he's battling his fucking arse off for me, he wants me to do the part and I'm making it so hard for him,' Brown laughs. Brown acquiesced and read the script opposite Cruise. That night, Donaldson told him the reading hadn't worked. He couldn't show the tape to the studio executives. He again implored Brown to learn lines for an audition. Brown refused and flew home the next morning.

A fortnight later, at the Tokyo Film Festival, a curious Brown rang Specktor, his agent, who said, 'If you'd rung me yesterday I would have said it's dead but I've got a feeling they're going to offer it to you.' Donaldson didn't show the executives the tape of Cruise and Brown reading together. He showed excerpts of Brown being himself between readings, the non-audition components of the tape. Furthermore, another actor pegged for the role bowed out due to his drinking habit. Brown won the role. He was forging a Hollywood career in spite of himself. Brown smiles. 'Roger would say that.'

'[Telling] Australian stories was going to be my sustenance'

Cocktail quickly became a hit but Brown was on the plane home the day after the premiere, when, he admits, 'I should have been there working the industry. To get anything you've got to put in the work.' Roles followed in Michael Apted's *Gorillas in the Mist*, opposite Sigourney Weaver, and a number of Australian projects, including *The Empty Beach* and *Rebel*.

'There's a certain amount of work I was prepared to put in and a certain amount I wasn't. The results are the results of that. I [realised] Hollywood was going to help me with my income and that was going to allow me to do Australian films. [Telling] Australian stories was going to be my sustenance.'

His Hollywood forays were 'good fun' because every film seemed to work but 'I was never there when it all had its impact'. Brown doesn't regret that: 'I couldn't handle all the arse licking that goes on.' He hired a public relations person for a week before he realised he didn't know why he needed one. 'I will say what I think to people. I don't need you to siphon it for me. I can't stand "The spokesman says". I throw up whenever I read that.'

'They're the prices you pay on all this shit,' he adds. 'You lose "you" and you become this other thing that everyone's speaking for. That's a part of the game that's really difficult. You could feel, going into a movie like *Cocktail*, it's like, this is all so fucking wrong; it's going to undo me.'

Brown came back to Australia for what turned out to be another massive Australian mini-series, *The Shiralee*. It remains Brown's favourite project, next to his 1996 film *Dead Heart*. 'When you do those sort of things you pray you don't fuck 'em up,' Brown says of the classic Australian story. He admits good fortune in also succeeding with *A Town Like Alice*. '*Eureka Stockade* we got wrong and it wasn't good. Luckily two of the three [were] done incredibly well.'

'He's a very clever actor. He always picks good projects,' says Matt Carroll, Brown's producer on *'Breaker' Morant*.

Brown's Hollywood career appears to have lost focus through the late 80s and early 90s. He contends otherwise; he had to prioritise his children, marriage and career. 'I was at that stage where if I'd been in Hollywood it [would have] all fallen apart. You only have to look around. You can't really have a marriage and a family life and pursue the stuff you pursue in Hollywood, you just can't and keep it together.'

Nevertheless, the couple did buy a house in LA's beachside suburb, Malibu, around the same time they bought in Sydney's Whale Beach. Then they realised they rarely stayed in Malibu. 'Whenever we finished a job we'd come and live here.' Essentially, Brown and Ward 'took ourselves out of the market'. Juggling two careers in their family was 'just a fact of life. A number of times I went, I can't work because she's working. Simple. Not a big deal.' And Ward's career was just as fruitful, if more selective, at that stage after the solid 1984 hit *Against All Odds*.

'Slowly you're moving down the list and then you're off the list for those big movies,' Brown concedes. 'Certainly [at] the time of *Gorillas* and *Cocktail*, if I'd bothered to pursue it in the right way, there would have been one or two movies every 12 months for sure, that's just how it works.'

He still received offers from American television and cable networks; some, such as Nic Roeg's *Full Body Massage*, in which he played a philosophising masseur, quite obtuse. 'That was an interesting idea, far more interesting than James Bond.'

In Australia, roles were scarce due to the perception that Brown was hackneyed, unsuitable for the tedious 'arthouse years' of Australian cinema in the 90s. International work was available and well paid. Five weeks' work would pay for a year at home working on Australian stories. Brown took more control of his own destiny by producing. 'I began using whatever clout I had to give me the opportunity to tell those stories and get into it myself.' *Sweet Talker* was his first real attempt.

Brown's desire to play as many Australian characters as possible extended to Hollywood. He managed to change the nationalities of all his characters to Australian: *Gorillas in the Mist*'s Bob was initially South African; *F/X*'s Rollie and *Cocktail*'s Doug were Americans. 'They hired me and I just started talking on the set as an Australian,' he says. 'No-one ever said to me "Tone it down" [or] "Will you do it American?"' Even so, he believes there was 'no question' that position excluded him from a number of US roles.

'I've just never seen a reason why I'm supposed to hide behind a bushel [about being Australian],' Brown contends. Leaving Australia – Panania, mind you – as a 25 year old forced him to assess his capabilities starkly. Brown recalls standing off stage at an English production of *The Tempest*, watching John Gielgud perform the last soliloquy and thinking to himself, 'You're really good at that but there's no fucking way you can play a boy from Bankstown.'

'He's limited, and I am limited; I can't and don't want to do that and he can't do this and probably doesn't want to. That was a significant moment [realising] I've been given a background and type of people I can play and within that scope there's a million of them.'

Brown had no reason to retain his Australian identity in Hollywood but in many cases it worked well for the piece. In fact, Brown was cast in the 2003 US film, *Along Came Polly*, starring Ben Stiller and Jennifer Aniston, precisely for that essence. Writer/director John Hamburg wrote Brown's character as an Australian due to the devil-may-care attitude of the director's Aussie friends. His comic love story about a risk analyst (Stiller) who's scared to gamble on love required another character who could tell him, 'Who cares about the risk?' He had to be Australian.

Brown and Paul Hogan are the only Australian actors to fashion a Hollywood career while maintaining their Australian screen identity. Not that Brown believes he suited the American idea of Australians: 'Paul Hogan fitted their view because he played into that,' Brown says. 'I just played contemporary characters. Doing things like *"Breaker"*, I wasn't out there catching kangaroos or wrestling crocs. Yes, he was a very Australian character but it wasn't because he ties his shoelaces a different way. It was just in the nature of the person, the irony, the disregard for authority, that sort of thing. That's all.'

Hollywood didn't try to change Brown although he admits he couldn't see where he'd fit. 'I saw I could have a bit of it but I couldn't belong. What I wanted to do wasn't there, simple as that. Not its problem, mine. I actually had some amazing opportunities in spite of myself. Still do.'

He wanted Australian stories. They've been his focus since the late 90s, projects such as *Dead Heart* and the Nine TV series *Twisted Tales* also introducing Brown to a new generation of filmmakers. 'Suddenly, instead of being an actor that had happened with Beresford, (Peter) Weir, (Fred) Schepisi in the 70s, I was thrown amongst the David Caesars, the Gregor Jordans, the Samantha Langs and relationships developed. That whole period of *Twisted Tales* and *Dead Heart* was really stimulating.

'There's 250 million Yanks; they don't need me to be one. There's only 20 million Australians, they do need each of us.'

And there's the difference; I do something like that and feel great and I do something like a *Cocktail* or *F/X* and I think, that was nice, thanks for the experience, but I don't feel anything.'

His generation views Hollywood differently to the next generation. In the 70s, Australian actors gained a voice they hadn't had, which is why he's so political today. 'I don't want to see that voice taken away,' he says. 'That voice is taken for granted by a lot of the young guys now and they go, fuck it, I'll go and be a Yank now, but that's a totally different thing for me. I can understand their thinking because they're taking it for granted. I've been there when it wasn't there and I know how fragile it is. It's a very bad thing to not have a culture of film and television. Very, very bad.

'I don't blame them but to get that voice was so thrilling. I've only got 20 more years until I die, I've gotta keep doing it. Besides, there's 250 million Yanks; they don't need me to be one. There's only 20 million Australians, they do need each of us.'

07

phillip noyce

Pivotal Projects

The Quiet American (2003), Rabbit-Proof Fence (2002)

The Bone Collector (1999), The Saint (1997), Clear and Present Danger (1994)

Sliver (1993), Patriot Games (1992), Dead Calm (1989)

The Cowra Breakout (1984), Newsfront (1979)

noyce

When Phillip Noyce first visited America the natives knew not much about Australian films and even less about Australians. It was 1978, the 'pre-*Crocodile Dundee*' era, which, in the history of US–Australian celluloid relations, meant the traffic was all one-way. Australians flocked to Hollywood movies. The reverse? Well, it was unimaginable.

'Oh, you're Australian? How funny you speak English,' Noyce recalls Americans saying to him on that early visit. He was there because his first feature film, *Newsfront*, was selected to screen at the New York Film Festival. Its inclusion was an unexpected honour, given that Noyce's story of Australia's 40s and 50s newsreel business was black and white, contained large chunks of grainy archival footage and featured accents that perplexed the Americans. 'There's a case to be made for English subtitles,' moaned one newspaper critic on seeing it. Others were more generous: 'An Australian film with uncommon gusto and feeling', cheered the *Village Voice*.

After the festival, *Newsfront* was released in some American arthouse cinemas, one of the first Australian films to be screened there. Meanwhile its 28-year-old director was fielding approaches by talent agents eager to share in the fortunes of what they suspected might be a thriving Hollywood career. He agreed to be represented by Joan Scott, an ex-New York theatre agent who had recently decamped to Los Angeles. 'I decided to let [Joan] represent me, not so I could work in America – because I wasn't interested in that – but rather in the hope she might be able to introduce me to some American money for films I wanted to make in Australia,' Noyce explains.

Such commitment to Australian storytelling appears quaint. These days, the move to America after your first film triumph is almost mandatory. Some film school graduates progress straight to Hollywood without even making an Australian film. Victorian College of the Arts graduate Robert Luketic burst upon the US scene with the Reese Witherspoon comedy *Legally Blonde* in 1999 while another Melbourne boy, Jamie Blanks, became known to Australians through his debut American horror movie, *Urban Legend*.

But in 1978, Noyce wouldn't contemplate it. *Newsfront* was his first movie (his previous film, *Backroads*, was sometimes described as a feature when screened through a slow projector). Besides, Australian directors in the 70s and early 80s enjoyed almost unfettered artistic freedom. Why wouldn't he stay? Audiences, unused to seeing themselves on screen, were 'in love with themselves', Noyce notes, and newly introduced government grants and an experimental 10BA tax concession system meant the industry was flush with money. Filmmakers could make the movies they wanted, more or less.

According to Australian press reports at the time, Noyce was due to direct several movies, including *Phillip and Bennelong*, about the friendship between Captain Arthur Phillip and Aboriginal Bennelong. Twenty years later this particular report fascinates him because he's been pursuing the tale lately but can't recall investigating it before. Another prospective movie, *King Hit*, a story of the 1975 dismissal of the Whitlam government, was eventually made as the TV mini-series *The Dismissal*. Noyce went to Taiwan to direct a war film, *The Z-Men*, but quit the project and was replaced by Tim Burstall four weeks before shooting, after disagreeing with the producers over casting. In Noyce's words, executive producer John McCallum and producer Lee Robinson 'were from a different era of filmmaking'. He objected to their plan to cast 'a guy who looked like a Taipei dentist' in the role of a 'wizened old rice farmer'.

He didn't regret the decision – 'I could see it was going to be a nightmare in every way' – and there was a significant upside. Noyce stayed in Taiwan for a couple of months with Christopher Doyle, an expat Aussie, fluent in Mandarin, who had been his translator on the movie. 'At the time he was one of those Australian expatriates who had run away and rein-vented themselves in Asia,' Noyce says. 'He used to say he was going to be a cinematographer but I thought he'd end up under a bar stool, and he did, but he also became a cine-matographer.' Noyce finally consummated his professional relationship with Doyle 21 years later on *Rabbit-Proof Fence* and *The Quiet American*. Doyle was by then an award-winning cinematographer.

Newsfront made its money back in Australia but it took Noyce four years to make his next movie. 'That was partly my own indecision but also the difficulty of running the gauntlet of government film agencies,' he says. Noyce finally returned with *Heatwave*, a drama about journalist Kate Dean's efforts to expose corruption in Sydney after the mysterious disappear-ance of activist Juanita Nielsen. It starred Judy Davis and was released in 1982, a golden year for Australian filmmaking, when local films accounted for more than 15 per cent of the total box office (in the early 2000s that figure has languished to nearer 5 per cent). The hit list included *The Man from Snowy River*, *The Year of Living Dangerously*, which launched director Peter Weir's Hollywood career, and Gillian Armstrong's zany musical comedy *Star Struck*. But the early 10BA system, which was introduced in June 1981 and allowed investors to reap a 150 per cent tax deduction, also resulted in some of the worst Australian films ever made. Typical was the film with no narrative, *Corpse*; and *Snow: The Movie*, a comedy shot at the Falls Creek ski resort in Victoria, complete with wet T-shirt contest. Noyce knew immediately the 10BA scheme 'wasn't going to last forever'. In fact, the government began winding it back soon after its launch. It exists today in a much-reduced form.

The mid-80s also saw the introduction of video and a resultant decline in box office attendance. 'I thought television would be my future,' Noyce says. So he began working with Dr George Miller and Byron Kennedy, who were producing landmark mini-series such as *The Cowra Breakout, Vietnam, Bangkok Hilton* and *The Dismissal* for Network Ten. Around this time Noyce was also attached to *Saigon*, a TV series intended for the Nine Network and CBS America that was eventually scuppered by CBS, which was wary of the drama's anti-Vietnam war stance. *Saigon* morphed into another script and eventually proved the trigger for Noyce to make *The Quiet American* in 2000.

The Dismissal managed to make the dry world of Canberra politics appear less dry. And, through directing the first two episodes of *The Cowra Breakout*, Phillip Noyce discovered his future lay in feature films of a particular genre – thrillers. *The Cowra Breakout* is a 'long story of escape by a thousand Japanese prisoners of war from the camp in the New South Wales countryside in 1944', as Noyce describes it. While researching the opening, he came across a story of two soldiers, the only surviving members of their warring Japanese and Australian units, caught in a clearing in the middle of the New Guinea jungle. He incorporated that story into episode two. 'So there I was directing a 47-minute film that featured a Japanese machine gunner, holed up inside his bunker with his dead comrade and facing, about 100 metres away, an Australian solider marooned in a shell hole with his dead comrade,' Noyce says. 'Neither could move for fear the other would kill them.' It was his first exercise in manipulating tension, creating a thriller. 'Two men, two guns and a cleared space in the middle of the jungle,' he says simply. 'By accident I realised I liked working within those restrictions, exploiting those tensions. And that led to *Dead Calm*,' the film that broke him in America.

Joan Scott also played a part. She had shown *Newsfront* to many people including Tony Bill, producer of *The Sting*, director of *My Bodyguard*, actor and famous LA restaurateur. He had tried unsuccessfully to help Noyce finance *Heatwave*. Some time later Noyce dropped in on Bill in Los Angeles. 'As I was going out the door he said, "Hey, wait a minute. You've got a lot of water down in Australia, maybe you'd like to do this"', and he threw me a manuscript,' Noyce says. It would prove career-making. It was a photocopy of Charles Williams's novel *The Deep*, which Orson Welles attempted to film in 1970.

'Welles, as became his habit, ran out of money', and only made a quarter of a film, Noyce explains. 'But it was even more complicated on this one because his star, Laurence Harvey, died of cancer [and] he tried to complete the film using a double but was not able to, there was too much footage to shoot.' Welles's salvage attempts appear doubly insurmountable considering *Dead Calm*'s structure – three actors (a married couple, played in Noyce's version by Nicole Kidman and Sam Neill, with Billy Zane as a crazed intruder) and two boats at sea with no land in sight. There's no covering for an absent actor there.

Bill had been trying, in vain, to secure the film rights to the novel for years, Noyce says. His efforts were thwarted by Oja Kodah, the Serbian actress who not only played Rae

Ingram (Kidman's role) in the film but was also Welles's de facto wife, and hence de facto widow after his death in 1985. 'Kodah jealously guarded the film rights from the Hollywood establishment, which she thought had persecuted Welles,' he says. Bill represented that Hollywood establishment.

Bill recalls, 'It was just very hard to get the rights.' He happily relinquished the struggle to Noyce. He was a fan of *Newsfront* and thought Noyce could make a fist of *The Deep*, despite it being a very different type of movie. 'I know a good director when I see one,' he shrugs. Noyce read the script and relayed the story to George Miller, himself already a dab hand at visceral thrillers. Miller 'loved it'. Bill let the Aussie duo run with it. 'George, being an outsider, an ex-doctor [and possessing] a wonderful bedside manner was able to convince Kodah we were not part of the Hollywood establishment,' Noyce notes. Ironically, Miller later sold the film to the Warner Brothers studio, very much the Hollywood establishment.

'It was probably a manuscript I wouldn't have been interested in before making *The Cowra Breakout*,' Noyce confides. Despite launching the careers of all its principals – Noyce, Kidman, Neill and Zane – *Dead Calm* earned remarkably little money in Australia: $3 million. Success came later on video and coincided with Neill's new-found international success in *The Hunt for Red October* and *Jurassic Park* (in which, Noyce gaily points out, he wears an outfit identical to the one he wore in *Dead Calm* – confirmation that Hollywood is the world headquarters of reinvention).

Warners released *Dead Calm* in the US a few weeks before Australia. Noyce says that's when 'the phone started ringing with amazing offers'. 'I was almost forty and I thought I really should finally take advantage of the opportunity to establish a beachhead somewhere else, particularly as before *Dead Calm* I had mainly been doing television,' Noyce recalls. For his part, Bill was thrilled with the outcome. 'He did a better job than I would have done,' he says magnanimously.

During the 80s, the potential for the Australian film industry exploded. The triumph of *Crocodile Dundee* had, at the very least, informed American audiences that Australians spoke English as a first language. Elsewhere, Miller, Weir, Fred Schepisi and Bruce Beresford had established their names in Hollywood. Consequently, Noyce's ambitions grew. 'Although we had great opportunities in Australia, no matter how much money was available, there still wasn't enough to go around for all the skilled filmmakers. Coming to America was coming to a meritocracy. You didn't have to play politics with committees, be judged by your peers, or worry about who you were nice to at cocktail parties [in case] they [were] deciding on your future,' Noyce says of the Australian industry as it was then – and remains. And Hollywood fascinated him, as it does many directors in Australia who limp from one grant to another, their careers governed by luck and resilience rather than talent. In Hollywood different rules exist, Noyce observes: if you make a financially or critically successful movie, there is a very good chance you will make another one. Of course, there was a chance he might make a film that was neither financially nor critically successful but 'I was willing to walk that tightrope. I wanted to make movies and I was being offered many of them.'

'The Americans [have] erected an incredibly ruthless system for distributing films [and] the result is constant production,' he adds. 'Perhaps [their] greatest achievement has been to convince us our lives are not full unless lived through the stories Hollywood sends out to us as filmed entertainment, be it television or movies.' That system resulted in Noyce's constant employment – he didn't stop making movies for the next ten years. 'As the antidote to being in Australia, it was the perfect medicine, maybe too perfect,' he says. 'I became satiated, I just went from one picture to the next.'

In many ways, *Dead Calm* was an excellent bridging vehicle: Miller was already working in Hollywood (he shot *The Witches of Eastwick* while Noyce was directing *Dead Calm*); Noyce's three actors hankered for Hollywood careers, which made them keen to promote the movie in the US; and the sale to Warners proceeded early, giving the studio a say in the film's final cut.

In Australia then, even now, distributors rarely had the clout to force changes to a film because only rarely would they have invested a sufficiently significant amount of money in it. Also, changes can be prohibitively expensive once a film is finished, sometimes costing millions of dollars. It is a very different situation in the US, where studios control projects closely.

'[*Dead Calm*'s] sale to Warners was dependent on us showing we were willing to work with them.' Noyce testifies he was fine with that. Besides, with Hollywood beckoning, it was time for the veteran of three features, numerous short films and several episodes of ground-breaking TV to become acquainted with compromise. He'd already left for the US to direct *Blind Fury*, a low-budget comedy action picture for the Tristar studio (subsequently acquired by Sony). Tristar executives had seen Noyce's *Cowra Breakout* jungle sequence. That was enough.

Seen within the context of Noyce's cranking career as a director of thrillers in the late 80s and early 90s, *Blind Fury* is a quirky diversion. Shot for about US$6 million, using non-union labour in Texas and Nevada, it stars Rutger Hauer as a Vietnam veteran and swordsman with almost supernatural powers. Noyce made it during the editing and reworking of *Dead Calm*'s denouement. He's sanguine about that movie being refashioned in his absence. 'I didn't know if it would be better or not. I didn't pay for the movie,' he explains. 'We debated it and discussed what we would do and it seemed as though we were not connecting with the audience. Worldwide cinema distribution was dependent on making the changes [which] were certainly in the spirit of the film, which after all was a thriller.'

In *Dead Calm*'s original cut, the bad guy (Zane) disappeared, presumed drowned although his corpse wasn't seen. In the final version, a flare fired by Sam Neill's character blazes a hole through his chest. Not so ambiguous. This new ending emphasised the upended relationship between Rae and her husband. Rae started the journey paralysed by the loss of her child and comforted by her strong naval captain husband. In the final scene, Neill's character is nursed by his now strengthened wife.

'That story still sort of existed [in the original ending] but after we finished the movie, we found audiences were expecting the Billy Zane character to come back,' Noyce points out. 'He had resurrected himself several times [already] and the so-called *Carrie* ending was in vogue – where someone you thought was dead suddenly sprang back to life, only to be dispatched yet again.' The original scriptwriter Terry Hayes (a Kennedy Miller stalwart) and Miller rescripted the ending and Noyce returned to Australia to shoot it.

In the 80s, research from test screenings gained influence, and publicity, when disgruntled directors argued with results. 'Over the last five years, increasingly people tend to make their own assessments of test screening findings,' Noyce says. But in *Dead Calm*'s time, 'research and test screenings, which had been going on since the late twenties in Hollywood, suddenly were enriched, or dumbed-down – depending on your point of view – by the addition of the computer. What previously had been based mainly on intuition, suddenly was tabulated and computer[s] spat out all sorts of pronouncements about what was needed,' says Noyce, still sounding shocked by the innovation. Essentially, processing results by computer meant the questions and answers changed from qualitative 'hows' and 'whys' to quantitative, or numerical, identifiers. Instead of asking someone what they liked about a film and why, now they were merely asked to rate the film on a scale of one to ten, for instance. Suddenly, a studio executive could see the morning after a screening that only 15 or 10 per cent of audience members would recommend the movie. Raw numbers are much bolder statements.

Joe Farrell's National Research Group revolutionised the research process. Its most famous success was *Fatal Attraction*, which had been testing disastrously. After Farrell's advice, director Adrian Lyne ensured the protagonist (Glenn Close) met a brutal end. Afterwards it tested almost perfectly and became a top-grossing movie. 'Suddenly all power was based in Joe's computer and the hundreds of nerds around Hollywood who attended these screenings,' Noyce says. But directors hate testing, they find it insulting.

'What you have to remember is right at the beginning of this whole process here in Hollywood I quickly realised that the machine is essentially a marketing machine,' he adds. 'It helps if the movies are good but it doesn't really matter, not really.' Noyce's early pragmatism was a key to his future success. Once ensconced in Hollywood, even more pragmatism is required. Budgets are bigger, stakes are high-

'It helps if the movies are good but it doesn't really matter, not really'

er, overpaid stars develop egos commensurate with their fees and there's always a studio executive or producer ready to step in and finish the film without you. In an interview with the *Bulletin* to mark the release of 1992's *Patriot Games*, Noyce commented, 'One of the advantages of making films in Australia was the freedom to make almost any movie you wanted. One of the disadvantages was that so few of these movies have been seen by anyone.' *Patriot Games* would be seen by more than 10 million Americans during its theatrical release.

In 1990, Noyce took a deep breath and leapt in. At the invitation of John Goldwyn, head of production for MGM, he moved the family to LA. 'We moved into the Chateau Marmont on Sunset [Boulevard], room 31. This amazing suite just above the foyer where we had three bedrooms, this huge balcony, a kitchen and bathroom all for US$100 a night because of the benevolence of the manager – an Irishman who liked the idea of having a family,' Noyce smiles. 'The family grew bigger because it became a way station for orphaned Australians. Kidman spent some time there, as did Ken Cameron, Cameron Allan the composer and others.'

The Noyces lived there for nine months, during which time Phillip was employed by Brandon Tartikoff – 'the whiz kid of American television drama' and then head of production at the NBC TV network – to make a pilot for a series called *Nightmare Café*. Shortly afterwards, Pike was appointed chairman of Paramount Pictures, which needed a director for *Patriot Games*, an adaptation of Tom Clancy's novel which was to follow the 1990 Clancy hit *The Hunt for Red October*. Alec Baldwin was set to reprise his role as the CIA analyst Jack Ryan in the sequel but he'd earned a reputation for being difficult, particularly on the film he'd just finished for Disney, *The Marrying Man*, in which he'd starred with his future wife, Kim Basinger.

'The studio and Alec were unable to reach agreement on some minor points of his contract and as it happened Harrison Ford was just about to star in a movie at Paramount which at the last minute was cancelled – the budget had come in too high,' Noyce says. 'So, suddenly Harrison had a contract to do a thriller at Paramount but no movie and Baldwin pulled out of *Patriot Games* as a negotiating ploy, saying he'd prefer to play Stanley Kowalski on Broadway in *A Streetcar Named Desire*. When he walked out, the studio didn't chase him and we immediately approached Ford, who agreed to play Jack Ryan.'

It was convenient for all but Baldwin, 'who walked away from what may have continued to be a successful series [for him]'. Ford was at the peak of his popularity, even if he'd just appeared in a relative failure, Mike Nichols's *Regarding Henry*. '[*Patriot Games*] was the ideal vehicle for Harrison,' Noyce notes. It was ideal for the Australian too. Its budget was reported as close to double the combined budget of Noyce's previous four films and because it was part of a studio franchise, a crucial summer release date was secured long before shooting began. It would become an 'event movie'.

When *Patriot Games* was released, Noyce spoke of the on-set fatigue he felt while clocking six-day weeks for five solid months. He didn't realise it was the beginning of what would be almost a decade of continuous production. 'From one picture to another, all of them with [US] summer release dates,' he notes. 'The day we decided to do the picture would be the same day they gave us the release date. I went from *Patriot Games*, had two weeks holiday; did *Sliver*, had no holiday; started *Clear and Present Danger*, had no holiday; and did *The Saint*, then had about six months off before starting *The Bone Collector*.'

It was an orgy of popcorn movies fit for studio tastes and they couldn't get enough of Mr Noyce. Nor could he get enough of it. 'The studio system is very spoiling,' he says. 'When people estimate a budget, it really is an estimate because there's always this studio that'll keep furrowing more cash in. In Australia we grew up having to make films for a price – and still do. There *is* no more money. If you go over budget you don't finish the movie.' In fact, Noyce went over budget just twice in his Hollywood career – on *The Saint* and slightly over on *Clear and Present Danger*. 'You wouldn't call it over budget in [Hollywood] terms, it was less than five per cent on each,' he counters.

'When we came to America, [Australian] directors and cinematographers in particular were seen as being very practical – shooting only what they needed, and lightning fast,' he says. Also, 'Paul Hogan did a lot for the mystique of Australians; everyone thought every Australian was a sort of Mick Dundee,' Noyce laughs. 'Which

'*Hollywood is like a vampire, just sucks the talent out of newcomers*'

was great, [so Americans] usually gave you more credit than you were due,' he adds. 'It's not nearly as ferocious as it is back in the penal colony' because Hollywood wants new talent and wants it to succeed. 'Hollywood is like a vampire, just sucks the talent out of newcomers. Whether it's making US$100 million movies, US$100 000 movies or television, it has a voracious appetite year-round.'

Noyce sated that appetite during the 90s. He delivered Paramount US$83 million box office for *Patriot Games* in America alone. He then took on *Basic Instinct*'s Sharon Stone in *Sliver*. Again, a Noyce ending was altered after test screenings. The original had the New York book editor (Stone) and her voyeuristic lover (Billy Baldwin) fly into an exploding Hawaiian volcano as 'the ultimate sexual act'. That was too enigmatic for audiences who wanted a villain.

It's often said that having final cut is proof of a director's clout. Noyce says it's not that simple. He had final cut on his

first three films and *Rabbit-Proof Fence* and *The Quiet American*.
Miller had final cut on *Dead Calm*. Noyce didn't have final cut
on the Paramount movies but all the final cuts were his: that is,
the studio didn't invoke its right to recut. 'They were frequent-
ly compromised but only because I listened to what people had
to say. You make the issue of final cut a non-issue by incorpo-
rating other people's ideas, or at least trying them out. The
screening process allows that to happen. You try something and
if it works, it ends up in the movie,' he explains. 'Having the
ingredients to market [is] the achievement.'

Noyce admits he has 'made movies that were good, bad
and in between'. Either way, 'it didn't matter to the studio. All
that mattered was how were they going to sell it? The publicity team were usually coming through the door a couple of
days after the production team and they were with you right
through the movie. So when you look back on those test
screenings it was the perfect illustration of the real preoccupation of Hollywood: which is [having] a product to sell.'

Noyce 'sold' Jack Ryan's character again in *Clear and Present
Danger* (for worldwide box office of US$122 million) before
directing a contentious adaptation of British spy series *The Saint*,
which had the potential to become a James Bond-type franchise
but didn't. 'Paramount didn't have confidence, they said, in the
actor but I think possibly they probably thought its worldwide
box office wasn't high enough. It cost US$58 million [and
returned US$68 million in the US, plus returns from the rest of
the world]; it would have made a little money but not much.' At
least, not enough to repeat the exercise.

Noyce rejected Russell Crowe's bid to play the Saint, ditto
George Clooney, who Noyce had wanted for the *Nightmare
Café* pilot years before. The studio told Noyce Clooney was
'one of a thousand pretty faces that's been hanging around in
the Hollywood Hills for years going nowhere'. 'In my incredi-

ble wisdom [I] chose Val Kilmer,' Noyce smirks. Kilmer had a
beyond-Baldwin reputation for indulgent behaviour. 'Val was
always tiresome but you had to admire his incredible talent,'
notes the director.

Only after Noyce had truly established himself did he have
the clout to cast unknowns, such as future Academy Award
winner Angelina Jolie, in *The Bone Collector*. The studio said
she and Denzel Washington were not big enough. Noyce retal-
iated by asking the executives to nominate what budget they
were worth. They said US$45 million. So that's what he com-
mitted to make the movie for. He also volunteered to cover any
cost overruns from his own pay cheque. The studio made him
confirm this deal in writing. 'We ended up making it for
US$42.5 [million], then worldwide box office was US$140 million. I think it was just profitable,' he deadpans.

'Whether I made good films, bad films or in between, they
always seemed to make money, which is what kept me going
from movie to movie,' he says. 'I might have started out making art movies in Australia but when I came to Hollywood I
quickly realised I wasn't making that kind of movie.' But there
comes a time when blockbusters and their higher fees lose
allure. 'Ultimately they're less rewarding, particularly as you
get older and realise there's a limited number of movies you
can make in the whole rest of your life,' he concedes. '[So] you
better make the right decision about how you're going to
spend 18 months. I figure I've got the energy, and if I'm lucky
and find the finance, to make maybe five more films. So I certainly don't want to waste time on the wrong ones.'

Thus his return to 'art' cinema with an assured Graham
Greene adaptation, *The Quiet American*, and a triumphant
return home with *Rabbit-Proof Fence*. 'I was sick of the star
system.' Far more appealing was 'the idea of having three little kids that surely must do what they are told, as opposed to

the movie stars I'd been working with, who you had to walk a tightrope of negotiation with,' he says with a wink. (On *Rabbit-Proof Fence*, one of the three young Aboriginal actresses, Everlyn Sampi, was prone to occasional truancy. Ironic behaviour given the film, a collaboration between black and white filmmakers, is about three Aboriginal girls who run away from their white-run school for domestic servants.)

Having made the switch, Noyce is hooked. He is developing adaptations of Tim Winton's *Dirt Music* and Phillip Roth's *American Pastoral*. Meanwhile, he directed an advertisement for Manulife Insurance to ensure cashflow for his company, Rumbalara. But in 1999, when Noyce told his old friend, *Newsfront* producer David Elfick, he intended to make *Rabbit-Proof Fence*, Elifick 'seriously doubted' it would ever happen. He doubted Phillip could relinquish the trappings of Hollywood, come home and, for a miniscule budget, make an 'Aboriginal film,' hitherto considered 'box office death'.

Elfick's doubts were unfounded. Noyce explains, 'Making a film that was not pre-sold, and therefore pre-masticated, was exciting; it was like being young again. The movies I'd been making were guaranteed to work because they had [advertising budgets] and big movie stars that would pulverise the audience so they couldn't exist unless they saw the movie. It was becoming too easy and too predictable. They'd find me a book, I'd find a star, they'd spend US$30 million and it had to come first at the box office. It seemed like a formula and that wasn't why I started making movies.'

Rabbit-Proof Fence allowed Phillip Noyce to 'reinvent myself'. 'Hopefully, in the nick of time I've managed to resurrect myself as a filmmaker because there's nothing worse than a Hollywood hack and [I was] on the edge of feeling I'd become one.' As creatively revitalising as those projects were, Noyce faced a battle on each release. Elfick, who executive produced

Rabbit-Proof Fence, says he had to find an extra $2 million to pay for three more filming sessions. Noyce also clashed with the Australian distributors over the trailer. A situation in which 'everybody lost', Elfick says.

In the US, Miramax decided to shelve *The Quiet American*. The studio had paid US$5.5 million to distribute the movie, which stars Michael Caine, in the US, UK and South America. Within months, Osama bin Laden had unleashed suicide bombers on the US and the mood in America shifted from one in which self-criticism was tolerated to a siege mentality. *The Quiet American* takes a caustic view of American foreign policy, and post-September 11, 2001 'was not a time to receive such a message in America', Noyce says. 'Previews went from OK, to bad, to worse, to disastrous.'

The following August (2002) he was not surprised to be told Miramax was not going to release the movie at all. That's when Caine stepped in and refused to publicise another Miramax movie, *The Actors*, if studio boss Harvey Weinstein didn't at the very least let *The Quiet American* screen in the upcoming Toronto Film Festival. Caine's action was part-altruism, part-selfishness – he knew his performance was possibly his last shot at an Academy Award nomination.

Noyce engaged a publicist who had blacklisted him during the Paramount blockbuster years but agreed to work with him again now he was making 'quality movies'. The publicist set about lobbying film writers. 'This created the potential for it to be well received because suddenly it was an underdog, a threatened species,' Noyce says. Weinstein eventually allowed *The Quiet American* to screen at Toronto where, lo and behold, it was lauded by critics. 'Suddenly people were rushing to defend the movie from censorship,' Noyce says. The campaign culminated in a *Washington Post* editorial, 'Let The Quiet American Speak', while fortuitously coinciding with a public debate on the need to go to war in Iraq. Miramax acquiesced and released the movie in December, within the Oscar qualifying period. Caine secured his nomination.

'The next time I saw Harvey he said, "I want you to pay me US$1000 for every time you've defamed me – but don't stop because it's working! You've positioned this film as the ultimate underdog so let's not let anyone think otherwise, at least until after it's been released",' Noyce chortles.

He still marvels at Hollywood's allure despite having seen its ugly side. Noyce recalls his children's babysitter when the family first arrived in LA, Miss Dee, who loved coming to their house where she could read 'the trades' (*Variety* and the *Hollywood Reporter* newspapers) to see what was in production or development. She was seventy-six but had come to Hollywood in the 30s, after being crowned beauty queen in her small town. The prize was a screen test in Hollywood, she'd done the test and many since but she never won a part. Yet she remained hopeful.

'The pot of gold is always around the corner, or the next corner'

'The [depressing] thing about being in Australia was to watch people around me, even at forty, giving up because of the lack of opportunity. They thought they'd exhausted the possibilities.' In Hollywood, he says, 'The pot of gold is always around the corner, or the next corner.'

08

frances
o'connor

Pivotal Projects

Iron Jawed Angels (2004), Timeline (2003), A.I. Artificial Intelligence (2001)

Bedazzled (2000), Mansfield Park (1999), Thank God He Met Lizzie (1997)

Kiss or Kill (1997), Love and Other Catastrophes (1996)

frances

Eight years ago, in a café overlooking Melbourne's Yarra River, Frances O'Connor was all giggles and charm. Then twenty-eight, she was excited about the future and seemingly content. Why wouldn't she be? It was a fresh spring afternoon and she was in that enticing place actors sometimes find themselves – not knowing what the future holds but optimistic they might realise their every dream. O'Connor had completed three Australian films in quick succession – *Love and Other Catastrophes*, *Thank God He Met Lizzie* and *Kiss or Kill* – earned AFI Award nominations for each and was suddenly Australia's 'It girl'.

Four years later, in Sydney's Sheraton on the Park hotel, O'Connor was a different person, every inch a star while promoting the English period piece *Mansfield Park*. No more giggles though. That day, she was a dazed star, in another galaxy, still coming to terms with a phone call confirming she had been cast in Steven Spielberg's *A.I.*, the film the master director assumed when Stanley Kubrick died. Interestingly, O'Connor and Eric Bana are the only Australians Spielberg has cast in major roles.

'In another world?' O'Connor asks two years later. 'Maybe I was just happy.' You can't begrudge her that. She aspired to be a film actor when young, chose that risky path despite her parents' doubts and learnt her craft on the Australian stage.

She was a fan, became an actor and is now a star.

O'Connor was born in Oxford, England, to a musician mother, while her research scientist father completed his PhD. They returned to Australia's western-most capital city, Perth, two years later in 1971.

Frances was the third of five siblings. They would later become a violinist, viola player, environmental scientist and botanist. Yet when O'Connor was a teenager her parents disapproved of her artistic aspirations despite her love of movies. In fact, as a 15 year old she wrote in her diary 'I've decided I'm going to be an actress and I am going to keep it secret and not tell Mum and Dad.' Later, fearing disapproval, O'Connor burst into tears when she told her father she wanted to be an actress.

'Most actors these days grow up with a film culture and it's very hard not to fall in love with it,' she says now. 'I love theatre and it will always be a big part of my life but I've always been in love with film.' Judy Davis's strength in *My Brilliant Career* was influential. 'It looked like an international film but it was ours,' she says.

O'Connor completed a Bachelor of Arts degree before spending a year teaching in Japan. On returning, she promptly enrolled at the Western Australia Academy of Performing Arts (WAAPA), the institution that also primed Hugh Jackman. O'Connor shone and prominent Sydney talent agent Robyn Gardiner agreed to represent her. Roger Hodgman, then artistic director of the Melbourne Theatre Company, directed O'Connor's final year production of Shakespeare's *As You Like It*. 'She had been non-democratically cast as Second Lord and I said, if you come to Melbourne we'll give you some work,' Hodgman recalls. O'Connor debuted at the MTC in *The Dutch Courtesan* with Geoffrey Rush in 1993. 'It was as random as that,' she says. 'I decided to live in Melbourne because I got a bit of work and just ended up staying.'

Hodgman nurtured O'Connor. *The Dutch Courtesan* was followed by roles in *The Herbal Bed, Kid Stakes* and *Much Ado About Nothing*, among others. The MTC proved a fertile acting ground with Rush, Hugo Weaving and Rachel Griffiths (whom O'Connor played opposite in *The Grapes of Wrath*) all starring there in the mid-90s. O'Connor was an assured stage performer not prone to drawing attention to herself. More of a classical actor, she was fine and deliberate. On screen she won minor roles in TV drama series such as *Law of the Land* and *GP*, with one performance in the forensics drama *Halifax f.p.* gaining her most attention.

A friendship with budding film director Emma-Kate Croghan proved crucial. Croghan believed O'Connor suited the role as the love-addled Mia in her micro-budget feature, *Love and Other Catastrophes*. Despite O'Connor's low expectations, the cute film about odd love on the Melbourne University campus became a cultish cause célèbre. It made a splash incommensurate with its size at a market screening at the 1996 Cannes Film Festival and eventually propelled O'Connor, Croghan and Radha Mitchell to Hollywood, although Croghan's film career has lost its early momentum.

'That was pretty surreal because that was the first film we ever did, we made it for no money and I remember seeing a rough cut and thinking, oh God, this is terrible, because I'd never seen a rough cut before!' O'Connor laughs. She was shocked seeing the final product and 'realising it was pretty good'.

Cannes was a frenetic, chaotic and seductive experience for the young actors and director, overawed by their first trip to the south of France, seeing stars they'd long admired and acquiring 'a taste of the international [scene]'. Not that O'Connor thought that scene accessible: 'I always wanted to work overseas but I didn't think that would be the film to do it,' she says. 'But it just struck a chord with a lot of kids our age.' And it won her an AFI Award Best Actress nomination.

Next was the romantic tragicomedy *Thank God He Met Lizzie*, opposite Cate Blanchett and Richard Roxburgh. 'It didn't end up doing that well but it's a good little film,' she notes. Director Cherie Nowlan's debut didn't garner any attention in the United States, despite its prescient casting. Bill Bennett's road movie *Kiss or Kill* did, though.

In the noir-ish thriller O'Connor played an Aussie femme fatale, Nikki. O'Connor's performance as the exuberant Jenny in *Thank God He Met Lizzie* is superior but *Kiss or Kill* was the critical favourite, with an Academy Award campaign for her performance even hinted. She laughs at those 'upbeat media stories' because the film only registered on the independent circuit in the US. 'A lot of people in the industry saw it and loved it. That's all I really needed to get my next gig. But no, I don't think the Academy members had heard of that one!'

In November 1997, O'Connor earned dual Best Actress AFI Award nominations for the two performances. Her votes probably negated each other and Pamela Rabe's performance in the tedious art piece, *The Well*, swooped for the win. It didn't matter. *Kiss or Kill* delivered on *Love and Other Catastrophes*' promise. Its genre and O'Connor's gritty acting ensured 'it was a huge calling card in America', she says. 'It got me into a lot of rooms for auditions; helped me a lot.'

O'Connor flew to Hollywood after her Australian agent organised the requisite talent agency meetings. She signed with the biggest, Creative Artists Agency (CAA) and Kevin Huvane, because she thought it would offer her the most opportunities. 'It's very corporate over there and sometimes it's about the individual [agency] but often it's about who's got the strongest network of people.' CAA has that and the power. O'Connor hasn't regretted her decision. She required someone who not only believed in her talent but would also push her cause.

Nevertheless, it took an English film to establish O'Connor as a Hollywood prospect. '*Kiss or Kill* and *Love and Other Catastrophes* put me in good stead overseas but it was in some ways like starting again,' O'Connor admits. 'It's a slight fabrication [to say] I did those films, then got snapped up in Hollywood and did some big movies. It took some work. I had to make contacts and in some ways it [was] like starting again. Nobody knew who I was.'

Thankfully, a number of English directors were willing to gamble on the unknown beauty. Thankfully, because O'Connor decided London would be a more comfortable home than Los Angeles. Her first two international opportunities came in England; the first, *About Adam,* was a wan romantic comedy co-starring Kate Hudson.

She retained her American agent though, and while doing her first auditions in Los Angeles and 'adjusting to the LA way of doing things – it was pretty full on', her British agent urged her to return to the United Kingdom to discuss a period film called *Mansfield Park*. She met the Canadian director, Patricia Rozema (*When Night is Falling*), 'and we really clicked'. Soon after, while readying herself to return to the Melbourne stage, Rozema offered her the lead role of Fanny Price. 'Fran is a real person, not a Barbie doll,' says Rozema. 'In the audition she had that kind of shy, nervous, intelligent energy that I could imagine for a writer, which was what she was in my film.'

O'Connor had conservative expectations of the small film, as is her wont. 'I don't ever think [what] a movie's going to do for my career,' she says. 'I'm just an actor and I get a job, work on the character, try and do what the director wants and enjoy the process. I don't ever think, is this movie going to put me in the A list?'

Mansfield Park didn't put her on the A List, but it did put her within reach of it. She delivered a sublime performance in a refreshingly creative retelling of Jane Austen's most difficult novel, what Rozema calls her 'colonial Austen'. It became a popular arthouse film with audiences and critics appreciative of O'Connor's performance. The *San Francisco*

'I don't ever think, is this movie going to put me in the A list?'

Chronicle noted, 'Rozema is good with actors, and in her hands O'Connor gives us a Fanny who is self-assured without being a feminist caricature.' Britain's *Sight and Sound* described O'Connor as 'radiant'.

Rozema admits O'Connor provided her own strong performance. 'Fran would go 40 takes if I let her, she loves to work. She was the easiest actor to deal with: full of ideas but open to direction, creative but disciplined, and very, very funny. I'd like to do an outright comedy with her one day.'

If *Kiss or Kill* and *Love and Other Catastrophes* catapulted O'Connor out of Australia, *Mansfield Park* catapulted her to Hollywood. That was the aim, she concedes, although she has a more romantic view of the journey. 'You always hope it will lead to more work. It comes from when you were sixteen and wanted to be a famous movie star,' she laughs. 'You're watching TV and think, I want to do that. On some level, that small little seed is there. For most people, maybe they wouldn't admit it, but that's true.' It can't be manufactured though. 'How do you explain when people ask why did you decide to do this film when often it's just because we want to work?' she asks.

Bedazzled was merely one of a number of US films for which she auditioned. She took it because she loved co-star Brendan Fraser in the arthouse piece *Gods and Monsters*, and the remake of Dudley Moore and Peter Cook's 1968 cult comedy offered the opportunity to play many different characters.

O'Connor wasn't nervous, she laughs: 'I was just glad to get my first Hollywood gig,' despite realising there would be opposition to the remaking of a classic. Moving to a light, commercial comedy was also a refreshing change. 'You think, I'm going to be in one of those films like *Working Girl*,' she laughs.

While film productions are similar beasts worldwide, the amount of money spent on them is not. After starting out in the reported $35 000-budget *Love and Other Catastrophes*, then the US$10 million *Mansfield Park*, O'Connor was suddenly on a US$35 million movie. And on a Hollywood studio lot. She felt like a tourist, the film's myriad historical locations and costumes adding to her feeling of being in an old 30s or 40s film.

Bedazzled was also a freer Hollywood set than O'Connor would become accustomed to, at least freer than her next film. '[*Bedazzled* director] Harold Ramis is just a hippy and a Buddhist at heart too, so it was relaxed on set,' she says. 'I thought it would be more hierarchical. *A.I.* was very secretive, I only got the script pages I was working on, never read the whole thing through once, had to read in a special room and the sets were very closed, no-one could visit, so it was all a little surreal.' As were the indulgent budgets. She soon saw how money creates monsters. 'You don't have to buy into that,' she adds. 'You've got a choice to either be professional or not. We're all the same, all making a movie, and no job is more important than another. I love that feeling you're all working on this thing together and the great feeling of community.'

'We're all the same, all making a movie, and no job is more important than another'

O'Connor's micro-community in Hollywood was working for her, Huvane's clout making a difference. Huvane gave another of his clients, Steven Spielberg, a tape of *Mansfield*

Park. That was enough for Spielberg. Rozema recalls later meeting Spielberg at *A.I.*'s New York premiere, where he told her, 'Oh, it's because of your wonderful film that I hired Frances.'

O'Connor laughs that her first meeting with the most successful director of all time was 'a slightly out of body experience. It would only be my second film in LA and to be told Steven Spielberg wants to meet you!' Prior to their meeting, O'Connor was overwhelmed by the idea she was about to 'meet Steven Spielberg'. At the allotted time she was ushered into his office at Amblin Entertainment. 'He was quite shy and in that kind of situation I can be pretty shy so it was hard,' she says. 'But when I actually got down to it, it was like meeting another director, a very interesting guy, fantastic to talk to and he has such a great brain . . . It was surreal though, because Tom Cruise turned up at the end to watch a baseball match with him. So I was, OK, there's Tom Cruise,' she deadpans. The 15-year-old fan stirred deep inside her. 'All those fantasies you have of ever making it, at that point I thought I'd fulfilled them in a way.'

O'Connor won the role as the adoptive mother of a robot boy (Haley Joel Osment) with minimum fuss, just a couple of meetings. The role was tough due to the plot's strong mother–son abandonment issues and the high stakes in almost every scene. 'I had this very strong story to act and I'm working for Steven Spielberg, so I had two things going on,' she admits. Due to a short pre-production, she had little time to talk about the role and worried about how she would realise it but 'as it progressed I felt more of a personal connection to [Spielberg],' she says.

The US$90 million movie was a stretch for multiplex audiences, a meditation rather than an entertainment, both mismarketed and misunderstood. But a disappointment for the master director, in this case global box office of US$235 million, is a success for most. And it placed O'Connor in a higher realm.

Yet *Mansfield Park* was still working for O'Connor: 'It all leads back to *Mansfield Park*.' Action director John Woo saw it and invited O'Connor to play a nurse in his war drama *Windtalkers*, but she wasn't available. Then another actor pulled out and Woo asked O'Connor again. This time she was available: 'It was six days work so I said sure, it'll be fun and I get to work with Nicolas Cage.'

After filming *Windtalkers*, which was delayed from release due to September 11 sensitivities before ultimately fizzling, O'Connor returned to London. The three US films meant she'd been away for a year. 'By the end I had a very different perspective on things – all you see is the business.' Her words echo other Australians who've lived in LA. Back 'in London I realised there are other aspects [to] life'.

It remains her preferred home due to its access to British and American work and her Scottish partner, Gerald Lepkowski, also an actor. 'It doesn't really matter where you live,' she says. In fact living elsewhere can be an advantage 'because it's like, "She's coming [to LA], let's get her to meet this person and that" rather than being constantly available and therefore taken for granted.'

While in LA, O'Connor had met the English director Oliver Parker. He later offered her the part of Gwendolen in his adaptation of Oscar Wilde's *The Importance of Being Earnest*. The offer, for her, was as momentous as the one from Spielberg. 'Just to be in the same room as Judi Dench, to sit and watch her work was fantastic,' she enthuses. So too with Colin Firth, Reese Witherspoon ('a brilliant comedian') and Rupert Everett. Not that she'd ever ask Dame Dench for advice. 'You have to be cooler than that. You have to think, I'm part of this. The best way to learn about acting is to watch someone do it.'

After *The Importance of Being Earnest*, which earned wavering reviews, O'Connor punted on theatre. Her agent advised against it because her three US films were generating 'a bit of heat' but she insisted on five months on London's West End playing Maggie in Tennessee Williams's *Cat on a Hot Tin Roof*. The role and the chance to work with Brendan Fraser again proved irresistible, even though the stunt casting of Hollywood stars on the West End was attracting ire. 'There will always be anti-American sentiment but the funniest thing was a lot of people thought I was American,' O'Connor says. 'I was, "No, I'm Australian but I was born here as well", but it was like "American film actress Frances O'Connor comes to London!"' American, British, whatever, O'Connor earned terrific notices, the *Guardian* stating she displayed 'exactly the right feline sexiness' and the *Independent* writing she was 'superbly pent up'.

'It was just fantastic, a great character and 900 people every night, packed out most of the time thanks to Brendan,' she humbly notes. O'Connor also used the season as a refresher course. 'It's a bit like going back to school in some ways, a lot harder than camera acting,' she says. 'They're different skills but you get to exercise your acting muscle a lot more [on stage].'

Her 'Hollywood heat' appeared to have survived her absence. She followed *Cat on a Hot Tin Roof* with two pieces that competed at the 2004 Sundance Film Festival (the HBO telemovie *Iron Jawed Angels*, with Hilary Swank and Anjelica Huston, and New York feature *Book of Love*, co-starring another Australian actor, Simon Baker) as well as Richard Donner's big-budget action adaptation of Michael Crichton's novel *Timeline*. Donner didn't even ask her to audition. Clearly a time for the head to swell.

'Well, I don't think I've reached a point where I'm so ultra-popular in Hollywood that I've had an opportunity to do that but I'm looking forward to that moment!' she laughs. Obviously, the division between jobs for art or money has become more distinct. O'Connor appears to be veering back to the art, with her 2004 booked by a number of smaller films, including the British period comedy *Piccadilly Jim*, co-starring Sam Rockwell and Allison Janney (and written by *Gosford Park*'s Julian Fellowes) and the Australian drama *Three Dollars*, opposite David Wenham and Sarah Wynter.

'Now I find it much easier to just get on with it, it seems much more like a job now whereas when I first started getting attention for *Love and Other Cat's* and *Kiss or Kill*, that's when I went, wow, this is amazing! and it was harder to keep my feet on the ground then, which is ironic. I think that's the story for everybody. Then, when you get to work with different people and become more established, it [becomes] more like, this is what I do,' she explains.

You also have the confidence to move to television, despite its occasional stigma. 'I'm not snobby like that anyway,' O'Connor contends. 'If it's a good part and you're working with good people, it doesn't matter.' One of those good parts was in Gregor Jordan's film *Ned Kelly*, but she couldn't schedule it. Her desire to do an Australian film remains strong. Not that she regrets her international work. 'Everybody has their moments but generally I've found it very stimulating, especially when you get to work with people like Anjelica Huston. When you're acting your pants off and having a great time, that's thrilling.'

It's all an actor can ask for: a career with satisfying moments. 'It's hard to have aspirations, you have to work with what's there,' O'Connor says. In many ways, training can't prepare you for those moments, she adds. 'You just have to go with it, see how you deal with it and hopefully you deal with it well. At the end of the day, you're working a scene and that can't be any more special than what you did at drama school. It's just another scene, just another director, and you have to think of it on that level. Sometimes it's different because there's politics involved or there's a different power structure because, say, you're working with a movie star earning US$20 million; then it's going to be all about them and you supporting them.'

O'Connor's not in that position, nor does she want to be. She's one of the more reserved actors one could meet, not one to feed off publicity. 'If I could just be an actor and do different projects with different people, I'd be very happy,' she admits. But the reality is, before they can become choosy, actors have to promote films and become valued faces that investors will back. 'No matter how good an actor you are, if your [box office] value's only so much, you're not going to get the part. It's totally financial and nothing to do with talent in some ways. It doesn't negate your work, who you're working with and what it's like on set working with good people but if you want to be in the film industry, that's a reality.'

Consequently, O'Connor retains a publicist, 'a necessity because there are so many commodities on the market'. And commodities need selling 'unless they're Nicole Kidman who's totally AA list and it's more about managing it. At my level it's more about keeping my profile up in the US' and 'poking you in the back to make you stand up straight on the red carpet', she laughs.

She seems content being known in the industry, being occasionally recognised but ultimately being able to lead a normal life. Media intrusion doesn't become a factor when 'I just don't read anything anymore'. Besides, she adds, 'because I'm regarded more as an actor than a movie star, people aren't as interested in twisting a story about me. It comes with the territory of being more a movie star than an actor.'

'I'm regarded more as an actor than a movie star'

As does the pressure for perfection. O'Connor concedes an industry based on aesthetics can be tough. 'If people don't want to look at your face, they don't want to look at your face,' she notes. 'In the Hollywood movie, the role of the woman is to be attractive to the male, it still very much exists on that level in the mainstream, so there are certain pressures. You have to make your own decision about how you feel about that. You've got to be true.'

'I would never have plastic surgery, I don't think. There's a culture that undermines women's beauty, and also men now too, so women never get to feel relaxed in themselves. American women kind of die inside because they're so worried about the exterior, whereas Australian and British women have more of a sense of their own value.'

Australian women also aided O'Connor's journey. 'They're so authentic, the ones who have made it,' she argues. 'They have a great sense of themselves, they're not girly-women, they're women. That tradition probably started with Judy Davis but I don't think they're copying her, it's just an innate Australian trait.'

'And because there are so many good Australian actors at the moment we are respected and seen as serious actors and good to work with. People want to work with Australian actors because we don't have an attitude.'

As for particular Australian traits that aid her, she concedes 'keeping it real and not being a wanker keeps you acting well, as does the Australian sense of humour'. Isolation helps, she adds. 'We develop our own sense of who we are. We look to America but we're very much our own culture.'

09
hugo
weaving

Pivotal Projects

The Lord of the Rings: The Return of the King (2003)

The Matrix Revolutions (2003), The Matrix Reloaded (2003)

The Lord of the Rings: The Two Towers (2002), After the Deluge (TV) (2002)

The Lord of the Rings: The Fellowship of the Ring (2001), The Matrix (1999)

The Interview (1998), The Adventures of Priscilla, Queen of the Desert (1994)

Proof (1991), Bodyline (TV) (1984)

hugo

Hugo Weaving's star has ascended with the rising fortunes of Australia's offshore film industry. He has become a Hollywood name by default. Without pursuing an international film career, or even desiring one, he co-starred in *The Matrix* and *The Lord of the Rings* trilogies, two seminal motion picture productions of the modern era. Will his blasé attitude towards 'Hollywood' spell the end of his Hollywood career now those series have run their course? 'Might well,' he laughs. 'I don't know. I probably do need to have a good chat with my agent ... I suppose.'

He doesn't seem to care. Weaving is an actor before a star, happier performing on stage in front of 500 than being projected to millions in a Hollywood film; happier on the set of an Australian film production than on a bombastic blockbuster.

When Hollywood came Down Under in the mid-1990s and early 2000s, at the invitation of the Australian and New Zealand governments eager to lure 'runaway' film and television productions and their apparent riches from the US, Weaving was ripe for the picking. He'd done the hard yards on stage and screen. The influx of made-in-Australia American productions — including *The Matrix*, *Pitch Black*, *Mission: Impossible 2* and *Star Wars: The Attack of the Clones* — brought new skills, brighter careers and money. They also initiated a boom or bust economic cycle that was dependent upon the largesse of capricious Hollywood studios and a weak Australian dollar.

Weaving was born in Nigeria and grew up with the South African rand and the English pound. He became an enthusiastic drama student, first inspired by screenings of *Lawrence of Arabia* and *Romeo and Juliet*. A South African school master stoked Weaving's enthusiasm with film screenings in the dining hall every second Saturday night. 'We saw some pretty great films like Lindsay Anderson's *if ...* and *Lord of the Flies*. To show these to 13- and 14-year-old boys was pretty cool.' He devoured any film he could watch.

Due to his father's itinerant work in the computer industry, Weaving's family briefly moved to England, where the student aspired to be a writer. Upon arriving in Australia in 1976 for his final two years' schooling, his interest in drama revived.

Weaving was accepted into NIDA, in Sydney, straight from school. 'I left the North Shore, came into town and hung out with a lot of students who were older than me,' he remembers. The 18 year old from an all-boys school suddenly found himself in coeducational classes where some students were a staggering 35 years old. 'Suddenly here I was with lots of gorgeous women. It was very liberating, a wonderful three years.'

After graduating in 1981, Weaving secured a two-year contract with the Sydney Theatre Company and then television work with the Kennedy Miller production company: 'They seemed to [have] better scripts when the films were really not good'. Through Kennedy Miller he secured roles in *Dirtwater Dynasty*, *Bangkok Hilton* and as the wily Douglas Jardine in *Bodyline* – all high rating, critically praised miniseries. He admits he learned on his feet though, due to NIDA's preoccupation with stage, not screen, training.

Despite film roles in *The City's Edge* (1982), *For Love Alone* (1985), *The Right Hand Man* (1987) and *Wendy Cracked a Walnut* (1989), he admits, 'It wasn't until *Proof* that I was involved in the sort of film I enjoyed seeing.' *Proof*, Jocelyn Moorhouse's 1991 drama of a blind man (Weaving) befriended by a free-spirited dishwasher (Russell Crowe), was the young actor's first taste of the possibilities of a well-constructed, warmly received movie. It screened in competition at the Cannes Film Festival (although Weaving didn't attend) and became an arthouse darling. Not successful enough for attention in Hollywood though.

'I'm very ambivalent towards the whole idea of working [in Hollywood], very ambivalent'

'When I'm in America now, they say, "Oh I really liked *Proof*", but at the time it wasn't something,' he says.

His real breakthrough came in 1994 with Stephan Elliott's gay fantasia, *The Adventures of Priscilla, Queen of the Desert*. The camp classic about three drag queens journeying through Australia's straight heart was a global box office favourite – 'cult huge, not massive', he notes. Hollywood beckoned and, after launching *Priscilla* in Rio de Janeiro, naturally, Weaving stopped off in Los Angeles for four days. 'I met some agents and a few people, hated it, couldn't wait to get out of there and came home,' he says matter of factly.

He was an innocent abroad in those early LA meetings. 'I didn't know why I was there and thought, well, Ann's [Churchill-Brown, his Sydney agent] arranged for me to see so and so, so I went along and sat there and went [passively] "Hi" ... I remember meeting one agent and she said, "I can't take anyone on or do anything, blah blah blah," and I said, "OK then", got up to leave and she said, "What are you doing? Siddown. Siddown!"' Weaving wasn't used to Hollywood's double-speak and posturing. She implored him to stay and chat about future possibilities.

'I didn't understand it at all and it took me many years to work it out. But even now I'm very ambivalent towards the whole idea of working there and going over there, very ambivalent.' The major cause of his ambivalence is the city itself. 'It took me a long time to feel like I could go to LA and just be me.' People were polite enough but Weaving 'didn't feel there was any substance to anything they were saying'. For someone more interested in European cinema and from an English culture that 'had generally looked down on American culture in only the way the English can', Hollywood was an anomaly. 'I've always felt more of a foreigner in LA than in Delhi or anywhere else. I don't feel that in New York or San Francisco, but Los Angeles, I've always felt, is an extremely bizarre conglomeration of cities. I always felt lonely in Los Angeles, dreadfully lonely, and wanted to come back and be with my family and work.' His tolerance for the place has grown, ever so slightly – he still feels more comfortable working in Australia or England.

'I've always felt more of a foreigner in LA than in Delhi or anywhere else'

Weaving celebrated *Priscilla*'s success enthusiastically, oblivious to its possible effect on his career. He admits being 'oddly blind' to foreseeing the fruits of his labour. 'I don't really see the potential in what I'm doing. I don't know why; maybe I don't give myself much credit or I don't chase opportunities.' He thought if his work was notable, the right people would seek him out. It took a long time to realise if you want to work in America, you must spend time there and really 'hustle'. 'And I never really wanted to do that.' Weaving is determined but not driven to succeed in the US.

Nevertheless, he returned a couple more times in the 90s 'on sort of agent-hunting trips' but, true to type, he signed with an agent in London instead, ICM. 'I was quite happy about that but I've never got any work out of it — that's because I've never spent time there! Similarly, my ICM agent in LA [Chris Andrews] would tell you that I'd be the worst client. I never ring him, or very rarely. So I'm my own worst enemy in that way, I don't really know what it's all for. I don't quite understand it ... so stupid.'

Hollywood, in the form of *The Matrix*, came to Weaving via his Australian agent, Ann Churchill-Brown, in 1998. While he was filming the slight comedy film *Bedrooms & Hallways* in London, she rang to tell him two Americans were casting in Australia for a substantial film: 'They're not LA boys, they're Chicago boys and they're really interesting young filmmakers – perhaps you should read this script.' They were in fact Larry and Andy Wachowski, brothers who'd made the lesbian noir thriller *Bound*.

Weaving's London shooting schedule didn't allow him time to read the script, if indeed he wanted to do so. He could do without an expensive science-fiction film shot in LA. Churchill-Brown rang again. The Wachowskis wanted him to record a scene. So Weaving finally read the script. 'I got to the scene they wanted me to put down and I thought, this is actually fun and funny and a really interesting character. I'll do that.'

The 'interesting character' was Agent Smith, the personification of a rogue computer program hell-bent on destroying rebel humans. These computers had conquered the planet and enslaved all but the rebels in an alternative reality, the Matrix. Weaving recorded the scene in which Agent Smith interviews Neo (Keanu Reeves) for the first time. The Wachowskis adored it (they were also fans of *Proof* and *Priscilla*) and asked Weaving to meet them in LA. Weaving recalls meeting 'two really lovely guys with their feet on the ground. I just really warmed to them.'

After running through some scenes, they asked if he'd be available for kung-fu training. 'I said, "Yeah, sure",' he laughs. 'Stupidly!' Their offer was waiting for Weaving when he arrived home. Despite his reticence to commit, he appreciated the film's novelty and thought the Wachowskis' personalities could result in 'a great experience ... It's a weird one because of all films for me to be involved in, a really massive-budget action film was a huge jump,' he adds.

Weaving also nailed the essence of Agent Smith in his first audition. While other auditioners tended to be robotic, he saw something humorous in the character. 'I just thought there needed to be something weird about him, I wasn't quite sure what, something human but not really human.' Ultimately, Smith mimicked a US Presidential Secret Service henchman and scored most of the best lines in the first film. As the trilogy wore on, the character became its only beacon of fun.

The production proved to be 'a great experience' and a 'challenge' like no other. Weaving spent five months in the US training for the film's athletic combat scenes, bonding with the Wachowskis and cast members Reeves and Carrie-Anne Moss. 'We all got injured together,' Weaving smiles. Upon moving to Sydney's new Fox Studios, he realised *The Matrix* crew was an agglomeration of every Australian crew with which he'd ever worked. 'So in many ways it was kind of a great way to start doing a big-budget film, but the first day was pretty scary.' Happily, it began with Smith's interrogation of Neo. Weaving was comfortable and it 'set the pattern for the rest of the shoot for me and Larry and Andy'.

It quickly became evident from storyboards, art department drawings and special effects how massive this film would be. *The Matrix* cost US$63 million, a figure given significant oomph by a devalued Australian dollar. It was a mini-masterpiece that earned US$460 million globally and became the initial blockbuster of the DVD age, the first to sell one million copies. No-one could have predicted it, although Weaving contends the Wachowskis' determination and attention to detail hinted the project was 'heading in the right direction'. Actually, its design and cinematography were copied for years to come – lovingly in films like *Shrek* and cynically in movies such as *The Transporter*, *Bulletproof Monk* and *Charlie's Angels*.

Weaving's recollection of his first viewing is hazy. He knew what to expect tonally but was astonished to find an exciting, amusing film, and the audience response? 'They went off.' He has a better memory of the 'bizarre experience' of launching the film and the surrounding hype. It was extreme. 'If I'd absolutely loathed *The Matrix* I would have had a nightmare at the time. It's easy to enjoy yourself if you're happy with the result.'

Weaving gauges films by what's on the screen, not by the box office figures. His partner, Katrina, watches the numbers, he smiles. 'To me, it doesn't mean anything because you can get amazing box office for a film that's really, let's face it, not great. I'm not saying *The Matrix* was not great, but box office to me doesn't mean great films. Nor does Oscar. There are so many films and performances that have Oscars or huge success attached to them that really don't ring through the ages, they don't say a great deal about who we are as human beings.

'I'm increasingly coming to feel that that's what I'm about as an actor and that's what I'm interested in, somehow illuminating something about who we are. I can have a bit of fun as well as the next person – I enjoy being in comedies and *The Matrix* – but success at a box office is certainly not my primary concern. I get more worked up about Australian films not doing well.'

The Matrix's success meant Hollywood approached Weaving, although not with anything sufficiently tantalising to lure him to LA. He's barely contemplated acting in another American film since. He read many scripts and met many directors in one six-week LA visit but couldn't bring himself to pursue any; Brian De Palma's *Mission to Mars* was on offer, among others. Fortunately, Australian director Rolf de Heer sent him the script of *The Old Man Who Read Love Stories*. They met in LA and Weaving beseeched him: 'Good, I'll do it, get me out of here.' There endeth Weaving's Hollywood tale.

'It just hasn't really worked out that there's been a really interesting role in a really interesting film there whereas here, that happens fairly often,' he explains. 'I have continually found more challenging work here. Which is not to say the end result's always been great but [because of] the initial script and the people [involved] I'd think, great, I'd love to do that role.'

Unfortunately, *The Old Man Who Read Love Stories*, an exotic drama filmed in French Guiana, was nobbled after filming by a dispute between its producers. Subsequently the film, also starring Richard Dreyfus and Timothy Spall, didn't benefit from a structured release pattern. No matter, Weaving had some unfeasibly large blockbusters heading his way. Again, they came to him rather than him chasing them. He's almost ashamed looking back, knowing he aspired to be involved in *The Lord of the Rings* but didn't tell anyone, not even his agent, because he thought it had been cast.

Fortunately, the elves were cast late, says *Lord of the Rings* director Peter Jackson, due to J.R.R. Tolkien's 'ethereal' description of them. 'We didn't quite know what to do with the elves for a long time, then we felt we wanted to cast people who had a very particular sort of physical type – high cheekbones, tall, elegant, slender. We wanted people who obviously had great emotional weight because the elves are very much like philosophers, so we wanted strong actors in those roles who had a certain physical type and we tested all round the world for those parts.' To no avail.

Rings producer Barrie Osborne says he knew Jackson and partner Fran Walsh were struggling to cast Elrond. 'I said, "Hugo?", and they said, "Yeah? Do you think we can get Hugo?", and I said, "Yes".' Osborne produced *The Matrix*, so Weaving was a phone call away. Better still, Weaving was familiar with the character after reading *The Hobbit*. Osborne invited him to New Zealand. 'I went onto the set and met a few people [including] Ian McKellen, and saw a 20-minute cut which had this strong sense of reality,' Weaving says. 'It was very strong, so I said yes.'

Weaving surmises Jackson wanted someone who 'he thought had a certain kind of gravity, I suppose. I don't know that I do but Elrond has a much greater light and darkness when you read it, a man with vast experience.' Jackson agrees. 'We found in Hugo, and Cate [Blanchett], these rather ethereal but very grounded types of performers.'

Weaving was a fan of Tolkien's series without expectations of high art, although Jackson's mammoth creation proved to be that. 'I just thought it would be fantastic to be involved in a re-creation of Middle Earth and a whole new world,' Weaving says. 'It would be quite fantastic, literally fantastic.'

It was the biggest film production ever, a US$300 million trilogy filmed as one. So it's perhaps forgivable that Weaving hesitated about committing to the only possible project that might rival it, the Wachowskis' completion of *The Matrix* trilogy. The actor surmised *The Matrix* was open-ended but it took Larry Wachowski 18 months after filming the original to call Weaving and tell him the sequels were definitely happening: 'Are you on board?'

Weaving wanted to see the script first. It wasn't written and Wachowski needed a commitment before writing, otherwise the script would alter dramatically. Wachowski promised the Smith character would develop in 'an interesting way'. Weaving vacillated. His agent advised him he could renege later if he hated the script but his greatest fear was the possibility of spending up to two years training and filming in LA or Canada. Sydney and London were other possible shooting locations, which suited his family's plans. When it became clear the sequels would film in Sydney, Weaving said yes. 'That was odd, saying yes to something that hadn't been written,' Weaving concedes. 'It went against everything I'd ever been taught.'

He laughs at the suggestion he leveraged a stronger financial deal: 'What power? Do I have any? I certainly got more money, better money for the second and third ones, but I'm sure not nearly as much as anyone else. But for me it was absolutely fantastic.'

Even Weaving realises his hesitation to return for *The Matrix* sequels was 'odd'. 'It does sound weird. The thing I ummed and aahed about was the idea of reprising a character and being in a trilogy. Because the first film was so successful, I did wonder whether it was a good idea to be *that* character, just that character. Maybe it's not a good idea. Look at Sean Connery, he's just James Bond. How hard was it for him to get out of that?'

The production was torturous. The training alone took close to six months and Weaving suffered whiplash, among other injuries. Filming began in March 2001 and concluded in August 2002. He loved the experience on set but resented the long stretches of downtime. Occasionally he skived off to shoot some scenes for *Lord of the Rings* in New Zealand, but only because Osborne pulled strings. 'I was twiddling my thumbs for weeks on end all the way through that last year but the set itself was great, although the [Wachowski] boys got flat and tired and it wasn't quite as positive as it had been by the end. Otherwise, there were great technicians, mostly Australian crew and really good people to hang out with.'

Such work isn't Weaving's raison d'être, though. He remains a committed stage actor who's lucked into two of the three largest, and certainly most ambitious, film trilogies of all time (the *Star Wars* sextet being the other). He confesses there were moments on both when he thought the whole experience absurd. 'But I think that on stage too; the whole thing's really bizarre. Acting's a very bizarre profession sometimes but fantastic [too]. There's something wonderful about it . . . Sometimes you're on set and it's totally mad, totally bizarre, and you need to have a laugh about all that and then focus in on what we're doing. What is required and what have I got to do?'

The two series cost in excess of $1 billion combined, enough to make 100 Australian films. Yet Weaving contends neither experience felt truly 'Hollywood': 'Certainly *Lord of the Rings* didn't feel American. Not at all. All the crew and creative people seemed to be not American and a lot of the actors weren't either. Everyone working on it had that Kiwi spirit – can do and we'll work from dusk till dawn and be paid nothing but we love it and we love Pete. An extraordinary energy really. *The Matrix* [felt American] probably because we spent so much time training there but again a lot of the key creatives were Australian. I don't think either of those experiences felt too Hollywood, whatever that is.'

2003 was a year like no other. *The Two Towers* powered through the New Year, Agent Smith resurfaced in *The Matrix Reloaded* in May and *The Matrix Revolutions* in November and Elrond closed the year in *The Return of the King* in December. In one year, the films in which Weaving featured earned more than US$2 billion globally, US$400 million more than the next 'best performers' that year, Geoffrey Rush (*Pirates of the*

Caribbean, Finding Nemo and *Intolerable Cruelty*) and Orlando Bloom (*Pirates* and *The Two Towers*).

'They're huge, aren't they?' Weaving asks. 'Both *Lord of the Rings* and *The Matrix* are so mammoth but it's funny because in a way I still don't love them in the same way that I might. They're just different, very different. I couldn't wait to finish *Matrix* – as we all wanted to finish it, it was just a long shoot – and went straight to a wonderful TV mini-series, *After the Deluge*, and I absolutely loved it. It had a small crew, was shot quite quickly and you just have to be there, you don't have to be someone with pointy ears or some weird alien. By that stage I was a bit over the largeness and the fantastical nature of both those projects and wanted to get back to doing something which was a – Australian; b – contemporary; and c – just human, really.'

The popularity of both series will manifest for years to come. Weaving could spend the rest of his life signing memorabilia at fan conferences. Fans write to him and call out his name in the street but he knows the Sydney suburb where he lives is a sanctuary. 'All that sort of stuff, it's very here one minute, gone the next. People live their own lives and they do forget; they get impressed for a short period of time and then they're on to the next thing, so I take it as it comes.'

It came rather extravagantly. A month-long press junket – in which actors and directors promote a film with interviews and appearances – for *The Matrix* is most actors' idea of a nightmare. Again, Weaving is not your average actor. 'I thought it was going to be hideous but it was great, flying around the world and staying in the best hotels. It was just a ball, I had a blast. I didn't sleep a wink, chatted all day – in five-minute interviews, ridiculous but, oh well, you do it – had a great time, sitting in the sun in the south of France!'

The lure of a glamorous lifestyle and celebrity is an

increasing drawcard for young acting wannabes. Weaving warns that fame 'does destroy people' before noting ambition must be backed up by talent, lest the industry merely see the ambition. Which is partly why Weaving looks quizzical when asked whether he'll take advantage of his role in the *Lord of the Rings* trilogy. His Australian co-star, Miranda Otto, made it plain in promotional interviews she hoped to capitalise in some way. 'I don't quite know what you

Fame 'does destroy people' could take advantage of, really,' Weaving says. 'I could be wrong. What I do is look at the character; I don't really look so much at the success of a film and think, this is a way to move up to another level. And I suppose for me the other level doesn't necessarily mean going to Hollywood.'

He remains committed to more Australian projects. That's more appealing than hanging out and hoping for a blockbuster in LA. 'I don't really know that I want to do that. Which is not to say if the Coen Brothers rang me I wouldn't go straight away!'

Weaving's family, his wife Katrina, their son and daughter, come before work. His 'career' takes second place — though he uses the word sparingly because he thinks it implies the ability to manipulate where you're going, 'and I've never thought like that ... What I do is very important to me. I work very hard and there are certain things I want to do but if it means spending an enormous amount of time away from a young family, being in a city [where] I get lonely and if it means working on material I'm not 100 per cent sold on, then I'm not going to do it. Or any one of those factors actually.'

It is conceivable Weaving's Hollywood career ended at the end of 2003, when both his amazing trilogies were released. 'Might be. Might well be,' he smirks, as though he hadn't even thought about it. 'We'll see where it goes. I should go to LA in

December–January and spend a month there making the most of the tide that is my career but there are other considerations ... Who knows? Maybe in ten years there'll be some young filmmakers who absolutely loved *The Matrix* and think Agent Smith is the coolest thing in the world and they desperately want me to play some weird old codger.'

Many actors would consider Weaving has missed his opportunity. 'Probably,' he agrees. 'To me, there are so many other opportunities in life, it's not all about going to LA and being in a big American movie. There's more to it than that. If in three years there's nothing happening for me here because there aren't many films being made or – I'll be forty-five – there aren't many roles because they want 23 year olds, maybe that will happen too. Maybe I'll just be doing a lot of theatre but I'll be perfectly happy doing that.'

Hugo Weaving didn't go to LA in early 2004. All six of the Lord of the Rings and The Matrix films remain among the top 50 highest grossing films of all time.

10
hugh jackman

Pivotal Projects

Van Helsing (2004), X2: X-Men United (2003), Swordfish (2001)

Kate & Leopold (2001), X-Men (2000), Erskineville Kings (1999)

Paperback Hero (1998)

hugh

Hugh Jackman was destined to be a star. At least in the eyes of Annie Semler, a self-described 'white witch' (and wife of Academy Award-winning Australian cinematographer Dean Semler). Yet his stardom could easily have been confined to the realm of Australian soap operas, not Broadway or Hollywood.

Annie Semler happened across the young Jackman working as a 'towel and locker guy' at a Sydney gym. While showing her around, he recalls, 'She looked at me with these crazed eyes and said, "You're going to be a big star. Don't worry, it's all going to happen so fast. Listen to me, I'm a white witch". And I'm like, "Yeah, all right, love. Do you want a three-, six- or 12-month membership?"' Jackman is still incredulous at the memory of that meeting.

Mrs Semler gave him the phone number of her friend, agent Penny Williams. Jackman phoned Williams the next day. 'I was eager to get a foot in the door,' he says. Surprisingly, at least to Jackman, Williams took him on and quickly put his name forward for a general audition at Grundy, the major Australian TV game show and drama production company. Within a week Grundy had offered him a two-year contract on its long-running soap *Neighbours*. 'The first thing I thought was, God, Annie Semler was right. She is a white witch!' he laughs.

Grundy made an attractive offer which, despite fearing the white witch's wrath, Jackman turned down. He had other plans; he was midway through auditioning for the drama schools, Sydney's National Institute of Dramatic Arts (NIDA) and the Western Australia Academy of Performing Arts (WAAPA). He was confident he could have filled the *Neighbours* job. The character, in Jackman's opinion, was 'me, just me. Apart from the fact the guy had to play the trumpet and was a lawyer, it was me.' And he knew that after 12 months on a soap he'd be adept at publicity, at playing himself on camera and hitting his mark 'but nothing else'. Also, he wouldn't have considered himself deserving of an audition for the Sydney Theatre Company after working on *Neighbours*. He wanted more. Jackman had the acting bug; he wanted to pursue the craft, not necessarily stardom.

But acting hadn't always been Jackman's goal. He was studying a communications degree at the University of Technology Sydney when he first seriously considered acting. 'I remember having Wendy Bacon as my tutor in the final semester on investigative journalism and hearing her talk and thinking, oh, my fuck, I'm twenty-one and I don't have a third of the passion that this woman has for her job. And I remember my dad talking about having passion for what you do, otherwise you'll regret it and be unhappy, and to find what you're passionate about – it doesn't really matter what it is. So it kind of dawned on me that I was getting a degree in something that wasn't ultimately going to be that thrilling for me.' But having realised his heart wasn't in journalism, he only took up acting classes 'to forestall the inevitable'.

Jackman's British background (his English parents moved to Australia in the 1960s) infused him with an interest in the Anglo theatrical tradition. This interest was then stoked after he completed his UTS communications degree, at WAAPA, by two teachers with English acting backgrounds, Lyall Jones and Nigel Rideout.

'I remember watching tapes of Ben Kingsley and Judi Dench, Ian McKellen and Alan Bates doing Shakespeare and just marvelling at them, and then going to England and seeing them on stage,' Jackman enthuses. When he was a second-year WAAPA student he had a photo taken of himself standing outside London's National Theatre, hands together in prayer and looking up to the clouds. 'That was more the holy grail than Hollywood. I thought that was the pinnacle of acting.' Soon enough, Jackman found his holy grail: Hollywood via London's West End.

Upon graduation from WAAPA in 1994, Jackman won a small recurring role (and met his wife Deborra-Lee Furness) on the ABC TV prison drama *Correlli*. He found true fame, however, in Australian musical theatre, drawing solid notices in *Beauty and the Beast* and exceptional reviews as Joe Gillis in *Sunset Boulevard*. Here was Australia's new 'triple threat', a towering and handsome singer-dancer-actor. His dominant *Sunset Boulevard* performance was noticed on London's West End. Trevor Nunn, arguably England's best director, cast Jackman as the likeable lead, Curly, in the National Theatre's revival of *Oklahoma!* 'I was in the dressing room that Ian McKellen had just vacated and I thought, this is it, this

'I was in the dressing room that Ian McKellen had just vacated and I thought, this is it, this is my dream, now what?'

is my dream, now what?' he recalls candidly. Jackman was the star of the production and earned glowing reviews. Female writers in particular found his handsomeness and sex appeal difficult to deny. In the pressure-cooker environment of one of the world's two hubs of English-language theatre (the other being Broadway), he stood out in what was a major musical.

Yet he blanched when on one occasion he saw himself labelled, 'Hugh Jackman, singer'. 'I was like, Whoa. It's a miracle I get labelled like that but I was worried about it, because I never wanted to be a singer, I wanted to be an actor. All of a sudden I thought musicals can be a one-way street, they're very hard to get out of sometimes. And it doesn't matter what you do in musical land, whatever they say, it's not respected in the film community.'

And the words of his one-time WAAPA mentor, Lyall Jones, were ringing in his ears. A few years earlier Jones had warned that though he may love the theatre, it was now very hard to pursue an acting career without considering film. So while Jackman describes musical theatre as 'one of the most uplifting forms of entertainment', he knew he could always cross back to it. 'Not in a mercenary way but just kind of in a business way, I want to be able to do as many things as I can.'

So Jackman tried film. It was a means rather than an end and he still regards it as something of a curiosity. But after three years of non-stop theatre work he was drained. 'I'd had enough of it,' he concedes. 'It's a pretty disciplined life and really tough, it takes it out of you.'

His first cinematic efforts were small Australian productions. The first, *Paperback Hero*, in 1998, was a fey romantic comedy starring Jackman as the amiable Jack Willis, a rural road-train driver attempting to hide his burgeoning career as a soppy romance novelist from his rough and ready mates. Co-starring Claudia Karvan, the film showcased Jackman's cinematic leading man credentials. The other Australian film, *Erskineville Kings*, made by Alan White in 1999, was a modest, almost humdrum tale of blue-collar Sydney men struggling to come to terms with altered family dynamics after the death of their father. Neither film earned much at the Australian box office but they nicely padded out Jackman's show reel. As did his AFI Best Actor nomination for his performance as Wace in *Erskineville Kings*.

Jackman had already signed with a US agent, Patrick Whitesell, by the time *Paperback Hero* was being screened at Hollywood studios. Whitesell told him: 'A lot of people are saying "We don't really dig the movie but this guy's a movie star",' he laughs. Hollywood rarely cherry-picks Australian talent without a hit or an internationally distributed film behind them. Regardless, Jackman believes his Australian films helped him get representation because 'as good as you might be on stage, unless they see you on screen they're not going to back you'.

Whitesell showed studio heads a compilation from the lighter *Paperback Hero* because it displayed how Jackman could hold his own on screen; and he always sent directors a 15-minute *Erskineville Kings* compilation because it showed his range. Jackman contends *Erskineville Kings* 'got me *Swordfish* and *Someone Like You*'.

But they didn't get him to Hollywood. The West End revival of *Oklahoma!* did. Jackman's London agent, Lou Coulson, suggested they meet a few people in Hollywood. Jackman had nothing to lose, and he had a hot agent: Coulson launched Alfred Molina, Tom Wilkinson and Minnie Driver in quick succession. Rather than swamp the market, Coulson carefully chose her moments to showcase her English clients in the US and earned a reputation for introducing talent worth considering. Jackman felt her influence as he met the heads, rather than the underlings, of Hollywood agencies. 'So it had been [thanks to] her as much as me, probably more her to be honest, that I got into the door,' he says. 'We met everybody.'

Jackman was amazed by the reception because neither of his Australian films had created a ripple in the US – 'I was a nobody really.' But *Oklahoma!*'s reputation was incredibly

weighty, and its influence for Jackman was aided by the fact
he had played Curly, an iconic American role. 'I remember
about three agents or managers that I met said, "Oh my god,
you were incredible in *Oklahoma!*" and I said, "Oh, you saw
it?" They said, "No, we never saw it
but we just heard great things",'
Jackman chuckles. 'That was
Hollywood for me. There was this
kind of buzz on me that was pretty
much totally unwarranted.' Only one

*'There was this kind of
buzz on me that was
pretty much totally
unwarranted'*

agent, Meg Ryan's, at ICM, was realistic enough to admit that
while he'd heard great things about the Australian, he didn't
have enough material to justify taking him on. To Jackman, he
was the only agent who spoke any sense. 'But every other
agent I met said they wanted to take me on.'

Jackman engaged CAA. It felt right, he says. '[I just] imag-
ined one day I would be at CAA. I had this very bizarre confidence going in there.' He appreciated that CAA was the titan
of agencies 'and unless you're Tom Cruise, there's no point
going there because you'll be ignored'. Its agents eloquently
spoke of how it gave great service to its 120 actors. This rang
alarm bells and Jackman decided to give the arrangement a
six-month trial 'and if it's not working out for either of us
we'll just move on'.

It was a bold but successful move. His relationship with
Whitesell endured and the actor even followed his agent when
Whitesell switched to the Endeavour agency. Jackman contends their meeting was fortuitous because when they met, the
agent had recently achieved 'star agent' status for pushing
Good Will Hunting forward by coaxing his client Matt Damon
to write a script.

But for some US cultural protectionism, Jackman might
have launched his American career with a Broadway produc-

tion of *Oklahoma!* Yet in mid-1999 he was denied that opportunity due to US union laws that forbade foreigners from starring in American theatre (a law he later overcame after his *X-Men* success).

His first Hollywood jobs didn't come quickly, so Jackman committed to Alan White's second Australian film, *Risk*, a white-collar fraud thriller set in Sydney. He auditioned despite believing 'I was not 100 per cent right for the part'. White convinced him otherwise. But on a trip to Los Angeles with his wife to meet with an adoption lawyer, Whitesell told Jackman that actor Dougray Scott's participation as the burly Wolverine in *X-Men* had been thrown into doubt due to delays on the *Mission: Impossible 2* shoot in Australia. Twentieth Century Fox wanted to meet him in case they needed a replacement. Jackman said he was committed to *Risk*. Whitesell knew that but suggested he do the meetings to, at the very least, keep his face in front of the US producers. Jackman met *X-Men*'s producer, Lauren Shuler Donner, who'd been convinced of his talent by his turn in *Oklahoma!* 'He just had that masculinity, sexiness, a sort of angry strength that Wolverine has,' she says. 'I was incredibly intrigued. Sometimes you have a gut reaction to someone; I had it with him.' Shuler Donner promptly introduced him to casting director Donna Isaacson, Fox Filmed Entertainment's then-president Tom Rothman, and chief, Bill Mechanic. Mechanic invited Jackman to visit the director Bryan Singer on *X-Men*'s Toronto set.

Alarm bells rang. Jackman made Whitesell tell Fox about his commitment to *Risk*. 'We were up front with them from the beginning but they said "Just please go and meet Bryan, we still don't know what's going on with Dougray." So I did,' Jackman remembers. Both actor and agent were comfortable they'd been honest with Fox and thought meeting Singer

Guy Pearce, Terence Stamp and Hugo Weaving in what Weaving describes as the 'cult huge, not massive' *Adventures of Priscilla, Queen of the Desert*.

Hugh Jackman's agent told the *Paperback Hero* star many Hollywood executives were saying, 'We don't really dig the movie but this guy's a movie star'.

Bruce Beresford on the set of *The Fringe Dwellers* with actress Oodgeroo Noonuccal.

Ski gloves and ushankas; Bruce Beresford on the chilly Canadian set of *Black Robe*.

Greta Scacchi, Pia Miranda and Anthony LaPaglia in *Looking for Alibrandi*, the film that reignited LaPaglia's love affair with his homeland.

Anthony LaPaglia and Kerry Armstrong rounded out Ray Lawrence's ensemble for *Lantana*.

'I turned down the audition three times because I thought, "I don't want to be an actor. What a fantastic life, being an out of work actor!"'
Portia de Rossi in *Sirens*.

Hollywood is expert at spotting talent, according to Fred Schepisi, here directing Meryl Streep on the set of *Plenty*. But once Hollywood has new directors in its grasp, it only wants them to reinvent standard Hollywood fare. 'You try and give them more and sometimes you give them *Plenty* or *Evil Angels* or *Six Degrees of Separation*.'

Naomi Watts, before what John Duigan describes as her 'purgatory in Hollywood', in the ABC mini-series *Brides of Christ*, flanked by Melissa Thomas and Kym Wilson.

Heath Ledger was already generating heat in Hollywood when he agreed to star in Gregor Jordan's Sydney gangster pic, *Two Hands*.

The most successful Australian at the Academy Awards, costume designer Orry-Kelly, with Judy Garland at Ethel Barrymore's seventieth birthday party.

Two-time Oscar winner John Truscott (here in 1967), saw his Hollywood career cruelled by his profligate ways.

could not hurt. It might augur well for future roles with the studio.

Jackman met a 'polite' Singer, 'but it appeared to me it was pissing him off that I was even there,' he admits. *X-Men* was already four days into filming 'and he was seeing this actor, this Australian, who he's never seen before, for a role which he's already cast, and the other guy's meant to be turning up in three weeks'. The Australian promptly realised Singer didn't want to humour him. 'I worried I was in the middle of this game between the director and the studio.' Jackman performed one cursory video read-through of a scene, Singer decamped to the set and the actor flew back to LA that night thinking he'd wasted his day.

'Bryan didn't see the initial audition that we saw,' says Shuler Donner. '[He] took some convincing. The thing that might have been a problem for him is in the comics, Wolverine is five foot three. Have you met Hugh? He's six foot three.'

Mechanic summoned him the following day. Back to Toronto he would go, this time for a full-scale test. The studio chief couldn't commit to Jackman without seeing him on the big screen. Jackman heard Scott had sustained a motorbike injury on *Mission: Impossible 2* and further production delays made his participation in *X-Men* untenable. Unbeknownst to Jackman, Fox had scoured every English-speaking nation for a suitable replacement – 'We cast our net far and wide,' Shuler Donner admits.

Jackman again returned to Toronto. He wasn't pressured, knowing he was heading back to make an Australian film. That attitude, he now believes, 'probably helped me because I didn't have all those nerves. I thought I was getting to the point where they went "Dammit, we can't have that guy. He's great, we're going to get him a part in our next film."' Furthermore, his wife had quietly suggested that a silly sci-fi film might not be the best way to begin a Hollywood career. He had his doubts too. 'Naturally I would have been better cast, I would have thought, in *Kate & Leopold* or *Someone Like You* than as Wolverine because my personality's not really like that. And in Hollywood first impressions are very much personality driven.'

He spent 12 hours waiting for the *X-Men* screen test. Thankfully, cast members Anna Paquin and Famke Janssen made him feel welcome and shared the midnight screen test with him. 'The whole crew responded to him,' says Shuler Donner. Singer wasn't so helpful though, impassively leading the Australian through a couple of scenes before walking away without even acknowledging Jackman. 'I was sort of left there on the set, and he was in a huddle and after about five minutes he came up to me, gave me a huge hug and said, "I'm so excited, man, I want you in the part."'

That day, Scott had officially exited *X-Men*. Jackman thought he would have to bail out too. 'I'm on the set of this huge US$100 million movie, looking around going, Oh my god, it's my big break and I can't do it.' Jackman spent the night in his hotel room elated but also depressed that 'my big chance had gone'. There was one more thing to mull over. An actor's fee is always negotiated before the final screen test so the actor cannot hold the studio over a barrel once they know they're a desired property. 'I was lying in the bed thinking they're going to pay me hundreds of thousands of dollars and I can't do it. This was just too weird, everything, just amazing.'

The next day, Jackman told Fox he had to return to Australia for *Risk*, for his buddy. 'Fox were like, "You don't have a contract. Just come and do our movie." I said, "No, you don't understand, no matter how successful I get I'm not going to walk into a cocktail party ten years from now and not be able to talk to Alan White because I screwed him over".'

Ultimately, Fox paid White in the order of US$500 000 to delay shooting until after *X-Men*, probably four months at a minimum. White was ready to roll, though, and had up-and-coming actor Tom Long on the shortlist anyway, so he took the half-million and proceeded without Jackman. A shrewd decision for Fox; Scott was likely to cost them twice that. Jackman is sanguine about the strongarm tactics. 'They're businesspeople but I have to say that in a way they must have accepted [my commitment to *Risk*] because they wouldn't have coughed up any money [otherwise]. I mean if they really thought they would be able to push this guy into it, when push comes to shove they would have. But I wouldn't have, and my agent was the one who told them that.' Whitesell stood by Jackman and told him, 'We were just pursuing this for relationships. So he was the one who pushed it with the studio and they coughed up.'

The actor barrelled into filming for the special effects-laden comic book adaptation. *X-Men*'s production crew soon realised they had the right actor to play Wolverine, even if others were still waking to his talents. 'He's so electric,' says Shuler Donner. 'Right after we cast him he sang "*This Is The Moment*" at this opening for Rupert Murdoch in Australia [the gala Sydney launch of News Corporation's joint venture Fox Studios in November 1999]. I think everyone knew about him then.'

His experience on set wasn't as smooth as he might have hoped. Many press reports at the time noted that Singer's job was on the line as he didn't handle pressure from the studio very well, and this manifested itself in spats with cast members, most particularly Jackman, who Singer felt wasn't displaying enough anger as Wolverine. *Premiere* magazine quoted Singer as telling him to 'find your inner Russell Crowe'.

Nevertheless, other cast members quickly embraced Jackman, says Shuler Donner. 'He's wonderful, so generous in spirit to other cast members and crew.' But she denies reports the Wolverine character was given more scenes during filming when they realised how well Jackman was taking to it. 'Not really, because Wolverine is a pretty big character anyway. He was always going to be the big character.'

That was confirmed in mid-July, 2000, when *X-Men* opened in North America. Its opening weekend of US$54 million exceeded the most optimistic expectations. Just as significantly, its positive reviews exceeded those anticipated for your standard comic book adaptation.

Jackman admits no-one knew how big *X-Men* would be. Even his agent implored him to sign up for another film before it could open and blight his future prospects. 'It was a big risky venture. Let's not forget Bill Mechanic, I think, left the studio a week before it came out [actually three weeks – he resigned on June 22] and that was one of the great mistakes in Hollywood history.' The US$75 million film would go on to gross worldwide more than triple its cost and subsequently spawn a sequel, *X2: X-Men United*, that was even more successful, earning US$85.5 million in its first US weekend, one of the top ten biggest openings ever. 'I'm not saying Bill was let go because of *X-Men* entirely but I'm sure that if *X-Men* had come out two weeks before Bill would still have a job. He was always behind that film and he really believed in [it]. It was a big risk. Comic book movies were not the done thing. It was a surprise to everyone.'

And Jackman's casting quickly over-shadowed that of Halle Berry, Patrick Stewart and Ian McKellen (the great Sir Ian whose recently vacated dressing room had given Jackman the thrills a few short years earlier), a late stroke of fortune for the production team, Shuler Donner concedes. 'Oh, 100 per cent, are you kidding? Hugh partly made *X-Men* the success it is today.' Jackman soon knew how successful it had been – the day after it opened. 'The weekend it opened I [was in New

York and] had phone calls at 7.00, 7.02, 7.04 — seven must be the acceptable time to wake someone up in LA. Mind you, that's 4am LA time.'

The new studio head, Singer and Whitesell all called him within the first ten minutes after seven o'clock Saturday morning, 'and they were still drunk, I think. That first day with 20 million bucks, no-one could believe it. It was very exciting and all of a sudden there was paparazzi. I was starting a movie in New York

'I was thinking, I wonder who they're taking photos of, without realising it was me'

on Monday [*Someone Like You*], and there's paparazzi on the street and I was thinking, I wonder who they're taking photos of, without realising it was me. Things changed very quickly.'

Initially the attention wasn't constricting, he adds, due to the obvious differences between Jackman and the comic book character Wolverine. That gave him at least a year in which no-one recognised him on the street. 'So my private life was like this real honeymoon of Hollywood because I had all these working opportunities that were amazing and I could get a good seat at a restaurant and yet I never got bothered. I could get courtside seats at the LA Lakers or the [New York] Knicks [basketball matches] and yet I lived with great anonymity. It was a wonderful time.'

Further professional opportunities quickly arose. Many saw *X-Men* as Jackman and Bryan Singer's film, despite its capable ensemble. The Australian was very much the revelation — quite an achievement in a film where special effects is the star. Even sober critics, such as the *New York Times's* Elvis Mitchell, enthused: 'The two-fisted Wolverine, well played by Mr. Jackman, is perhaps the only other semi-rounded character who animates the picture besides Xavier and Magneto.' Others, such as *Rolling Stone's* Peter Travers, were more effusive: 'What sizzles? Start with Hugh Jackman as Logan, the X-Man known as Wolverine. The Australian actor has snagged the juiciest role in the US$75 million epic as the mutant with the short temper and the long metal claws. Jackman energizes *X-Men* with power doses of fire, flashy humor and sexual heat.'

But the Australian realised to be typecast as Wolverine would be career death, even considering its monstrous success (*X-Men* went on to earn more than US$300 million internationally). His next role was as Ashley Judd's mischievous flat-mate in the slight, stagey romantic comedy *Someone Like You*. It barely registered, just earning back its US$40 million cost during its theatrical release. 'My feeling is it's a better film than it will be remembered as,' Jackman notes.

He auditioned for the historical drama *Quills* (the role went to Joaquin Phoenix), *U-571* (Matthew McConaughey) and the lead role in *Moulin Rouge!* (which went to Ewan McGregor). The glossy thriller *Swordfish* became the hit he needed. Jackman was the protagonist of the film starring John Travolta and Berry, in a role that emphasised his leading-man capabilities.

And Jackman knew it. At the time, he described himself as being in the vestibule of the A list, having to find the key to get in within the next year or he's out. While most reviews were damning of the film, it played extremely well. Jackman promptly had the two Hollywood hits one needs to build a career upon. Next came James Mangold's romantic comedy *Kate & Leopold*, in which he played an 1870s duke who's transported by time travel to contemporary New York. On paper, the concept sounds naff, but with Jackman pairing with romantic comedy queen Meg Ryan, its prospects were far more positive. Jackman admits he felt like he was back at drama school given the advice and encouragement from Ryan. 'In rehearsals I was amazed by her and I think even I'd maybe underestimated that talent a little bit because you get so used to her putting in that performance. You realise how crafted she is as a comedian and how she can craft a scene rhythm-wise.' Nevertheless, *Kate & Leopold*'s premise blighted it, even if Jackman enhanced his reputation as a horse-riding, upright leading man.

Jackman began toying with a return to the stage. He was the obvious choice to headline the risky production of the Australian-made musical *The Boy From Oz* on Broadway (now his 'international status' allowed him to work there). At the time, he conceded 'It seems crazy I'm talking about a year away but I feel like with my film career things are getting to a good point where I can take some time off. But there is a certain point where it's detrimental to get off the bus because you're actually building a profile.'

He was committed to *X-Men*'s sequel, *X2: X-Men United*. Wolverine's status grew, as did the sequel, which earned more than US$400 million worldwide in 2003. But he wanted his own film. Stephen Sommers, director of the hits *The Mummy* and *The Mummy Returns*, offered him the role of the vampire-slayer Gabriel Van Helsing, in the gothic horror film *Van Helsing*. Finally Jackman had the Hollywood vehicle he yearned for. In May 2004 the film conquered tepid reviews to earn more than US$105 million in its opening weekend alone.

But just as swiftly, he headed to Broadway for the 2003 launch of *The Boy From Oz*. Hollywood blanched. Playing the little-known Australian Peter Allen in a parochial musical seemed to many a potentially disastrous risk. 'As a friend, I'd say definitely go ahead because he needs an outlet for that incredible talent,' says Shuler Donner. 'As a producer, the business side of me would say it was a gutsy move, although it was only a year. It was a risk but a very good risk. I don't think he had much to lose and everything to gain. His film career was solid enough.'

He gained more than he could have hoped. *The Boy From Oz* was panned by Broadway's harshest pens, yet Jackman's Broadway debut was celebrated as the finest in decades. *Variety*'s Charles Isherwood noted, 'Hugh Jackman makes it all look easy. On stage as on film, he exudes warmth and a friendly sexuality. *X-Men* fans may not care, but he sings like a dream too, and dances with a carefree exuberance.' Jackman's performance and popularity single-handedly turned the widely panned musical into a qualified hit, playing at above 90 per cent capacity during its first six months and earning him a Tony Award for Actor in a Musical (he beat another Coulson discovery, Alfred Molina). The combination of blockbuster film appeal – he's even met a New Yorker with a full-colour Wolverine tattoo down the middle of his back – and prodigious talent worked beautifully on Broadway, where he has twice hosted the prestigious Tony Awards. Ironically, he also consolidated his reputation as a singer with the release of his own album in 2004.

Jackman's one-year Broadway contract concludes in late 2004, when he will lead again in another Hollywood film, Darren Aronofsky's time travel adventure, *The Fountain*. His abilities have ensured a prosperous international film and stage career, but it is his amiable, accommodating personality that distinguishes him from many A list film stars.

He admits, though, that his communications degree may have been more influential than he realised at the time. 'I think I had probably a slightly better understanding of the shoes journalists are in. I know some actors who say to me "I can't believe a journalist asked this question. For 20 minutes they talked about my film and then the last five minutes they quickly snuck in something about having another baby and then that's the headline!" ... I understand that every journalist has a line to pursue which is not necessarily the one they want to pursue but it's one given by an editor. So when I'm sitting at a round table and there's a journalist who I know writes for *New Idea* or *Women's Weekly*, I know at some point they're going to go [quickly], "So are you and Deborra going to have another kid?" I kinda giggle and don't get so annoyed. Maybe I just understand that a little more.'

11

bruce beresford

Pivotal Projects

Double Jeopardy (1999), Paradise Road (1997), Black Robe (1991)

Driving Miss Daisy (1989), Crimes of the Heart (1986), Tender Mercies (1983)

Puberty Blues (1981), The Club (1980), 'Breaker' Morant (1980)

The Getting of Wisdom (1977), The Adventures of Barry McKenzie (1972)

beresford

After directing six feature films on two continents, Bruce Beresford's seventh film, *'Breaker' Morant*, was his calling card in the United States. The court-martial drama, set at the turn of the nineteenth century in South Africa's Boer War, was filmed over six weeks in 1979, for $800 000.

'We had so little money,' Beresford recalls. In battle scenes, 'We used the same soldiers attacking the fort as defending it. We put them on horses, then when we were finished with that shot we dressed them in British uniforms and put them behind the guns. The same group of men!' Discipline and ingenuity of this kind have earned Australian filmmakers a reputation for resourcefulness. In Hollywood, with America's vast population hungry for entertainment, production budgets are rarely so slim.

Obviously Beresford, like his peers Peter Weir, Fred Schepisi, Dr George Miller and Gillian Armstrong, would feel the pull of Hollywood. Not that he went there, as such. At least, not initially. His first US movie was made in Texas and New York (not Los Angeles), and outside the studio system (albeit released by a Hollywood studio, Universal). Plus, after *'Breaker'* he made a further two films in Australia – *The Club*, an adaptation of David Williamson's hit play about footy politics, and *Puberty Blues,* adapted from Kathy Lette's popular beach babes coming-of-age novel. When Beresford did finally go to the US he maintained a home in Australia; always has. '*Breaker*', and its fine lead performance by Jack Thompson as the defence lawyer, was the trigger, however, for a steady stream of up to 200 scripts sent from abroad. 'None were particularly interesting until I got sent the script of *Tender Mercies* and [it] was so good, I thought, I can't *not* do this,' he remembers. The project was driven by its writer, Horton Foote, and Robert Duvall, who intended to star and co-produce. *Tender Mercies* was one of a handful of collaborations between the pair, the most famous being Foote's script for Harper Lee's Southern racism novel, *To Kill a Mockingbird,* in which Duvall portrayed Boo Radley. Foote saw *'Breaker' Morant* in New York and, according to Beresford, said, 'I want him to direct *Tender Mercies*'. 'They sent the script and I called them,' he says. 'There's never any more to it than that.'

A US$4 million budget was assembled on the strength of Duvall's commitment to play Mac Sledge, a divorced, alcoholic and inarticulate country and western star who finds love in the arms of a Vietnam war widow who runs a motel on a lonely Texas highway. A pair of New York documentary-makers, Mary-Ann and Philip Hobel, were engaged to produce the movie but according to Beresford, Barry Spikings and John Cohn, who ran EMI, became 'its driving force'. The only thing missing was a director.

Beresford learned much later other directors had passed on the project because Foote refused to allow them to make changes to the script. Beresford says he 'edited and reshaped it a bit because it was very long but I didn't rewrite it. You couldn't, Horton Foote has got such a distinctive style it wouldn't match.' Duvall, who reserved the right to approve the director, vetoed other candidates and his own chequered history of on-set cantankerousness ensured others took them-

selves out of the running. The thrice Oscar-nominated star of
pics including *The Godfather* and *Apocalypse Now* had publicly admonished some of his previous directors. It would take
someone who was supremely confident, thick-skinned or
unaware of this fact to sign for the job.

Beresford was unaware of this fact. And a little self-
assured; he'd just delivered four films in three years in
Australia. Blithely oblivious to potential problems, he took the
job confident Duvall had approved the decision. With hindsight Beresford says, 'He wasn't happy for anyone to direct, he
wanted to direct it himself.' (Duvall has in fact since directed
a number of marginally successful films.) Predictably, the pair
didn't gel. Beresford concedes there were 'a number of rows'
during filming 'which tended to have not much to do with the
film. When working on the film he was fine, apart from that,
he was a nutty guy. He finds it very hard to deal with people
on any level at all.'

Beresford was dismayed by what he dubbed the 'caste system' in the US, which allowed Duvall not to fraternise with
other cast and crew. 'In Australia,'
he said at the time, 'when you're
through shooting, all the actors and
crew go off for a drink. There's no
social division as there is here. I'm
surprised because film is such a collaborative medium. Actors look as
good as they do because of the people around them on set.'

> 'Actors look as good as they do because of the people around them'

When *Tender Mercies* was released in 1983, Duvall apparently threw a celebratory party at his house. Beresford cannot
recall attending and wonders if it ever occurred: 'Bob would-
n't throw a party, he's too stingy.'

In an interview published in Australia on the movie's
release, Duvall said Beresford was 'aloof' but nevertheless, 'a

very talented guy and he's going to be very successful'.

'*Tender Mercies* was a very prestigious film,' Beresford adds, 'but it didn't make any money'. It impressed the critics. The *New York Times's* scribe Janet Maslin began her review: 'What better proof can there be of the distinctiveness of Australian filmmaking than *Tender Mercies*, a film by Bruce Beresford that manages to be thoroughly Australian though it features Texas settings and an American cast?' Maslin's justifications for this statement? The film's 'hauntingly spare look'; 'it is set on a prairie as barren as Australia's', and features 'characters as silent and unyielding as the landscape'.

Tender Mercies garnered five Academy Award nominations, including one each for Beresford, Foote and Duvall. Foote and Duvall won Oscars.

Beresford's introduction to Hollywood was swift and successful but this wasn't Beresford's first Oscar nomination. For '*Breaker*' *Morant* he received a screenplay nomination in 1980, with co-scribes Jonathan Hardy and David Stevens. This was a watershed. Never before had an Australian feature film been nominnated for an Academy Award. Gillian Armstrong's *My Brilliant Career* also received a nomination that year, for costume designer Anna Senior.

'*Breaker*' producer Matt Carroll says, '*My Brilliant Career* paved the way for "*Breaker*" in the US. *Mad Max* enjoyed some success the previous year but it was a genre film – a road movie – and the Australian accents were dubbed into American for the US release.' According to Carroll, *My Brilliant Career* 'was an incredibly important film in America' because it made the Americans take notice of what was being made in Australia. 'I don't see "*Breaker*" *Morant* as that pivotal.'

After *My Brilliant Career*'s US release, '*Breaker*' screened in competition at the Cannes Film Festival and the jury voted lead actor Jack Thompson best actor. The film captured the attention of international buyers and was sold all around the world, according to Carroll. It opened in Australia the same month and went on to collect $4.7 million, slightly less than *Mad Max* and *Picnic at Hanging Rock*, the two highest grossing Australian movies ever at that time. Goldwyn and New World shared distribution in America. Beresford wasn't there to launch it, he was too busy working in Australia. The film opened in all the major US cities although Beresford says, 'it got a terrible review in *Time* magazine [and] they pulled it out of all the cinemas the next day. I said, "It's had good reviews everywhere", but the studio said to me, "You can't survive a bad review in *Time*".' Carroll, who was tracking the cheques, demurs: 'For a foreign film it did very good business [an estimated US$7 million] and there was a colossal sale to pay TV. The big audience all saw it on pay.' Beresford says, 'All the opinion writers seemed to see it. It had a reputation way beyond its audience.'

According to Carroll *'Breaker'* was released at 'a particularly political time, just before Westmoreland sued CBS'. A journalist with the major American television network had, in a documentary, accused Vietnam War General William Westmoreland of deliberately falsifying information to his superiors. It launched huge public debate on war ethics. *'"Breaker" Morant'*, says Carroll, 'was the first film about the morality of war since *Paths of Glory* 20 years earlier, which we were very influenced by.' As a result, 'It had a resonance in the American conscience we were utterly unaware of.' Carroll contends that even now, 'Everybody in the American industry remembers it.'

During this period President Ronald Reagan invited Beresford to the White House for dinner but he declined the invitation. 'I didn't want to be involved in anything to do with politics,' he says. 'I suspected Reagan may have liked the film because in a way it excused, or provided an explanation for, the Calley massacre in Vietnam. This might not be unreasonable in itself as I'm sure Calley was under the same pressures as Morant, but I didn't want to see myself promoted as someone who pardoned the slaughter of civilians. In the long run I'm sure Reagan was happy, as Bryan Brown substituted for me.'

So Beresford rode into the US where, he's adamant, he encountered few cultural differences. He was by then in his early forties, and had directed ten feature films. He had spent two years making films for the Nigerian government during his twenties and secured a job running the British Film Institute's Film Production Board before his thirtieth birthday. While at the BFI he oversaw about 30 films of various kinds and directed six. After returning to Australia to make the first fully publicly funded Australian movie – *The Adventures of Barry McKenzie* in 1971 and its sequel *Barry McKenzie Holds His Own* – he'd returned to England to shoot a musical comedy starring Barry Humphries, *Side by Side*.

Beresford believes he was forced out of Australia. 'The *Barry McKenzie* films put me out of work,' he says of the raucous comedies about beer-guzzling parochial Aussies. 'The critical reaction was so hostile it was a disaster.' The hostility died down after a couple of years and he returned to direct the similarly raucous, albeit political, film of David Williamson's classic election night play, *Don's Party*. So by the time he arrived in America he was a veteran of the Australian film industry, plus he imported a core team of Australians: cinematographer Russell Boyd, editor William Anderson and composer George Dreyfus. 'Making films is the same everywhere,' he contends. Except more money is available in the US, which raises the

'Making films is the same everywhere'

consequences but allows for longer shoots. 'Things have changed. The studios, I've found out in the last five years, are much more interfering than they were then.'

'One of the reasons I started doing some work in America is that I did a whole lot of films in Australia for which I never earned any money at all. In America, on the other hand, I earned a good fee.' The Americans also know how to sell films, he says, so there's a much greater chance many people will see them, which in turn boosts directors' work prospects.

After the renaissance of Australian film in the 1970s, led by Beresford, Armstrong, Schepisi, Miller and Weir, there was considerable alarm in the early 80s when they absconded to the US. At the time, Beresford rejected the charge they were being seduced by Hollywood studios. 'Our directors are flaunting themselves – they're running up with their pants down.' He also argued they would and could return. In 1985 he thundered, 'It's not as if one is a refugee from Eastern Europe who can't go home. Reading the Australian newspapers you get this message you can't go back, which isn't true. I'd like to be able to go back and forth between Australia and Hollywood.' That's exactly what he did.

Almost as soon as *Tender Mercies* was in the can, Beresford committed to his biggest challenge yet, the US$24 million biblical epic *King David*, which was set to star Richard Gere. It was a huge step up from his previous projects. The movie was initiated by Michael Eisner and Jeffrey Katzenberg who were at that time president and president of production, respectively, at Paramount Pictures. They decided there hadn't been a big biblical movie for many years and they considered David a dramatic character yet to be exploited by Hollywood. They offered Beresford the chance to direct and commissioned English writer Andrew Birkin to devise a script. Beresford describes Birkin as 'the most engaging and charming guy'. But trouble lay ahead: 'I realised after working with him for a while, he's not a particularly interesting writer. All his astonishing originality, charm and wit went into his life.

'I should never have approved the script. I'm always very careful about not starting until I'm convinced the script is correct [but] that was a huge juggernaut rolling down the hill and I couldn't stop it. I knew it was wrong.' Beresford asked Birkin at one stage what he thought the script was about. The writer replied it was about the relationship between David and Jonathan. Correct. 'But I pointed out there were no scenes between them. You've got a two and a half hour film with not one scene between the two protagonists. He said, "Oh". I said, "I think you better write some". He did and they were hopeless, only one ended up in the film.'

Scouting locations also proved epic. 'We found all the locations in Morocco, then we never got permission to film there,' Beresford notes incredulously. 'Then we were in Israel, [which] was completely hopeless. Why [do] they shoot those movies in Israel in the desert? The reason they fought over [Israel] for thousands of years is because it's very fertile. The bit that's not fertile, where they always film, there isn't anyone there now and there never was. I said, "This is absurd, why would we film here in the desert, we'd be much better off going somewhere like Italy or Sicily". That's what we did, we went to Sardinia.' It was more expensive but it was authentic.

'Had I been objective I'd have realised biblical films have been the death knell of directors. You could actually make a list of directors who, after making a biblical film, never worked again. I did. One of the most famous American directors, George Stevens (*The Greatest Story Ever Told*), did this huge biblical film and not only was it a fiasco, he was actually dead within the year.' Sure enough, *Solomon and Sheba* was King Vidor's final film, *The Ten Commandments* and *Samson and*

Delilah were Cecil B. De Mille's two last films, Nicholas Ray had a ten-year hiatus soon after *King of Kings*, Robert Aldrich's career declined in the 60s after *Sodom and Gomorrah* and *The Bible* was arguably John Huston's worst. Presumably Mel Gibson's *The Passion of the Christ* is the exception that proves the rule.

Beresford survived but *King David* took two and a half years, during which time the studio breathed heavily down his neck. Not that pressure is unique to Hollywood. On *Sydney, Story of a City*, a $7 million IMAX film sponsored by the City of Sydney ahead of the 2000 Sydney Olympics, the mayor Frank Sartor wouldn't let Beresford include a scene featuring a stage coach hold-up outside Sydney University 120 years ago. '"People will think they're not safe",' Beresford recalls Sartor saying. 'He said, "If you put that in I'll take you to court".' The scene did not make the final movie but Sartor, who became a minister in the New South Wales Labor government, cannot recall the conflict. He says the only time he argued with Beresford was when the director wanted to walk away from the project after interference by the council's staff. Sartor insisted he fulfil his contract and complete the film. 'There would have been lots of disputes on details,' Sartor says. But, 'I really did not edit the film'.

On *King David*, Eisner and Katzenberg insisted Gere play David. The actor was riding high following the success of *American Gigolo* and *An Officer and a Gentleman*. Beresford wanted to make the movie without a star. Studios always want to hedge their bets by casting names but 'stars bring baggage', he says. And Gere's two recent films had been very sexy, contemporary, a world away from a biblical epic. Beresford wanted Daniel Day Lewis, who he'd seen on stage in the UK. No-one else knew of him. Paramount refused. (Four years later Day Lewis rocketed to international attention with his starring role in *My Left Foot*.) Beresford says, 'Either I accepted Richard Gere or someone else directed the film.'

Matt Carroll describes Beresford as 'a director junkie, nothing [makes him] happier than going from one picture to the next'. But Carroll, his producer on *Money Movers*, *'Breaker'* and *The Club*, contends Beresford 'needs to be strongly produced ... He's a wonderful director of performance [but] he tricks himself out sometimes by casting actors who are inappropriate in the belief he'll be able to bring them around.'

Beresford rejects this notion. 'If the decision was entirely mine, with all of them, the casting would have been quite different.' In *Last Dance* (1996) he wanted to cast Sarah Jessica Parker (pre *Sex and the City*) but the studio insisted on Sharon Stone. This was a mistake. Similarly his desire to cast Emmanuelle Seigner as Alma Mahler in *Bride of the Wind* was vetoed. Much later, Beresford was apprehensive about Dan Ackroyd playing Jessica Tandy's son in *Driving Miss Daisy* but acquiesced because nobody else wanted the role. Ackroyd proved to be a revelation.

Time has been kind to *King David* but the reviews when it was released were savage, especially about Gere, who was unanimously deemed miscast. An Australian newspaper report at the time summed it up thus: '*King David* opened in New York last week and if the reviews are anything to go by, it could well close next week' (*Sun Herald* 7 April 1985). The studio interference took a terrible toll on Beresford, who said after the shoot: 'I've learnt it is a mistake to get involved in super-productions, as the money gets bigger, the interference gets greater. They're naturally scared of losing everything and they put terrific pressure on you to do all sorts of things.' With hindsight he says, 'the best films I've done were the ones where the studio [was kept at arm's length].'

His next film was *The Fringe Dwellers*, about an Aboriginal clan's adventures in the public housing system. With a pre-sale to UK distributor Virgin Films, producer Sue Milliken raised the rest of the budget from the Australian and Queensland Film Commissions. The $1 million movie appears to be a reaction to the vastness of *David*. Beresford says, 'I don't really think like that, I just think it's a story I'd like to do. I never think in terms of it being small or big; or in Australia or America. All I think is, would I like to do it? All other things are not relevant.' That said, 'It was nice working with all those Aboriginal actors, that was fun.'

Beresford continued to follow his nose for projects, flipping between Hollywood and Australia. In 1988 he was devastated when his $17 million sci-fi extravaganza *Total Recall* with *Dirty Dancing* star Patrick Swayze fell over when veteran Hollywood producer Dino de Laurentiis went bust. In 1986 de Laurentiis set up an Australian production company and set out to build an $5 million studio complex in Queensland. It was the first such attempted marriage between Hollywood and Australia. Another Beresford project, *End of the Line* with Bryan Brown, was to be de Laurentiis Australia's first project but it all ended in tears two years later, having produced nought. Beresford was so frustrated by the experience he charged across to Hollywood and demanded his agent find him a movie, 'Now.' He found *Her Alibi*, a forgettable comedy about reclusive writers starring Tom Selleck and Estee Lauder model Paulina Porizkova.

Having diffused his pent-up frustration, he then set to work on the movie for which he would earn his highest acclaim, *Driving Miss Daisy*. 'I had been telling everyone for five years the script was wonderful and virtually nobody agreed. The only person who liked it was Richard Zanuck, the producer. I sat down once with him and said, "The only two people in the world who think this script has any merit are you and me". He said, "And we're the only two who are right".' Nobody wanted to finance it, or distribute it. 'They said, "You've got three people talking in a house, two of them are really old. To actually sustain an audience's interest with such limited material it's going to have to be directed so well it is virtually impossible.'

Zanuck and Beresford eventually eked US$5.25 million from a Canadian investor called Jake Ebert and persuaded Tandy, Morgan Freeman and Ackroyd to star. Warners invested another US$2 million but showed no real interest in it. Then a funny thing happened. 'We'd finished the movie [and] I suddenly got a call from the publicity guy for Warner Brothers [who] said, "Where's that film you made with the old lady and the black guy?" I said, "Oh, it's here".' The bloke asked to see it, immediately, so a curious Beresford bundled a print into the back of his car and drove to meet him. 'We got to the theatre and he was the only one there. I said, "Who's going to see it?" He said, "Just me".' So the odd couple sat down together but within a quarter of an hour the publicity guy jumped up and left. 'So I followed him and when I got out to the lobby he's all excited and said, "We can sell this!" I said, "You've only seen 15 minutes". He said, "It doesn't matter, is it that good all the way through?" I said, "It's fantastic". He said, "Great".'

At this point Beresford demanded a reason for his behaviour, strange even by Hollywood standards. The publicist explained Warners had been hit hard by the failure of Norman Jewison's *In Country* and needed a Christmas release. 'They needed something quickly [and] the next thing I knew it was everywhere. It was so rapid I couldn't believe it. There were posters up, and trailers, it was promoted like hell. They would never tell you this story, they would always say they were planning a big release. That kind of thing happens with a lot of films,' Beresford confides.

Driving Miss Daisy unspooled across the US on 13 December 1989 and rapidly garnered nine Oscar nominations, including Best Film, but not one for the director. It ended up collecting the trophy for Best Film, plus another four. 'I wasn't even invited!' Beresford blurts. 'Well, they don't invite you unless you're nominated.' With clear memories of how so many people had advised him that *Daisy* was 'virtually impossible' to make, when it became so successful Beresford assumed he was a shoo-in for an Academy Award nomination. 'Then I think it looked so effortless on screen they all thought it wasn't directed at all. It backfired on me,' he says. When the night arrived he was far away, directing *Mister Johnson* in Africa, and it was the best thing. He became the cause célèbre of Oscar night 1989 (held in March 1990).

> Driving Miss Daisy 'looked so effortless on screen [everyone] thought it wasn't directed at all'

Master of ceremonies Billy Crystal dubbed *Driving Miss Daisy*: 'The movie that apparently directed itself.' Tandy, accepting her best actress trophy, called him 'that forgotten man!' Zanuck, collecting the Best Film statue, said, 'We're up here for one very simple reason, Bruce Beresford is a brilliant director.'

So Beresford could write his own ticket? 'No. I think Hollywood in general regarded it as a kind of freak show, a one-off peculiar thing that'll never happen again. So it didn't really help me at all but I'm glad I made it because I did think it was a very good film.'

Beresford continued to make very good, if enigmatic, films. He helmed *Black Robe*, a dark, violent epic about Jesuit missionaries and Canadian cannibal tribes in the 1800s and later made *Paradise Road* (for $25 million) in far north

Queensland in 1996. The tale of allied women who form a choir while imprisoned by the Japanese during the Second World War starred Glenn Close and a young Cate Blanchett.

Beresford then anchored a blatant US$45 million Hollywood potboiler, *Double Jeopardy*, which effortlessly returned US$112 million at the North American box office alone in 1999. He still seems embarrassed that it's his most heavily promoted, and consequently most successful, film.

12
anthony lapaglia

Pivotal Projects

Without A Trace (TV) (2003–), Lantana (2001), Looking For Alibrandi (2000)

Sweet and Lowdown (1999), Murder One (TV) (1996–7), Brilliant Lies (1997)

The Client (1994), One Good Cop (1991), Betsy's Wedding (1990)

Frank Nitti: The Enforcer (1988)

anthony

Anthony LaPaglia didn't want to become an actor, not at first. Like so many Australian boys, he wanted to be an athlete, and as the son of an Italian father and Dutch mother, his sport was soccer.

He grew up in an Adelaide housing development then called Beef Acres, making good on his superior football talent. The Juventus club signed the 15-year-old LaPaglia to understudy its, and Australia's, goalkeeper Roger Romanovitz. LaPaglia had a few chances to impress in Australia's premier league but he admits he choked when presented them.

His motor mechanic father insisted he stay at school but 'I wasn't a particularly good student. The only thing I was interested in was sport. I didn't care about anything else, hated drama class with a passion.' At twenty, he retired from soccer and took up some new hobbies: among them, smoking cigarettes and drinking coffee. He had no idea what he wanted to do with his life. After graduating from Norwood High School, LaPaglia tried, and failed, to work with his father before 'drifting' into teachers college. Upon graduating, he was assigned to rural South Australia. 'I knew I wasn't going,' LaPaglia says. 'Adelaide was small enough.'

He found a job selling shoes with Florsheim in downtown Adelaide's Rundle Mall. His part-time job became full time and, after he showed some promise as a salesman, the company posted him to its Chicago head office for six months to learn the business from the ground up. Big things awaited him when he returned to Australia, including a transfer to Sydney.

'So that became my job at the ripe old age of twenty-one and I hated it,' LaPaglia says. While working in Bondi, he took a shine to a woman working in the clothes store next door. She was reluctant and would only agree to a date if LaPaglia took her to the theatre. 'I didn't care, I'd never been to a play, I just wanted to go out with this girl,' he admits.

They saw William Congreve's sixteenth century restoration comedy, *The Way of the World*. Produced by the Sydney Theatre Company at the Sydney Opera House, it starred Ruth Cracknell and Hugo Weaving. It was a revelation to LaPaglia. 'The light bulb went off,' he recalls. 'I sat through that play and at the end of it I knew what I wanted to do.' And most of it didn't have much to do with his date.

Weaving smiles at the recollection. 'I don't think there was anything particularly great about that production, in fact I saw a recent [version] that was much better than the one we did. And my performance was rotten!'

After weeks of enthusiastic banter, his now girlfriend implored him to audition at Cronulla Arts Theatre. LaPaglia was petrified. He once attended an acting class in Adelaide to help a friend but was thrown out after three sessions for 'completely fucking around'. The teacher said, 'You'll never be an actor.'

At Cronulla, he lucked onto a role in John Van Druten's play *I Am a Camera*. 'I think I was the only male that showed up.' Director Ray Ainsworth nursed him through the season. By the end, 'I got a little better and could walk and talk without hitting the furniture; but I'm sure I was appalling.' One cast member, Sarah Chadwick, suggested he audition for

NIDA. Why not? LaPaglia was clueless but with a blossoming career as a shoe salesman from which to escape, he was desperate to learn.

With a sheepdog's audacity, he memorised his monologues and fronted up to NIDA. He progressed through a number of sessions before a teacher advised him to return next year because, among other shortcomings, he had poor vocal quality. 'I looked at the guy and said, "That's why I'm here. If I was [already] good, I'd be a working actor". He looked at me stunned,' LaPaglia chuckles. 'I was naive but truthful.'

He decided not to wait the year, he'd learn elsewhere, and so another 'NIDA reject' myth was born. Once LaPaglia became known, the press found great joy in chiding NIDA for failing to recruit him. 'I never felt NIDA did anything wrong,' he shrugs.

Sydney didn't offer much else for actors then. And as a TV-addicted child, weaned on black and white movies, he was fascinated with American icons: New York, Spencer Tracy, Katharine Hepburn and Gary Cooper. He'd also heard marvellous tales about his grandfather's 1910 migration to New York.

'So I made this completely irrational decision, within three days of being rejected by NIDA: I'm going to New York.' He couldn't leave fast enough. Racism weighed heavily on the 'wog'. 'I've never spoken to my father about it but the truth is I watched him suffer a number of indignities at the hands of "Australians". I used to feel ashamed of being Italian and would do everything I could to eradicate it from my persona in an attempt to fit in, but it just never really worked. If your last name ended in a vowel you were fucked and there was a certain expectation attached to that.'

As a first generation Australian, it was impossible to disregard how few ethnic acting roles there were in Australia. His decision was easily made. His parents couldn't believe it but his ticket was in his hand and they were 1000 kilometres away, in Adelaide. In quick time, LaPaglia resigned, sold his car and everything in his apartment and flew to New York with a suit-case and $500.

'I was so naive. I showed up in New York in the middle of winter [wearing] a pair of Dunlop Volleys and no socks,' he laughs. He had no friends there. He blundered through his first days bumpkin-in-the-big-city style. 'It was so insane and so different from anything I knew.' He camped at the YMCA in Chelsea before discovering a basement apartment and scrounging tax-exempt jobs bartending, waiting, 'whatever I could get my hands on'. After six months 'it was just so hard I couldn't cope', so he hit the road for Los Angeles with anoth-er actor who posited life would be cheaper, easier and warmer there.

It wasn't. LaPaglia despised LA. Granted, the 80s was not the city's finest decade. Drugs and crime were rife as the rem-nants of its earlier glam eras disintegrated, and on his first bus trip, LaPaglia witnessed a stabbing. Somehow, he remained dogged. 'My general m.o. everywhere I went [was to] meet people and ask them questions,' he says. One of his questions elicited information about an acting school run by an old Russian woman called Madame Olenska. 'It was like a bad film,' LaPaglia laughs. Sitting behind an imposing desk flanked by her two great danes sat a woman who, in LaPaglia's estimation, 'must have been a hundred and five'.

'Apparently, with very little qualification, I had the right stuff to enter her school.' He signed a contract for about US$600, a considerable sum for someone with no money. After three classes, LaPaglia realised he was in a hell presided over by a failed third-rate soap opera actor fond of spewing bitter bile at anyone with potential. He told the Madame he wanted out and his deposit returned. She demanded he pay for the entire course or she'd take legal action. A nervous LaPaglia penned a letter to Madame Olenska saying he'd moved back to Australia, 'so come and get me'. He sent it to his mother and asked her to send it from Australia. Welcome to Hollywood.

Within 18 months, LaPaglia left LA, which constricted him, and returned to New York. 'For the first eight years I didn't achieve much as an actor in the United States,' he concedes. His first job was as a soccer player in a milk commercial. No stretch. He also scored minor roles in TV shows including *The A-Team* and *Magnum P.I.* but 'honestly, if you looked at it from the outside, you'd say this guy's got no shot'. Nevertheless, roles such as Mechanic #2 in *Amazing Stories* or Punk #1 in *The Twilight Zone* earned him enough money to attend some of New York's classier acting schools and perform, gratis, in off-off Broadway theatre productions.

Not all his work was 'legitimate', LaPaglia confesses. The US has a quaint name for his type: 'illegal alien'. 'It was not cool. At that point I was so convinced I wanted to be an actor in the United States I took some very big chances. If I miscalculated, I would get kicked out and never be allowed back in again.' He was prepared to take the risk.

He was the typical struggling actor. To massage his American accent he even recorded and replayed Al Pacino's dialogue from long overdue rental videos of *Serpico* and *Dog Day Afternoon*. He tried a voice coach but couldn't master phonetics. He kept studying and took to crashing auditions. Eventually he secured an agent, albeit an 85-year-old Irishwoman, Maureen Oliver, who was so deaf and addled, she'd forget he was on the other end of the phone line.

Finally LaPaglia gained legitimacy, in the form of membership to the Screen Actors Guild, the card permitting him to work on film and television productions. He received it for performing one line in a Dolly Parton and Kenny Rogers

Christmas TV special: 'Sing us another song, Dolly.'

'Believe me, you weren't looking at my career thinking this guy's going to rocket to the top!' he laughs. Nevertheless, LaPaglia felt he'd won the lottery. 'I still remember the elation anxiously waiting [for it] to air on TV.' When it did, all he saw was a tiny speck in the background earnestly yelling that unforgettable line.

'In a lot of ways, the way I started was good for me because it taught me humility, the value of hard work and of persistence,' he adds. 'It did- *'It didn't come* n't come easy, I tell ya.' In fact, his story is dis- *easy, I tell ya'* tinctive because he entered the US without a body of work or hit film behind him. 'I came dead cold, which is why people always assumed I was an American, not an Australian.'

Not that he forced the issue. After six years, his Aussie accent was falling away, just at the moment Paul Hogan became ubiquitous. LaPaglia endured 20-minute discussions about that lovable 'shrimp on the barbie guy' at every audition. He'd even have to say 'shrimp on the barbie' before performing, only to be informed there were hints of 'Ossie' in his American accent. 'I thought, bullshit, my American accent was really good and they were just predisposed to hearing an Australian accent.'

Frustration reigned until LaPaglia found his first big US agent, Michael Bloom. A friend had asked LaPaglia to perform opposite him at an actors' showcase. His friend happened to be tall, blonde and handsome; apparently Bloom only attended because he had a crush on the blonde. One actor reneged though, so LaPaglia filled the hole with the 'coalminer' monologue from English comedy revue *Beyond the Fringe*, with Peter Cook and Dudley Moore. The crowd loved it; Bloom signed LaPaglia but not the blonde.

Bloom found LaPaglia a role in the New York production of the popular comic play *Bouncers*, John Godber's collection of monologues by nightclub doormen. Prominent casting director Mary Colquhoun saw the play and requested a meeting with LaPaglia about projects for the ABC TV network. One of them was a TV movie about the mobster *Frank Nitti: The Enforcer*. Colquhoun flew LaPaglia to LA to meet the producer, Leonard Hill, about the lead role. LaPaglia hatched a plan. 'I wasn't going to tell the truth because it never worked in the past.' He decided to say he was an American, born and bred in Chicago's Riverside, Nitti's stamping ground.

Hill was anxious because Stanley Tucci dropped out of the role two weeks before shooting, the producer says. 'And boom! There's Anthony who tells us he's from the outskirts of Chicago and he reads brilliantly.' They took him to another reading in front of the ABC TV executives who had final approval. 'He didn't seem to need reassurance,' says Hill. 'Most actors in this situation are testing the limits of their antiperspirant but Anthony's unfazed, he's just a kid from Chicago.' He fooled the execs too, one of whom said he lived ten miles from LaPaglia. 'His lie was so brazen it was appalling,' Hill laughs.

LaPaglia avoided the requisite conversation about shrimps on the barbie and won his first lead role in a telemovie – in anything. Early in the shoot, Hill walked into LaPaglia's trailer and heard the actor talking to an Australian friend in a convincing Aussie accent. 'I was thinking what a nice guy to make his friend feel so at home by speaking his language,' says Hill.

'He looks at me and says, "Mate, I am Australian".' Hill hit the roof. LaPaglia asked Hill if he'd have cast him if he knew. Hill said no. LaPaglia was vindicated. 'I almost wet my pants because the question was maybe he could pull it off in a reading but could he do the movie because he had to acquire and evolve an American street dialect. The lead actor had to go through a 40-year time span in a 20-day shoot,' says Hill. 'I was trepidatious but I had no place to turn. The gift is he was so well prepared and extravagantly blessed with talent he pulled it off.'

It took six months to find his next acting job, so he resorted to bartending. *Nitti* didn't pay well; the opportunity was considered an honour. Colquhoun saved the day again by inviting LaPaglia to a reading of Alan Alda's new script, *Betsy's Wedding*. Johnny Depp already had the role but wasn't available for the reading, so LaPaglia stepped in.

After two readings, producer Martin Bregman asked LaPaglia if he wanted the role. LaPaglia was stunned, disbelieving, and left thinking Bregman was only being polite. Three weeks later, the role was his although Alda and Bregman had to fight the Disney studio to cast this unknown 'Brooklyn actor' opposite Joe Pesci, Molly Ringwald and Ally Sheedy. 'If it wasn't for Marty Bregman and Alan Alda I'm not sure I would have even had a film career,' LaPaglia

'Success is lightning in a bottle, it has nothing to do with you'

concedes. 'Now that I'm older I understand success much better,' he adds. 'Success is lightning in a bottle, it has nothing to do with you. It helps if you're prepared but you don't have to be particularly talented to be successful; it helps, especially for longevity, but basically the finger of fate points down at you and says, "It's your turn."'

So it was with *Betsy's Wedding*. He totally understood Stevie Dee, the character landing in his lap – Stevie was the American version of a former Adelaide workmate. In a star-studded ensemble, LaPaglia shone, the *Chicago Sun-Times's* Roger Ebert writing that LaPaglia 'provides the movie's best moments'.

It was a heady time but the actor still didn't realise how lucky he was; he thought, 'Of course, I've been struggling for seven or eight years, this is how it should happen.' Then an acquaintance from school, now a journalist, 'blew the whistle' on the 'New Yorker'. LaPaglia began his deception as a Chicagoan but later claimed Brooklyn as home 'because I look like I'm from Brooklyn, I'm Italian and I sounded like I was from Brooklyn because I was doing Al [Pacino]'. No-one challenged him. 'This guy completely blew my cover but the weird thing was people didn't believe it,' he says. Twenty years later, some Americans still don't realise he's Australian.

'I was young, ambitious and I wanted to succeed,' he admits. He adopted his American persona for what he thought were the right reasons although reading articles about Australian actors succeeding in Hollywood frustrated him. 'They had flowery accolades about how brilliantly they had managed to do the American accent yet I never ever got that kind of credit. Ever. Not that I think I deserved credit for it but that's the kind of weird stuff that goes through your head.'

After filming *Betsy's Wedding*, LaPaglia returned to Sydney and sought Australian representation. 'They told me to fuck off,' LaPaglia says bluntly. 'They didn't believe I was working in the United States or that I had just done a film with Alan Alda.' One agent told him 'Sweetheart, I've got my star, I've got Gary Sweet.' He's moved on such that he can recount dismissals like these with mirth rather than bitterness. Nevertheless, LaPaglia felt like a star after *Betsy's Wedding*. Disney even signed him to a three picture deal that fizzled after three years because he didn't like any of the movies offered. Unwisely, LaPaglia concedes. 'I can say this retrospectively: I didn't understand the business, all I knew was I'd succeeded from *Betsy's Wedding* and I wanted to be more selective.' He also avoided publicity because he considered himself 'a real actor' yet he didn't know how to parlay *Betsy* into a more substantial career.

It was easy to be cocky, the roles were finally coming. LaPaglia enjoyed *One Good Cop* with Michael Keaton, more so *29th Street*, which suffered when its studio, Twentieth Century Fox, moved its promotional budget into Bette Midler's struggling *For the Boys*. LaPaglia's selectivity amounted to choosing characters rather than projects, 'so I ended up being good in a bunch of bad movies because I didn't look at the other actors and director, I just looked at the part'.

One bad movie holds particularly dire memories: *Innocent Blood*. LaPaglia didn't like the script but his agent talked him into it, saying he was out of his mind turning down a lead in a studio film directed by *An American Werewolf in London*'s John Landis and starring *La Femme Nikita*'s Anne Parillaud. LaPaglia quickly developed 'personality conflicts' with Landis and was vocal about them. Then he told Warner Brothers he wouldn't promote the film after Landis yanked LaPaglia's name from the promotional poster. 'I realised later by saying no to press [commitments], I'd blackballed myself for a couple of years at that studio. The irony is I'm working there now [on the TV series *Without a Trace*],' he chuckles.

LaPaglia's outspokenness occasionally causes other minor ruckuses. He's unrepentant but wary. 'The truth is half the time there's a percentage of people you work with that you would like to shoot because they were arseholes, not collaborative, didn't care and were a pain in the ass but you can't say it publicly. You could but it's not accepted practice.'

Then there are the times the actor must promote a film that went wrong, for whatever reason. 'You feel like a hypocrite because you're asking people to devote not only their time but their money to see something you wouldn't go and see,' he admits. 'Everybody's expected to play ball. Anybody who thinks they're bulletproof in Hollywood is really wrong. You can be bulletproof for a while but if you screw enough people over and don't play ball, you'll get written off eventually.'

LaPaglia admitted in one 1993 interview he'd become so obsessed with success during that time he almost subverted his career. His four-year marriage to model Cherie Michan disintegrated in 1990. 'I wanted to become famous more than I wanted to be a good actor,' LaPaglia says of the tumultuous period. 'Now I'm more objective about it and I realise whatever road I've had to take to get to where I am, that's the road I needed to take. I don't want to sound too Zen, but that was my path. And I've ended up in exactly the place I needed to be.'

'I wanted to become famous more than I wanted to be a good actor'

He returned to Australia in 1992 to co-star in a small cop thriller directed by John Dingwall, *The Custodian*. Taking the role meant turning down a big offer to star in *Judgment Night* (later starring Emilio Estevez and Cuba Gooding Jr) and LaPaglia was understandably reticent. 'There was a struggle going on inside me between the person who wanted to be an artist and the person who wanted to be a star. It was a big struggle, very difficult to be both without compromising yourself in a lot of different ways.'

Ultimately, he couldn't ignore Dingwall's enthusiasm or the opportunity to co-star with the actor who initially inspired him, Weaving. 'It's an OK film but John's tenacity, I admire that in people and I'm attracted to passion. My theory is if somebody is truly passionate about something, they're much more likely to do a good job. His passion lured me back.'

As it happened, LaPaglia met his future wife, Gia Carides, on that visit. A memorable return. Soon after the pair starred opposite each other as newlyweds in the forgettable romantic comedy *Lucky Break*. They re-teamed in 1996 for *Brilliant Lies*.

The mid-90s also saw him work on stinkers including Nora Ephron's *Mixed Nuts,* some minor hits such as Thomas Schlamme's *So I Married an Axe Murderer* and Steve Buscemi's *Trees Lounge*, and the big hit, *The Client*, which consolidated his reputation. He says he turned down 'a tonne' of television jobs during this period 'because I was hell-bent on becoming a movie star'.

At that time, television was the movie stars' graveyard. It wasn't until George Clooney's successful jumps between *ER* and movies that actors truly considered careers in the two mediums compatible. LaPaglia wasn't achieving what he wanted in film so he relented and took the lead role in the second series of *Murder One*. LaPaglia was the main character, Jimmy Wyler, in the sharply written, high quality legal drama. He surmised he could use the series to reinvigorate his progress. 'Once again it was the wrong reason to choose something,' he notes. 'But even if I choose something for the wrong reasons, once I'm in it I'll commit 100 per cent. I can't tank anything. Even when I realise I've made a mistake and I'm not enjoying it. That's a good lesson I learned. I take credit for the good and the bad things that happen to me [and] don't blame anybody for anything.'

Murder One performed well. Then he took on Broadway. Theatre remains a constant in LaPaglia's career. 'It's the only place you can't fake it. Movies you can fake it, a good editor can save your ass half the time, but once you're up on stage you're either doing the job or you're not. And people sitting in the audience know it. I love that about the stage, for two hours it's yours, nobody yells cut, nobody says I want you to do it this way.' LaPaglia contends theatre roles require responsiblility, a discipline he loves. 'I'd rather make my own mistakes. I'd rather be the one responsible for fucking up; I can live with that. I can't live with taking somebody else's advice and fucking up.'

LaPaglia loved Arthur Miller's play *A View from the Bridge* for years. He often utilised scenes from it in acting class and dreamt of being old enough to play the 50-something Eddie Carbone. 'So when I was thirty-eight I thought, I'm old enough, I can play this guy!' LaPaglia's different take on Eddie meant youthfulness would bring more sexual tension to his relationship with Catherine. He pitched the idea to Miller, who shared LaPaglia's New York agent, Sam Cohn. Cohn convinced Miller to allow LaPaglia to stage a reading with Frances McDormand and Chazz Palminteri, among others. LaPaglia then found a director, cast and theatre for a 15-week run. The show sold out its 500 seat theatre, moved to a 1200 seater and ran for another 11 months. He won a Tony Award, Broadway's highest honour, for his performance. 'The award meant a tonne in New York,' he laughs. 'It meant nothing in LA. It was a nice bauble I could wear on a big chain around my neck in LA!' But in 1998 it cemented the notion he was an 'actor', not just a mob character for hire.

'I've always kind of been considered a quality actor,' he notes. 'Even bad films I've managed to survive, not always, but most of the time. I've been in some movies nobody could survive.' He has committed one review of *Company Man* to memory: 'It would have been more interesting watching the actors suffering from food poisoning than watch them suffer through this film'. Ouch.

Broadway was 'an amazing experience' similar to his *Betsy's Wedding* ride. 'It basically took ten years to enjoy that kind of success again and I realised how fleeting it can be and how lucky you are to taste it once, let alone twice.'

The quality of LaPaglia's film projects swiftly elevated. Roles in Spike Lee's *Summer of Sam*, Woody Allen's *Sweet and Lowdown* and Terence Davies's *The House of Mirth* became standard rather than exceptions. Then two Australian films came along that his agents advised him against – an Italian coming-of-age story popular on school curricula, *Looking for Alibrandi,* and an ensemble drama from director Ray Lawrence, *Lantana*.

LaPaglia liked them too much to refuse. 'I said to my agents, "You show me something better and I'll do it". They didn't and couldn't.' He felt a connection to the Adelaide-Italian father in Melina Marchetta's script for *Alibrandi*. *Lantana*? Despite 'zero support' from his US reps, the movie, which co-starred Geoffrey Rush and Barbara Hershey, was an 'incredible working experience' and 'a major turning point' for LaPaglia. He knew it was something special during filming. He told Carides, 'After this film I should retire, it's not going to get any better than this.' LaPaglia testifies Lawrence provided 'the greatest working partnership I've ever had'.

His agent ignored him while he was shooting in Australia 'thinking I was off playing in the sandbox or something'. Upon his return to the US, LaPaglia said, 'You didn't call me for 15 weeks, didn't call to see how the film was going, how I was doing, nothing, and I pay you ten per cent for that?' He fired him.

Somewhat surprisingly, LaPaglia contends *Lantana* had more impact than any of his films. 'I can't tell you the list of people who just adored that film. There isn't a week that goes by where somebody doesn't stop me and go, "That *Lantana* is one of the best movies I've ever seen".' It performed well at the box office everywhere but America, earning $11 million in Australia. 'It was everything American movies can't be by the nature of the business here – character-driven, no explosions, no green screen (special effects). And there was this unified spirit between crew and actors, no delineation, no star, no pecking order, everybody had an equal voice on that film. I had the same experience on *The Bank* with Robert Connolly.'

LaPaglia won the 2001 Best Actor AFI Award for *Lantana* only months before collecting an Emmy for a guest perform-ance in US comedy series *Frasier*. He'd reconnected with Australia and spent eight months promoting *Lantana* 'at every festival and pothole I could possibly go to'. He doesn't feel obligated to return and make Australian stories, 'more a great desire'. 'It's like a breath of fresh air; in many ways I prefer it. I've developed a whole new relationship with Australia, a new love affair going on for a couple of years now.' He appreciates Australia's individuality against America's homogenisation, among other things. 'I'm not America-bashing at all, I like it here and America has afforded me an incredible career that I may not have had in Australia but I'm aware of America's shortcomings as well.'

In 2001, LaPaglia was offered the lead role of Jack Malone in the missing persons drama *Without a Trace*. He played hard to get, providing producer Jerry Bruckheimer with a testy list of demands before he'd commit. LaPaglia had done episodic television before and knew its requirements. He didn't shun the hard work, merely the predictability and the hours.

'It's about organisation,' he says. Television is quick, much quicker than shooting film, and that suits this 'not particular-ly patient' actor. 'But half the time television is a little bit dis-organised and they figure if they're paying you, they can keep you waiting around all day for two lines.' LaPaglia structured a deal where his schedule wasn't disorganised. A four-day working week with no more than nine hours a day is a luxu-ry in US network television. 'I got the John Travolta deal for TV,' he laughs contentedly. 'I'm very happy with that.' Even happier because the drama became a solid hit, powering into a second season while giving its all-conquering competitor, *ER*, a run for its money and delivering LaPaglia his first Golden Globe award for Best Performance by an Actor in a Television Series – Drama. After *Betsy's Wedding* and *A View From The Bridge*, this would be LaPaglia's third phase of success?

'I've been hot and not and written off about 12 or 13 times since I've been in Hollywood,' he laughs before asking to revisit his story in two years. 'I'm more wary of success now, I'm also more appreciative of it and I never used to enjoy it.' Now he most definitely does. He's no longer frustrated about his work either. 'It reaches a point where if you do enough things that have satisfied you, the results aren't really that important anymore, particularly as I get more into it as a producer [on the 2004 film *Winter Solstice*], you see the other [financial] side of it and what a crap shoot it is ... The Hollywood I came into and the Hollywood I'm in now are really different,' he adds. 'It's really fucking brutal now. If you thought three chances weren't a whole lot in my day, now it's even fucking worse. You get one or two shots at it.'

LaPaglia believes his Australian upbringing helped in this regard. Tougher and more pragmatic by nature, Australians don't over-analyse. 'Americans over-think shit and it hurts them in the end,' he says. 'What we do is not rocket science. Stop over-thinking it, just do it. That's the one thing that I've taken away from being an Australian.'

Also, like Bryan Brown, he didn't take rejection personally, some feat considering his eight years in the wilderness: 'I always thought it was their loss. Even if that's arrogant, that's how I really felt.' Americans tend to blame themselves when told they weren't good enough for a role. When LaPaglia lucked out, he merely thought producers 'didn't get it; it's their project, they're entitled to see what they want to see ... When you realise what goes into choosing actors to finance films how can you take it personally?' asks the man who, thanks to *Innocent Blood* and *Lantana*, is now big in France. His new TV series hasn't hurt his profile either, with 20 million Americans watching him every Thursday night.

'I have a great life,' he enthuses. 'I get up in the morning, go and do a job I love, have a wife and beautiful baby daughter I'm incredibly in love with, get to play soccer twice a week – you know what? My life's fucking perfect!'

He's struck the fine Hollywood balance of being known but not annoyed by media intrusion because he's 'not in the Ben–Jen business', although unflattering photographs of him disrobing at a soccer match did appear in an Australian women's magazine in 2002. 'I looked at them and said, "Well, that's you, that's your gut, that's the shape you're in and they took the photos",' he says. When he called the magazine's editor, it transpired the photos only ran because he didn't agree to pictures with his newborn baby. 'I believe in confronting people when I think that they're doing something cheesy,' LaPaglia notes. He told the magazine to pay a charity $2000 as a quasi-apology. 'And I said next year you can take a shot of my ass for $10 000,' he laughs.

'I can't deny that's who I am. I've got a gut, that's me. If I wanted to be skinny, I'd make the effort to be skinny but I don't care. I work anyway, it doesn't matter, fat, thin, whatever. The irony to prove it doesn't bother me, the first season finale of *Without a Trace*, I showed my gut to 22 million people!'

He's content and he's struck a balance between art and commerce, Hollywood and Australia. It only took a couple of decades.

13
portia
de rossi

Pivotal Projects

Arrested Development (TV) (2003), The Night We Called It A Day (2003)

Ally McBeal (TV) (1997–2002), Too Something (TV) (1995)

The Woman in the Moon (1995), Sirens (1994)

portia

Portia de Rossi began her acting career in Australia but a chance meeting with a movie mogul in London forever changed its course. After shooting her first film, *Sirens*, about painter Norman Lindsay, in which she appears as one of his three life models, she flew to London.

'I had no agent when I got there,' she recalls. Getting work would have proven difficult. One night the cast, which included Hugh Grant and Tara Fitzgerald, and director John Duigan went to dinner with Miramax co-chief Harvey Weinstein after a screening of the film. Miramax was distributing the movie.

'[Weinstein] was kind of an important type of guy,' says de Rossi with deliberate understatement. He even took the trouble to tell her as much. Weinstein is undeniably one of the most revered and feared men in New York. Unlike his brother, Bob, with whom he runs Miramax (and its mainstream offshoot, Dimension Films), Weinstein is big and intimidating, although he is also known to treat favoured actors very well. The company at that time had a burgeoning reputation built from distributing movies like *The Crying Game*, *Cinema Paradiso* and *Sex, Lies and Videotape*. 'Harvey', as he's universally known, has since become famous for backing expensive promotional campaigns that ensure his films and actors always feature during Oscars season.

So de Rossi was looking forward to the dinner. 'But there

were a lot of people, it was a very large table and I was sitting three chairs down from him on the same side. I remember thinking, if I'm going to do this dinner with Harvey Weinstein then I may as well talk to him. So I got up off my chair and sat directly in front of him, across the table. He was in the middle of a big story, stopped dead and said, "Hey, did you just move chairs so I could see you?" I said, "Yeah, I did, Harvey, because we're here for you and I'd like to meet you." And he thought that was hysterical and laughed and said, "Girl, you're gonna go far, I'm gonna get you an agent". The next day I was with the best agent in London at ICM.' Ms de Rossi was just 21 years old.

'Both of them noted one another,' John Duigan grins at the memory. 'Harvey has an eye for talent and he makes a mental note of those to look out for. Portia's also somebody who would have been always making a note of people who might be useful to know in the future.' Weinstein called Michael Foster, then with International Creative Management, and told him, 'Take Portia de Rossi.'

'I had nothing to lose,' de Rossi states. 'I was in law school, I'd deferred, done this movie, I liked [acting]. What the hell? It wasn't so precious to me.' She says her fresh and full-on approach came from being Australian. 'I think when you're living [in Los Angeles] and you want to be an actor, you try really hard [and] you just get more nervous that you could make a mistake. If he thought it was obnoxious and ridiculous of me to do that – whatever?' Heath Ledger describes possessing a similar devil-may-care bravado when he first arrived in LA yet the opposite is true of Naomi Watts, who took forever to break through and whose agent, at one stage, pulled her aside to warn that her desperation was making people nervous.

De Rossi attempted to find work in London but faced snobbery on two fronts: she was Australian and lacked formal training. She returned home and hooked up with agent Barbara Leane. 'She really did me the best service anyone has ever done my career,' de Rossi recalls. 'She took me aside and said, "Look, Portia, you're not gonna work here, you're gonna work in Los Angeles". She got my energy, understood me.' Nevertheless, de Rossi remembers being shocked by the information. 'She made me feel better when she said, "I said the same thing to Nicole Kidman".'

De Rossi now fully agrees with Leane's edict that some actors are better suited to working in the United States, or England, or Australia. 'In Australia I [was perceived] to be a model. I wasn't considered a serious actress after *Sirens* because I was such a newcomer.' Playing alongside well-known models Kate Fischer and Elle Macpherson reinforced this perception. 'The Americans don't care about what your credentials are, just that you're right for a job,' de Rossi says.

After being a model for ten years, she quickly took to acting. Her performance in *Sirens* as the young, prudish Giddy is more accomplished than Macpherson and Fischer, admittedly both novices as well. Despite having a much lower profile than those two and being much younger, Giddy's role was significantly bigger.

'I was a girl Kmart model [and did] general Melbourne catalogue work.' Magazine spreads followed, she explains. 'In the 80s there was a lot of catalogue work to be had. I was very busy and making pretty good money for an 11 year old,' she laughs. 'I looked pretty much like I do now and I was an ambitious little thing. I liked it [and] the money it gave me. We lived in Geelong [an hour southwest of Melbourne] and when I got it into my head that I'd like to model, my mother was taking time off work and driving me for auditions. She was great, the good old stage mother. She thought, while you're having fun doing it and while your school grades are good, why not?'

That said, de Rossi was socially ostracised during the crucial high school years. Students at her elite Geelong Grammar School were particularly brutal. 'To never be at school because you're off modelling for *Dolly* magazine is a big deal when that's the magazine on everybody's desk. And I changed my name during that time. You don't want to do that as a 15 year old who wants to fit in.'

Amanda Rogers began her transformation clumsily. 'Kids are really cruel,' she says. 'I had an ego the size of Texas. I felt mature for my age because modelling is a pretty harsh world and you have to know how to handle yourself. I probably thought all my little friends were very provincial. I was very ostracised and probably a pain in the arse to everybody. It was good though, because it made me grit my teeth and want to succeed.'

'I had an ego the size of Texas'

She moved to Melbourne and Melbourne Girls Grammar for her final two years' education but only managed a year before convincing her mother to let her leave. She'd pursue modelling full time on condition she would consider returning to school the following year. The deal worked perfectly. De Rossi recalls being so bored by the end of that year, she couldn't wait to hit the books – this time at a progressive school, Taylor's College. She studied incredibly hard and earned exceptional grades to qualify for the prestigious Melbourne University law degree.

At university she eschewed the drama clubs and student companies and continued modelling. 'I didn't even think about acting. I did less print [modelling] and more television work [including] on-camera commercials, such as "the girl in the fast food joint".' Occasionally, she was given lines in the ads. 'So I didn't realise I was kind of acting and I loved doing them, they were fun. I got a script and I got to interpret the

lines; I could sell a piece of chicken like I was no-one's!'
Gradually she became known to casting directors, so when the
queen of casting, Liz Mullinar, received the script for *Sirens*
(which required three actresses to portray Lindsay's muses, or
sirens), de Rossi, the model, seemed a natural fit.

'I turned down the audition three times because I
thought, "I don't want to be an actor. What a fantastic life,
being an out-of-work actor!"' Then she learnt Sam Neill would
play Lindsay and discovered she liked the script. 'There was
something magical about it, so I finally went in and it was
probably the most gruelling process I've ever come across in
my life.' In ten years as an actor nothing has come close? 'Most
definitely.'

John Duigan, the director, 'loved an ingenue. As a director he really is drawn to that kind of naivety, the freshness
people have as young kids, so he likes working with first-
timers. I was lucky,' she acknowledges. But he insisted on
intense training. 'Workshops over the weekend, improv, theatresports.' Duigan confesses he needed 'certain physical
requirements' of the sirens, to physically intimidate Tara
Fitzgerald's English character, 'a very demure small woman'.

De Rossi was one of about 40 to audition in Melbourne. She
performed well, Duigan recalls, so he shortlisted her for the
intensive three-day audition. 'The interesting thing about her
was she plays this character, Giddy, who's quite naive and guile-
lessly sensual and it's a very, very different person to Portia,
who was an extraordinarily single-minded young woman at the
time,' Duigan adds. 'From very early on in the process, she told
me she was quite keen to try out in Hollywood. She was very
bright and ambitious. It was very impressive how easy [acting]
was for her and how completely convincing she was [as] this
character. As an untrained actress to be able to do that, it was
quite interesting and amusing really.'

Sirens was a watershed for de Rossi. 'I discovered how wonderful acting could be [and] realised I really wanted to pursue it.' Duigan, who wrote the screenplay, gave Giddy the most remarkable line. 'I'm quite ambitious,' she says to Fitzgerald, playing the prim English minister's wife.

'You want to be a model?' Fitzgerald's Estella asks.

'No, modelling is just to get known. No, I'm going to be quite a famous actress. People will get to know me through Mr Lindsay's paintings, I hope, and then I'll move on to stage and screen.' Quite an ambition for a 20-year-old Australian girl living on a property in rural New South Wales between the World Wars. Or for a 21-year-old model from Geelong. Duigan laughs: 'I was aware by the time we came to shoot it there was a certain resonance about the line, although I think my awareness of that was not quite as complete as it would be now.'

Sirens didn't set the world on fire critically or at the Australian box office, where it collected $2.8 million. It fared better in the US where it earned US$8 million, only slightly less than *Strictly Ballroom* (US$12 million) and *The Adventures of Priscilla, Queen of the Desert* (US$11 million) a couple of years before.

De Rossi attended its well-received premiere at Robert Redford's Sundance Film Festival in Utah. On the strength of that screening she was offered a role in *The Woman in the Moon* – 'A *very* low budget independent feature,' she says. In 1994, she flew to Tucson, Arizona for the shoot.

'After that movie I remember sitting in the airport and I had a ticket back to Australia via LA,' she says. She took out a pen and paper and plotted the pros and cons of returning home versus stopping in LA. 'It was the hardest few hours of my life.'

Other actors on the movie, who lived in LA, had invited her to crash on their couches. 'Actors over here are pretty generous to each other because we all go through hell. No matter how successful you are or how much work you get, you're still going through hell in one way or another. If you're getting offered scripts it's "Which one am I going to do to keep my career where it is?" or "How much money is he getting and he's my co-star? I should be getting the same". So I got to LA, got off the plane, had my luggage taken off. In the end, it was "Why not?"'

The decision spelled the end of her law studies. Fortunately, her acting friends did supply couches for a couple of months and because she was represented by ICM in London, the agency automatically represented her in LA, though she was assigned a junior agent. De Rossi began auditioning and 'as luck would have it I booked a job a couple of months in'. Initially, she didn't have a 'green card', the qualification that allows foreigners to work in the US, so the production company applied for a visa, which took a couple of weeks.

Her first job was in 1995 on the Fox TV network comedy series *Too Something*. The network only aired seven episodes but shot 22, so de Rossi was essentially paid for a full TV season's work. That enabled her to survive financially until the following pilot season, the period in which TV networks produce new programs.

'I read for a half-hour pilot called *Mixed Nuts* by *some* guy called David E. Kelley (famed producer of *Ally McBeal* and *The Practice*) and I'm so oblivious,' she says. 'I didn't know who David Kelley was but I went in and read and David Kelley wanted me to do the pilot, which was amazing but I couldn't get a visa in time to do it.'

'Usually there's enough time to petition and get the paperwork together, it takes two to three weeks, but it was Friday afternoon and we were shooting Tuesday – which on television happens a lot. So I had to pass, which was great for me because David Kelley, who's so used to getting what he wants, was so pissed off about it he always kept me in mind.'

Mixed Nuts didn't make it to a series. Meanwhile, Kelley's *Ally McBeal* and *The Practice* were becoming two of the most popular and talked about shows on US network television. 'He brought me in, he didn't even know what he wanted [and] he said, "I've got *The Practice* and I've got *Ally McBeal*". I remember him turning to his partner and saying, "I think she'd be better for *Ally McBeal*." That's how it happened. He wrote the character Nelle Porter [a foxy attorney at Ally's firm] after the meeting.' According to de Rossi her experience with Kelley was not unusual. 'He does that a lot, writes parts for people.'

De Rossi was a recurring guest initially. She then joined the show permanently in January 1999, midway through series two, and stayed to the series end in May 2002. As the TV machine cranked into action, de Rossi's life changed very quickly with media interviews, paparazzi and scurrilous speculation about her private life.

'I never thought it would be great to be a big, fabulous movie star, I wanted fortune but I didn't necessarily want to be famous. It was such a shock,' she notes. 'I was so highly embarrassed, the first year. With a show that was so loved and watched, people are really intent on scrutinising you and I was the new girl; it was a crazy, crazy time.'

'I wanted fortune but I didn't necessarily want to be famous'

Gossip and entertainment media relished de Rossi's relationship with Francesca Gregorini. She is sanguine about the attention but says it's tough on the people close to her, who did not necessarily choose public life. 'It's not just me, it's natural to want your mum to be proud of you and sometimes you can't. My mum, for example, would really like to see me always dressed beautifully, glamorous and a big Hollywood star. And I'm not, that's not my truth, so occasionally she'll say, "Nicole Kidman always dresses so beautifully". I'm like, "Well, she does and she looks great but unfortunately I have a lot of paparazzi that tend to love me more when I'm at the supermarket, which is most of the time … You can't turn your back on it but keep acting. If you keep acting you keep all of it,' de Rossi says. The paparazzi, the demands for interviews, the websites, glossy magazine stories … are all part of the package.

'I have a lot of paparazzi that love me more when I'm at the supermarket, which is most of the time'

De Rossi faced tough decisions in 2002, when Kelley shuttered production on *Ally McBeal.* 'I panicked,' she admits. Should she pursue films? Would anyone cast her in another TV show? Did she want that? Television, she says, 'takes up so much of your time and so much of your identity, I wasn't Portia de Rossi, I was Portia from *Ally McBeal.*' She mentally sifted through a list of previous television regulars, asking herself: 'Where are they now?' 'It's rare for TV stars from one show to jump onto something else but I'm not worried about that anymore.'

She isn't worried because she was chosen by Ron Howard's Imagine Entertainment to co-star in *Arrested Development.* The half-hour weekly comedy launched on Fox in the US in 2003 and became the season's biggest new hit. A darling with the critics, *Variety* newspaper even theorised *Arrested Development* could fill the void that will be left by *Friends* in 2005. Audiences were less enthusiastic, so this remains to be seen. De Rossi portrays a 'shopaholic brat' in an extended family of nutty, once-wealthy characters coming to grips with newfound poverty. 'Of course, if I had not been successful in [the 2003] pilot season we might be having a different conversation!' she laughs about the fickle nature of her business.

Once, there was a huge divide between film and television makers – actors, directors, producers, all. Television people were seen as the industry's workhorses and their actors were beamed daily into viewers' homes. Those viewers, the argument went, would never pay to see the same actors at the cinema. Jennifer Aniston, George Clooney, Robin Williams, Tom Hanks, Will Smith and many others have changed that. The industry's best film producers and directors are now also working in TV; Jerry Bruckheimer and Steven Spielberg, to name two, have added spectacular television successes to their stellar film careers. As the budgets for major films soar and studios demand more conservative storytelling, so they can reach the broadest possible audience, television, especially cable TV with its niche audiences, is increasingly the home of creative, challenging work. It's now fashionable for the industry leaders to switch between the two.

De Rossi credits Kelley as a major force behind the new brand of TV. 'The whole tone of Ally was different,' she says. 'It came out of the blue and inspired people to write more interesting television ... Doing features isn't that important to me,' de Rossi explains. 'If a great feature comes my way, fantastic, I'll do it, if it doesn't and this great television show lands on my lap, I'll do that.'

Her TV career is flourishing as she flits in and out of film roles, some of which – *Women in Film* and *Who Is Cletis Tout?* – were interesting though unsuccessful. In 2002, her career finally came full circle when, almost a decade after being cast in *Sirens*, she returned home to portray a journalist insulted by Frank Sinatra while he toured Australia. The 1974 incident resulted in cancelled gigs and Sinatra being stranded in Sydney by trade unions demanding an apology.

'I had been trying to do a film in Australia since *Sirens*,' de Rossi confesses. Why, with such a consistent US career? 'It's a very emotional thing, I just [wanted] to do a movie at home. *The Night We Called It A Day* landed on my lap and I was very excited. The script was interesting and fun; it's hard to find that quirky sensibility in American [projects] and it's so business-oriented here. When we were shooting *The Night We Called It A Day*, no-one was focused on the demographic and the potential box office. Of course we wanted it to be successful but there's a whole element of Australian filmmaking that is for the pure enjoyment of making art which is really lost over here. The whole thing is so bloody serious and it's such big business and to me it seems like it's lost its desire to make good, nice little stories.'

The only problem with that approach was that few critics supported *The Night We Called It A Day*. It was a surprising disaster at the Australian box office and enjoyed little activity elsewhere. It was one of many Australian films released in 2003 that led the local industry to throw up its hands in dismay. Arguably, other films poisoned its prospects.

De Rossi was nervous returning to make the film: 'I just didn't know where I fitted in. We had big American actors [Melanie Griffith and Dennis Hopper] and Australian actors [Rose Byrne and Joel Edgerton] and I'm somewhere in the middle.' De Rossi was a link between the two sides but fully settled with neither. A stranger in her own land. 'When it was green-lit, I started working on my accent. I'd just start speaking with an Australian accent to get used to it and I realised very quickly it wasn't like riding a bike, I had trained myself so thoroughly to get rid of it.'

Despite de Rossi's frustration, *Sirens* director Duigan believes her convincing US accent is symptomatic of her career. 'It's a testament to her sense of focus. When she went over there the first thing she did was become absolutely fluent in an American accent and she did that by speaking all the time in an American accent. Portia's decision was to immerse herself as completely as possible in that culture so there would be no question that she'd be speaking to the casting director in an American accent from the very beginning.'

In preparation for *The Night We Called It A Day* she urged herself to try harder to reinstate her native accent but she lacked Australian stimuli and had no other Australians to bounce off other than her brother, who was living in Venice Beach, LA. 'So I'd call him up just for a little conversation, wouldn't tell him what I was doing and afterwards I'd say, "How was that?" And he'd say, "Waddyamean?" "I was speaking with an Australian accent." And he'd say, "No you're not." It was scary.'

She did likewise when chatting with *The Night We Called It A Day*'s Australian producer, Emile Sherman, and director, Paul Goldman. 'Then halfway through the conversation they'd say, "So how's that Australian accent coming along?"' De Rossi groans, recalling her frustration.

Unable to bear the thought of hiring an LA dialect coach to teach her Australian, she placated herself with the thought that when she touched down in Sydney, it would come back to her. Nope.

She eventually met with a dialect coach ... who was English. 'The last thing I want is to be ridiculed for being an Australian and not having an Australian accent,' she confesses. But true to form, her astonishing determination won out. There's not a hint of 'LA' in her performance in *The Night We Called It A Day*.

14
fred
schepisi

Pivotal Projects

It Runs in the Family (2003), Last Orders (2002)

Six Degrees of Separation (1993), The Russia House (1990), Evil Angels (1988)

Roxanne (1987), Plenty (1985), Iceman (1984), Barbarosa (1982)

The Chant of Jimmie Blacksmith (1978), The Devil's Playground (1976)

schepisi

'Hollywood is always looking for people with talent – but actually what they're looking for is people who will freshen up their genres.' So says Fred Schepisi, who discovered this the hard way. He was first among the 1970s directors – the so-called Australian New Wave – to go to Hollywood but as he tells it, it was an excruciating time.

After almost 20 years' directing advertisements and two feature films, Schepisi was celebrated but he was also broke. In 1976 his debut full-length feature, a coming-of-age drama set in a catholic seminary, *The Devil's Playground*, had been well received at the Cannes Film Festival and was a hit in Australia. His follow-up, an occasionally violent exploration of white–black relations, *The Chant of Jimmie Blacksmith*, enjoyed some critical support overseas. But local critics hated it and audiences stayed away. 'We weren't ready to watch Indigenous Australians on screen then,' he muses.

Schepisi was shattered. He had invested a large chunk of money in both films. Buoyed by the returns from *The Devil's Playground*, he doubled his investment in 1978's *The Chant of Jimmie Blacksmith*. 'The budget of *Jimmie Blacksmith* was something like $1.2 million,' at the time the most expensive Australian film ever made, and it included $250000 of Schepisi's own money. He also charged a minimal fee to keep costs low. 'I charged $11000 to write and bloody direct and produce. How stupid can you be?' he asks. Facing his fortieth birthday, the father of six, despite running a successful advertising production company, was feeling the pinch. He recalls thinking, I can't keep just throwing money in like this. But moving to America wasn't a simple solution.

Hollywood was circling but the outspoken director had backed himself into a corner. For longer than he cares to remember he'd advocated – especially loudly when drunk – that to maintain integrity, artists should stay in Australia: 'I thought we should stay at home and do films in our own voice and in our own culture,' he says, 'without interference.' It was a fine opinion, no doubt appreciated by his fellow filmmakers, but the reaction to *Jimmie Blacksmith* had stung Schepisi's wallet and his ego. It was time to be pragmatic. 'Maybe there were things I could learn and if I made a name for myself, that would make it easier to make other pictures. Also I'd get paid,' he recalls thinking.

He'd advocated – especially loudly when drunk – that to maintain integrity, artists should stay in Australia

He kick-started negotiations with US studio Twentieth Century Fox, then managed by Alan Ladd Jr. Fox was cashed up from its recent spectacular success with George Lucas's *Star Wars*; it also owned the Hoyts cinema chain in Australia. Ladd recalls Fox, through Hoyts, had 'invested in some movies, among them was *Jimmie Blacksmith* ... It didn't work in America at all [but] I did admire it very much and thought [Schepisi's] direction was quite excellent [so] I commissioned him to do something else.' Ladd is surprised to learn Schepisi was the first Australian director of that era to accept an offer from Hollywood. He says it was as common for the studios to employ talented outsiders then as it is today.

In the 30s Hollywood drew heavily on European filmmakers. Then, according to Schepisi, 'at the same time we were going over there, so were a whole group of English filmmakers'. He believes Hollywood executives are expert at spotting fresh talent. They lure it in and kid themselves they want to encourage more movies in a similar vein but what they really want is for the directors to reinvent standard Hollywood fare. 'You try and give them more and sometimes you give them *Plenty* or *Evil Angels* or *Six Degrees of Separation*', he says.

Before arriving in Hollywood Schepisi had written a vaguely autobiographical relationship drama called *Bittersweet Love*, about a twice-married man. He planned to produce and direct it but 'just as I was about to go over (Ladd) was marched off the lot under police escort'. Ladd's explanation for the rough handling: 'When I started, the company was at US$4 a share and when I left it was US$64 a share, so they weren't too happy when I quit.'

Fox Studio vice president Sandy Lieberson was promoted into the top job. 'So I rang him and said, "What the hell's going on?"' Schepisi says. Lieberson asked Schepisi to wait two months, then fly to Los Angeles. The director agreed. He didn't have much room to argue. He'd already sold his house. 'It was a little disturbing,' he deadpans. 'I gave him two months, then we jumped on a plane and when we got to the other end, *he'd* been sacked.' Sherry Lansing replaced him.

This personnel revolving door was an early taste of what lay ahead. With creative personalities, swelling egos, huge amounts of money at stake and the major studios (and 'mini-majors') sourcing funds picture by picture from wherever they can, everything is volatile and nothing is guaranteed, ever. 'When I did *Roxanne*, from the start of Steve Martin doing the screenplay to the distribution of the picture, [there were] five different [studio] heads at Columbia,' Schepisi notes.

Hollywood lore dictates 'You're only as good as your last movie' but for studio chiefs that's problematic. According to Schepisi, 'the next guy who comes in doesn't want to know the last guy's [projects]'. If they fail, the new studio chief can be fired but if they work, the

'You're only as good as your last movie'

chief can't bask in the full glory of success either. So executive turmoil freezes financing and stifles production. *Roxanne* halted twice as new studio personnel equivocated over who should co-star.

Schepisi and Martin wanted Columbia to sign Sigourney Weaver before *Aliens* was released. It didn't. *Aliens* was a hit, Weaver's fee rocketed and they lost her completely. Eventually Daryl Hannah, an equally big star at the time due to *Splash*, was signed. Schepisi intones, 'and of course it cost us as much as it would have cost to get Sigourney Weaver in the first place'. But that was later.

Years before *Roxanne,* Schepisi struggled to begin his first American movie. 'I waited for [studio head Lansing] to read [*Bittersweet Love*] and after about three weeks I thought, this is damn silly, so I said, "I don't care whether you've read the script or not, have a meeting with me".' Lansing agreed, though Schepisi probably employed more subtle language when he actually made the request.

Fox owed him money for a rewrite of the script, so he said, 'Why don't we make this simple? Set me up with an office, give me the oldest secretary on the lot, who knows the routine, I'll do my rewrite, give it to you, you give me my money, you don't even have to read it, we'll just say goodbye. If you want to read it and it tickles your fancy, fantastic, if not, we're both off the hook.' Lansing liked the idea so much she actually tracked down the oldest secretary on staff and assigned her to him. The lady 'really was great, she got me Bette Midler's office [and] executive dining privileges'. Schepisi laughs. 'Then I spent the loneliest two months of my life.'

Hollywood newcomers talk of feeling isolated. In recent years, for some actors at least, the loneliness has been cushioned by the swelling ranks of Australians in LA.

Some Australian actors and directors even wangled a toehold in Hollywood without leaving home. But there were no friends – long lost or brand new – awaiting Schepisi in sprawling Los Angeles. 'Some people came and went, some people stayed,' he says of that time in the late 70s, early 80s. 'A lot of people who you don't really hear about went over and they just fell foul.'

He says the system is innately wearing, particularly the litany of meetings where you think something is actually happening but it's not. 'Then suddenly months go by and you're no further advanced. You've got four projects and think you're doing something, then one day you realise, "Actually, this isn't going anywhere, this is all smoke and mirrors". It's very, very hard to get a contract concrete. There's a thing there called being "kissed out the door".' In a Californian accent, Schepisi mimics air kissing: '"You're such a great talent, I'm just so looking forward to working with you". What they mean is: "Can you get the hell outta here, I've got another meeting".'

'I often come across people who've made one film, or haven't even made a film and they're over there [boasting], "God it's great, I've got a meeting for this and that ...",' Schepisi continues. 'I try and assess who they are and I say, "You know what? You should go home, you're gonna crucify yourself here", and you can. Maybe I was pretty close to it.'

In 1982, Schepisi nearly packed his bags. With seven projects amounting to not much, he had one foot on that Qantas jet outta there. 'Sometimes you can break through and it's good for you and sometimes it just isn't,' he says. 'You may not have the moxie or that extra bit of talent they're looking for or you may [have it] – and they don't give you the chance. It's all of those things.'

Schepisi submitted the draft of *Bittersweet Love* to Lansing as agreed. It was never produced but now he was in the loop. He was offered two movies – a depression-era story called *Raggedy Man* with Sissy Spacek, who was hot following the success of *Coal Miner's Daughter* and *Carrie*. The other was a western buddy movie called *Barbarosa*.

Then came his crash course in the next level of Hollywood politics. Despite committing to *Raggedy Man* and reworking the script extensively, the producers refused to make Schepisi 'pay or play' until Spacek signed. 'Pay or play' guarantees a pay cheque whether or not the film is made. It's the clause that allows some directors to live quite well in Hollywood without ever having to make a movie, though its use is rare these days, for obvious reasons.

Schepisi continued beavering away at rewrites but Spacek, despite indicating she was keen to make the movie, still refused to sign. The Australian couldn't shake the gnawing feeling her tactics related to him and he confronted the producers with his fears. They denied its veracity.

Meanwhile *Barbarosa* was firming. Willie Nelson and Gary Busey had signed to co-star and there was a firm start date but to make it meant walking away from *Raggedy Man*, on which Schepisi had done so much work. He gave the producers until the end of the week to make him pay or play. They didn't, so Schepisi quit that Friday afternoon in late 1980. 'I got the most extraordinary amount of abuse from the studio [Universal] and the producers,' he says. 'I would know better how to handle all that now, but you don't know all that stuff [when you're new to Hollywood] ... It was rather significant that by the Monday morning Spacek's husband Jack Fisk [was] made pay or play.' Schepisi suspects, despite the abuse, his exit suited the studio. 'Fisk was a very good production designer who Universal had promised to make a picture with and they hadn't found one. [So] it seemed to them to be a very good fit – to honour a contract and to hook Sissy Spacek.'

So Schepisi started work on *Barbarosa* for Marble Arch, a mini-major studio that then collapsed during the course of production. 'Guess where the picture ended up? Universal! And the joke is, the Universal management, who were being rather unkind to it, had all gotten fired. It's a pretty constant process,' he laughs. Futhermore, Bob Rehme, who'd assumed the top job at Universal, called Schepisi into a meeting to tell him the studio had no faith in *Barbarosa*'s box office prospects. Was this one of those instances where incumbent studio chiefs distance themselves from projects inherited from others? According to Schepisi, Rehme said, 'It's got Willie Nelson, he's failed' [in his previous movie *Honeysuckle Rose*]. Even worse, he added, 'It's a western and it's got Mexicans in it.' That was studio-speak for 'double box office death'. 'We're gonna give this a one-week release across the southwestern drive-ins and if it doesn't work, it's history.'

Schepisi asked, 'If you did that with *Honeysuckle Rose* and it didn't work, why would you do it with this? Why don't you let me take the picture to New York and get [the *New Yorker*'s] Pauline Kael and various critics to look at it? If I can give you reviews, don't mass release it, let me put it in one or two places and let it build.' Rehme replied, 'If you go to New York and you don't get the reviews, I'll never release the fucking thing.'

Kael, the most influential American critic at the time but no fan of Australian movies, had previously dubbed Schepisi's *The Chant of Jimmie Blacksmith* 'magnificent'. He was confident *Barbarosa* would also please the reviewers. It did. But Rehme wouldn't budge from his original plan of only releasing the film in the south. So at Schepisi's urging, critics Gene Siskel and Roger Ebert, of the high profile, syndicated TV show *At The Movies*, helped out. They regularly dubbed bad films Dog of the Week. 'They gave Universal a Dog award for not releasing *Barbarosa* and [promised] to give them one every week until they gave it a release. The critic at the *Washington Post* drove 130 miles to a tiny town and a tin shed to see it and wrote a one page rave about it.' Reacting to this bad publicity, the studio shunted *Barbarosa* into a theatre in Manhattan's Upper East Side, 'with no back-up or advertising', according to Schepisi. It screened for not much longer than a week.

During this tussle, Schepisi signed to direct, for Norman Jewison's production company, *Iceman*, a science-fiction movie about a Neanderthal man frozen in ice who is then resuscitated. Ominously, Universal was due to distribute it. When Schepisi was appointed director, Rehme wrote him an apparently sincere letter, congratulating him on getting the job and offering to be of assistance where he could. Not one to let sleeping dogs lie, Schepisi fired back an identical letter to Rehme, congratulating him on his job and also offering to help out in any way he could.

It would be too easy to conclude Rehme buried *Iceman* because Schepisi was so cantankerous. 'On the opening weekend I was doing publicity,' Schepisi opines. 'Does something seem wrong there? Usually you need two months lead time.' Having self-released *The Devil's Playground* and worked closely with distributors on the US releases of his Australian films, Schepisi was well schooled in the business of film distribution.

'I had a whole theatre wanting to rip the screen down. That's a great reaction.'

His next lesson was in the brutality of test screenings. 'There was one scene in *Iceman*, I had a whole theatre wanting to rip the screen down, that's how angry they were. That's a great reaction, that's what it was meant to evoke, it was an injustice, they all had to react like that.' This is vintage Schepisi; *The Devil's Playground* had a similar impact on audiences. 'It used to clear cinemas,' he adds with a grin. 'I could stand outside the cinema door and tell you what scene was playing by the number of people who were coming out.' Schepisi admits this reaction was 'not great, but it was having an impact. The violence was meant to be anti-violent, so I guess I had to expect that was going to happen.'

But test screenings, Hollywood's new weapon against the unpredictable, resulted in *Iceman* being watered down. The studio was nervous and then compounded its problems by releasing it against Hugh Hudson's big, highly expensive, *Greystoke: The Legend of Tarzan, Lord of the Apes*. Schepisi is still stupefied by the decision. In the mid-80s schedules were less crowded than they are now, that is, fewer movies were released each week so there was less competition for media attention. These days scheduling is the key to a film's chances of success. For example, distributors don't release two teen romantic comedies in the same week. The release dates for mass-appeal action movies will jostle until there's a month, either side, wherein no similar picture is released, if possible. Also, similarly named films should be avoided; in 1996, the simultaneous release in Australia of *Dead Man* and *Dead Man Walking* – two vastly different films – baffled audiences. Movie-goers expecting to see Johnny Depp in black and white were instead being confronted with Susan Sarandon as a nun in full colour.

So, releasing a sci-fi movie about a hairy Neanderthal man the same day as a film about another hairy guy who was raised by wolves and lived in the jungle befuddled audiences, to say the least. 'It was the stupidest decision, the confusion was amazing,' Schepisi says. Still, *Iceman* performed well enough and heralded Schepisi's entry to mainstream Hollywood. So what did he do? He took off for London to shoot *Plenty*, an adaptation of David Hare's stage play starring Meryl Streep. It is telling that Schepisi's journey through Hollywood was incremental. His preference for interesting movies over ones that generate massive box office has ensured his career longevity. 'If I was making highly commercial pictures and they weren't highly commercial then I'd have been dead in the water very quick,' he offers.

Schepisi was hankering to make a comedy but the studios wouldn't risk an unproven comic director. 'Finally, Steve Martin and producer Dan Melnick wanted a filmmaker rather than a comedy filmmaker', for *Roxanne*, their comic reworking of the classic play *Cyrano de Bergerac*. It was a huge success that ironically saw Schepisi inundated with comedy scripts. The movie remains a highlight of Schepisi's Hollywood career, which was happening everywhere, it seems, but in Hollywood. *Iceman* shot in Canada, *Barbarosa* in Texas, *Plenty* in England, then it was back to Canada to make *Roxanne*. His four children from his first marriage were living in Australia, so he was also juggling trips home as often as possible.

In 1987 he settled in New York but the money soon came through for him to make *Evil Angels*, the movie based on the infamous disappearance of baby Azaria Chamberlain from an Uluru campsite. Schepisi was jetting to Australia again, his dream of using Hollywood money to make an Australian movie finally realised. After 30 years as a director, including a decade being buffeted by the American system, he was on home ground, removed from interfering studio minions but making a movie with their money, about the biggest legal–media case in contemporary Australian history.

　　The $16 million, Warner Brothers-backed film featured some known and emerging Australian actors but starred an American and a New Zealander (Sam Neill) in the lead roles. Australian critics and local actors were outraged by Schepisi's casting of Meryl Streep as Lindy Chamberlain. The director says, 'I understand but in this case she was a huge collaborator [they'd previously worked together on *Plenty*]. I don't believe I would have been able to do it without her – or someone of that kind of ability – and it would not have been made with that kind of money.' Almost 20 years later Australian directors are spoiled for choice with legions of talented, experienced and world famous Australian actors.

　　The studio didn't interfere with *Evil Angels* during filming and the test screenings were relatively painless. The film earned just US$7 million in America and although Schepisi says 'Australians stayed away in droves', homeland box office was a respectable $3 million – Phillip Noyce's *Dead Calm* took $2.4 million the following year. But $3 million was less than Schepisi would have expected, given the cost and calibre of the project. It remains the thirty-first highest grossing Australian film ever.

　　'In America I hated the poster, I hated the way Warners handled it,' Schepisi notes. 'The big studios, they've got formulas, they're a machine, but they're not very good generally at handling special product that needs careful releasing and building.'

　　A quarter of a century after he left for Hollywood, Schepisi still spends a great deal of time in Australia. He's come full circle and is now focused on developing and producing his own projects rather than playing the Hollywood system. 'In the end, sure, I got to do something like *Evil Angels* but the way you think it works at any given time doesn't last very long nor [do] the people you form relationships with,' he says. 'You're constantly having to renew relationships, understand new situations and find other ways of getting money to get films made.'

Yet there are the moments when it all clicks. 'Some films are like serendipity, they come out of nowhere, everything falls into place, and they happen,' he smiles. *The Russia House*, Tom Stoppard's adaptation of John le Carré's spy yarn, was one of them. Schepisi's agent became le Carré's agent, they took the project to MGM, where Schepisi's old acquaintance Alan Ladd was now working. He committed to a certain budget if they could nab Sean Connery. Schepisi met with Connery in an airport while both were in transit, gave him the script, had a chat and sent him on his way. As soon as Connery disembarked from his flight, he phoned Schepisi to commit. The film made US$23 million in the US and has been particularly enduring on television and video.

Schepisi's slice-of-life dramatic comedy, *It Runs in the Family*, also proved smoother than a film starring Michael Douglas and his 86-year-old, ex-stroke victim father might have been. The script was sent to Douglas's company as a writing sample but he decided it would be a wonderful film in which he could play alongside his father and son. At the suggestion of one of the film's producers, who had seen Schepisi's recent adaptation of Graham Swift's novel, *Last Orders*, Douglas invited him to direct it. 'And from November to November the whole thing was done, despite all the obstacles with insurance [for Kirk] and all that stuff, it was done in a year,' Schepisi says. 'That's damn near a record, I tell ya.' Even the weather was perfect, unseasonably so, on *It Runs in the Family*. 'For some things, Huey the Movie God says "This one's going to be mine", and you'll get good weather when you need it and bad weather when you want it to be bad, this is how it'll be made. You have no say in it.'

There's no sure recipe for success in Hollywood but that's the case everywhere. Schepisi says his Hollywood journey was fuelled by 'ignorance' and 'chutzpah'. Other motivating factors were money and the sense that he had little to lose. He admits being wounded by the Australian industry's savaging of *Jimmie Blacksmith* but now understands its context. Australians used to always ask him about *The Devil's Playground* yet foreigners were more interested in *Jimmie Blacksmith*. 'Now that's changed here, now I get asked about *Jimmie Blacksmith* as much as *Devil's Playground*,' he says. 'It's not a reflection on *Devil's Playground*, it's a reflection on *Jimmie Blacksmith*. Australians couldn't take it when it first came out, just couldn't take it. There was a lot of vitriol directed towards me and now they see it differently. Now they're looking at it as a film rather than as something that stirred their social conscience at the time.'

'I was thrilled to see Phil Noyce's *Rabbit-Proof Fence* was so well attended, it's a wonderful move forward for Australian audiences; anything with Aboriginals usually just kept them away.'

In the 70s, it made sense that Schepisi wanted to go to the US, where *Jimmie Blacksmith* was better received. The irony that *Blacksmith* was his entree card has never left him. For the first 18 months after leaving Australia for Hollywood, Schepisi says, 'every time I answered my phone to an Australian journalist the first question [was] "Why did you sell out?"'

15
naomi
watts

Pivotal Projects

King Kong (2005), I Heart Huckabee's (2004), 21 Grams (2003)

Ned Kelly (2003), The Ring (2002), Mulholland Dr. (2001), Tank Girl (1995)

Gross Misconduct (1992), Brides of Christ (TV) (1991), Flirting (1989)

naomi

The story of Ned Kelly, the rebellious, bog-Irish bushranger, says much about the Australian character. Equally, *Ned Kelly*, Gregor Jordan's 2003 film, says much about the so-called Australian 'invasion' of Hollywood.

The film, shot in the Victorian countryside, tells an Australian story but was bankrolled by Hollywood's Universal Studios through Working Title, its English production house. The $30 million budget came together on the strength of its high profile but predominantly Australian cast, including Heath Ledger, Geoffrey Rush, Rachel Griffiths and Naomi Watts. Watts almost pulled out. Exhausted from shooting three movies back-to-back, she flew into Melbourne's Tullamarine Airport to fulfil her six-day commitment to the project. 'I was like, my body cannot take this. I was thinking of ways I could get out of it but once I got here I thought, OK, this is the right thing to do, I'm glad I came.'

'It's so wonderful [Ned Kelly was] made with Australians playing Australians rather than having to pull in American movie stars just based on their box office appeal.' But ask if she's one of those Aussies with 'box office appeal' and she tries to laugh it off. She will never be entirely comfortable with her own success after more than a decade's frustration endeavouring to attain it.

'Define success?' she asks defensively before venturing, 'To me, success means not having to audition.' She laughs before catching herself, lest anyone notice she's too big for her boots and, therefore, un-Australian. 'I'm happy to audition now because it'll be different, not having to walk in at ten past one as just another actress. [Now] people know who I am, know my work. It won't be such a test where you're set up to fail. That's how auditions used to seem for me and that was tough,' she adds before returning to the question. 'Success is being invited to work with people I've always admired or newly admired — incredible directors you know will teach you and inspire you and bring out the absolute best. I want to take risks and I'm sure to make mistakes again.'

'To me, success means not having to audition'

The mistakes will be public now. 'Sure, but I'm going to allow myself to do that because taking risks can have huge pay-offs. Obviously.' Obviously. Watts's story is all about risk and a huge, albeit belated, pay-off. Her path to that pay-off was tortuously long and obstacle-ridden; a path many would have abandoned. Watts prevailed and finally consolidated her talent in Hollywood in 2001, 16 years after being cast in her first movie, a decade after playing her first lead role and eight years after taking the greatest risk of all: packing up, leaving Sydney and moving to Los Angeles.

The project announcing her to Hollywood almost came crashing down as so many others had before. Watts quietly rejoiced when, in 2000, she was cast to co-star in a pilot for *Twin Peaks* creator David Lynch. *Mulholland Dr.* was touted as the new *Twin Peaks* and working with the famous *Blue Velvet* director carried greater credibility than almost everything she had ever done. What more could she ask for? She could ask that America's ABC network didn't baulk at Lynch's idiosyncratic result and can the series. Lynch being Lynch though, found French producers who bought the rights forUS\$7million, US\$1 million less than ABC spent on it. It gave Lynch two weeks to reshoot some scenes and refashion his pilot into a film.

Mulholland Dr. eventually premiered spectacularly at the 2001 Cannes Film Festival. Later that year, it upended the end-of-year awards season and earned Lynch an Oscar nomination. Inexplicably, and despite heightened industry speculation, the Academy ignored Watts's career-changing performance. It didn't matter. *Mulholland Dr.*'s profile was reward enough and she was sufficiently driven to make the most of it. A lead role in Gore Verbinski's blockbuster thriller *The Ring* followed.

Watts's career was not devoid of opportunities. She was poised for stardom almost from the outset but early movies, such as *Gross Misconduct*, fell short. In the late 90s, her American TV series *Sleepwalkers* was axed abruptly. After *Mulholland Dr.*'s axing, she contemplated throwing in acting – again. Or returning home.

Did she have a true home though? The British-born blonde moved to Australia aged fourteen, after a brief stint in Wales. Her father, Peter, a sound engineer for prog-rock band Pink Floyd, died when she was seven, three years after her parents had separated. Her mother, Miv, has since returned to Norfolk, England.

In England, Watts confesses she 'always liked to show off and draw attention to myself'. She first tasted theatre's magic as a four year old watching her mother play Eliza Dolittle in a Shoreham amateur production of *My Fair Lady*. She featured in *Mary Poppins* aged five and joined the local theatre group at six. At her admittedly free-spirited home, Watts loved dressing up and playing with make-up. She also liked inventing characters and concedes she was something of a tomboy.

The family moved out of London due to the recession in the early 80s. The transition to Sydney was unsettling, as might be expected for any teenager, particularly one with a single mother and elder brother. Again, she tried a few acting schools and picked up occasional modelling work while her mother found work in film art departments and married a musician.

'I trained but not in a formal way,' Watts says of her nascent acting. 'I did many different courses from fourteen right up until I left Australia.' But she admits she didn't feel particularly creative compared to her mum, brother and stepfather. She hated school and had trouble making friends. Aged fifteen, at an audition for a swimwear advertisement, she met another aspiring actress who would later become a solid friend, Nicole Kidman. They shared a taxi home and crossed paths many times in Australia before their friendship consolidated when Watts later moved to LA.

Watts left Mosman High School after Year 11 despite her mother pleading with her to complete her final year. She knew school offered little that would assist her career, particularly as she was already studying drama and had nabbed a couple of minor screen roles.

Despite its tribulations, her teenage years in Australia were useful both personally and professionally. They gave her, at the very least, a working knowledge of disparate accents. 'I consider myself both English and Australian,' she confesses. 'At times I feel so Australian and I go back to England and I'm around my family and I feel English. My dad passed away when I was a kid, all my aunties are here [Australia] and most of my friends are Australian because I moved here when I was fourteen and that's when you start creating long-term friendships. Although I lived four more years in England than I did in Australia [she left Sydney aged 24], I really do feel a good combination of both. Long before the Australian invasion happened, I said I'm an Australian actor because this is where I started my career, did my training.'

That training also included a stint in Tokyo (aged eighteen). Displaying the chutzpah that later propelled her to Hollywood, Watts secured a modelling agent, despite being a diminutive five foot four and a half. Tokyo was unfulfilling and depressing. She swore to herself she'd never work in front of a camera again and returned to Sydney.

She secured an advertising job in a department store before finding work at two fashion magazines. But shortly afterwards a friend urged her to make up the numbers at a weekend drama workshop. It was there she realised she'd denied her calling. On Monday, a re-energised Watts told her doubting boss she was quitting in order to act.

Almost immediately, the 20 year old met director John Duigan at 'a couple of parties', he recalls. He told her she'd suit a role in his next film and recommended she call his casting director, Liz Mullinar. Duigan cast her in the schoolgirl drama *Flirting*, a sequel to his acclaimed *The Year My Voice Broke*. Watts was only a support next to Kidman and Thandie Newton but it was her biggest role yet.

'She had no experience at all at that point,' says Duigan. 'I was happy to find that she had a real natural gift for acting and had this very engaging freshness and a sense of subtle sensuality underneath it, which was great for that role. I put her in glasses because I wanted to just make her not as obviously pretty as she was! She was fantastic in it.'

Other roles arrived in spurts, including a guest role on TV sitcom *Hey Dad*, commercials, and a bit part as a paraplegic in the soapie *Home and Away*. Then came the moment other actors might regret – she turned down a regular role in the popular night-time TV drama *A Country Practice*. She brooded

about that decision for the next six months but with hindsight, she says, it was a learning experience.

Eventually, in 1991, she scored a role in the hit ABC TV
mini-series *Brides of Christ;* a small part as an aspiring movie
star in Joe Dante's warm US drama *Matinee;* and the TV adventure mystery, *Bermuda Triangle,* before Duigan cast her again
in the Pacific Island period misfire, *Wide Sargasso* Sea. 'I said
do you want to come over and do this little role and I think she
enjoyed the break over there,' Duigan says. 'Then began her
purgatory in Hollywood.'

Watts stayed in LA sporadically but hadn't committed to
a particular home base – her family was in the UK and her
highest profile roles were coming out of Australia. Most
famously, Watts played the girl who turned down a date with
Tom Cruise in preference for her mum's roast lamb dinner. By
then, Watts had met Cruise through his wife, Kidman.

What should have been Watts's big break came with a call
while in London. *The Man From Snowy River* director George
Miller wanted her to audition for his sexual harassment
thriller, *Gross Misconduct.* Duigan, by now a friend, directed
and acted in her screen test for the lead role opposite *LA Law*'s
Jimmy Smits. 'We saw it and just went "Yes".' recalls Miller.
'There was nobody else we wanted, she just gave a terrific performance.'

Nevertheless, casting a relative newcomer against Smits, at
the peak of his power, was a leap. Miller didn't see it that way.
'In the Australian film industry, sometimes we have the luxu-
ry of casting the actor who's right for the job rather than by
their "Q-quotient" [a market-researched number specifying
appeal and profile]. She was easy. I found her readings so often
left me very little to say in terms of direction.'

The stylish film's tight focus conspired against mass audience appeal though. It appeared Watts's time would never

come. Again, her tenacity in the face of rejection revealed itself. In 1994, after a small role in John Dingwall's *The Custodian*, starring Anthony LaPaglia and Hugo Weaving, she packed her bags and headed for Los Angeles.

Admittedly, she hit Hollywood 'pretty wide-eyed and naive' and, by Australian standards, ambitious. Her friends there helped, particularly actress Rebecca Rigg and Kidman. 'She's been a constant source of inspiration and has handled herself so graciously and done so well, so I've always looked to her.' They rarely talk about business, she demurs, perhaps disingenuously given that Watts's Academy Award 'campaign' for *21 Grams* closely mirrored Kidman's for *The Hours*. Watts scored all the right magazine covers in all the right months – and won an Oscar nomination.

Kidman's friendship occasionally meant Watts had a place to stay or a gown to wear but she also experienced Hollywood's supercilious side. She received employment promises from people who knew her connection to Kidman. Promises promptly forgotten. Yet her move to LA appeared to pay off immediately. In 1995 she nabbed the co-lead role of Jet Girl in the comic book adaptation *Tank Girl*. It tanked. Her purgatory continued. She scraped by with television movies such as *Timepiece,* the straight-to-video horror flick *Children of the Corn IV: The Gathering* (aka *Deadly Harvest*) and George Hickenlooper's *Persons Unknown*. Her American TV series *Sleepwalkers* was axed midway through its debut season, despite Watts garnering warm reviews.

In 1997 she returned to Australia for Graeme Rattigan's limp *Under the Lighthouse Dancing,* shot on Rottnest Island and not released outside Western Australia. The hard times rolled on. She was living in a two-bedroom guesthouse and practising her beloved yoga to cleanse herself of the despicable auditioning process. Yet she maintained her focus on acting and refused to take other jobs to pay the rent. The years were passing and Watts admits her bags were often packed and she was 'fed up'.

'I had moments of really, really just wanting to pack it in [but] just as I was about to go through with it something would hook me back in.' Nothing substantial, though. She hung in because 'I just loved acting. I loved the form of expression, it was in my bones and something I wanted to do and, believe me, I second-guessed myself all the way. I kept thinking of what else I could do and couldn't come up with much,' she laughs.

The offers trickled in but the projects kept failing. In 1998 Marshall Herskovitz's camp costume drama *Dangerous Beauty*, starring Catherine McCormack and Rufus Sewell, and Emma-Kate Croghan's *Strange Planet*, with Claudia Karvan, both ran off the rails dramatically. Watts's expectations of the US TV movie *The Christmas Wish* were never high. Kidman kept advising, 'One great role, just one great role is all it takes.'

'Yes, it was one role in the David Lynch movie that turned me from total obscurity to people suddenly ringing me and asking me to be involved in their projects,' Watts observes. 'It changed things really significantly, turned everything around.'

The David Lynch movie nearly wasn't her watershed moment. Watts admits that by 1999 she was damaged goods, having been rejected so often, she couldn't shine. Luckily, Lynch didn't like auditions. The enigmatic creator of *Twin Peaks* merely glanced at resumes and head shots. He and Watts spoke at length on consecutive days – during which Lynch admitted he'd not seen one of her performances. Two weeks later he cast her in *Mulholland Dr*.

She quickly sensed something special. And she brought something incredibly special to the most memorable scene in the occasionally befuddling movie. The 'audition scene' wherein Watts, as the desperate actress, delivers a knockout audition that floors both the clumsy onlookers in the room and the cinema audience, had industry folk abuzz from Cannes to Hollywood and beyond. The irony of that scene mirroring her situation at that time is not lost on her. She says generously that every actor in the room 'brought something really special to either their annoying director or their cynical casting director or hopeful producer'. They all had personal experience of just such a belittling scenario, 'so when we shot it there was magic in the room'.

Not enough magic for the US ABC TV network though, which canned the pilot. Meanwhile, Watts was at her wit's end. This was too much bad luck to be considered luck anymore. She enjoyed falling in with Lynch's creative posse and spent time working with them on unseen projects but *Mulholland Dr.*'s on-again, off-again status proved oppressive. She continued to audition until her agent told her people were sensing her desperation. Casting directors felt Watts was too intense and hard-nosed about the work. Then came the clincher. Her agent asked if Watts was worried about her age. She was thirty-two. She burst into tears.

As *Mulholland Dr.* lurched from go to whoa, Watts had to face the fact her dream might be over. She gave up hoping the movie would ever be seen but two months later, in May 2001, *Mulholland Dr.* premiered at the Cannes Film Festival. The film world lauded the return of Lynch and the arrival of Naomi Watts. 'People [were] wanting to meet me, that was all,' Watts notes dryly of the instant change in her circumstances. 'I haven't [auditioned] since then. [*The Ring*] was the last audition I did.'

Lynch had Watts play two characters: Betty, a plucky actress arriving in Hollywood whose journey is derailed by an amnesiac, and then Diane, an embittered Hollywood wretch. It was wonderful casting, if only because for Betty's pluck you could substitute Watts's tenacity, for Diane's shattered dreams, Watts's. Yet it wasn't her first such role. In 2000 she made a 16-minute short film, *Ellie Parker*, with Scott Coffey that was passed around Hollywood, played the 2001 Sundance Film Festival and caught the attention of many directors, including *21 Grams'* Alejandro Innaritu.

Coffey, Watts's 'very, very good friend', was exasperated with acting and wanted to write and direct so he suggested Watts play a harried aspiring actress in his short film. The digital film was cheap – 'all our friends were in it' – and popular. Watts played the young actress hurrying from one audition, and character, to the next. 'So there's the transformation, physically and emotionally while driving from one place to another, late, stuck in traffic, on the freeway, changing clothes, make-up, learning lines, checking phone calls, bad news, good news – chaos. A day in the life of an actor in LA, a starving, unprivileged one.' Despite its heightened comedy, 'there was a lot of truth in there too'. She knew all about the truth.

But thousands more saw *Mulholland Dr.* Critics were unanimous in their praise of Watts's performance. *Rolling Stone's* Peter Travers's response was typical: 'The relatively unknown Watts and [Laura Elena] Harring are sensational in ways that go beyond the call of babes-in-distress duty. And Watts . . . is a revelation. Her performance, nailing every subversive impulse under Betty's sunny exterior, ranks with the year's finest.' Yet Watts inexplicably missed a 2001 Oscar nomination. She contends it didn't faze her, although 'The trouble is all the time leading up to it with the predictions in the newspapers and friends telling you you'll do well, it's hard not to invest a little bit of hope and believe them.' After her 2003 nomination for *21 Grams*, she said, 'This time I had a little bit of preparation.' She tempted fate and watched the nominations live on television, figuring 'It's anyone's guess [who'll win] so why not just watch it on TV like everyone else?'

Mulholland Dr. could have been a flash in the pan but Watts consolidated that success with a box office hit – an even more important attribute in Hollywood. No-one anticipated Gore Verbinski's reinterpretation of the cult Japanese horror hit, *The Ring*, to succeed as it did. It took US$250 million at the global box office. Somehow the cold thriller about a videotape that kills its viewers resonated with the audience. Watts relished the 'kinda risky' idea of playing a character who's 'a bit of a pain in the arse in the beginning'.

Despite confidence in her work, Watts knew *The Ring* was the real test for her longevity. 'Because of all that attention with *Mulholland Dr.*, people are waiting – "What's next?" And there's a real fear of people judging me too harshly because the second film is always the most harshly judged and people are thinking, did she just get a great role? Maybe it was a fluke. Can she really deliver anything again? So when I found out the movie had done well and 70 per cent of the reviews were good, it was a huge relief,' she sighs. 'And I'm still thinking, eek! Because you can't just rest on your laurels.'

Watts remembers charting *The Ring*'s box office figures attentively. She wasn't so attentive with *Mulholland Dr.*, primarily because she hadn't been there before. *The Ring* was different. 'My face wasn't on the poster, there is no star in this movie. I am known in the industry but the public is not aware of me – they are not going to see a Naomi Watts film,' she says. 'Having said that, they did put my face on the poster in the week preceding the release and I am the lead in the film, I am the protagonist, and if the audience is not interested in her then it's going to affect their interest in the whole story. So I did feel a certain sense of responsibility even though I was going to protect myself that if it didn't work, it was the plot!' she laughs.

The long haul clearly resonates with Watts. Confidence still hasn't taken hold though. 'I get encouraged and um, yeah, no, I'll always be someone – no matter what level of success I experience – who has self-doubt; that's just part of my make-up.'

The Ring should have eliminated that doubt. The only way she's been able to keep doubt, and that niggling question of age, at bay has been by working. Prolifically. An intense two years had their disappointments, such as the flaccid British comedy *Plots With A View*, and its successes, *21 Grams*. The Ismail Merchant–James Ivory romantic comedy *Le Divorce* fell somewhere in between, a well-reviewed film starring Watts, Kate Hudson and Glenn Close that found a middling but appreciative audience. Merchant says Watts 'showed her greatest gift' in *Mulholland Dr.* 'We were very much focused on her and she met with James Ivory, he liked her and she had wanted to work with Merchant–Ivory, so it was very much a mutual admiration. She's sensitive, beautiful and very talented,' he adds. 'She's very hard-working and learned French impeccably and we were all very impressed with her.'

Watts was Innaritu's only choice for *21 Grams*, the drama co-starring Sean Penn and Benicio Del Toro. 'Her ability to be like an innocent, a tender little fragile woman and then so full of rage, that is not easy,' he observed at the Toronto Film Festival. Watts researched her role as a grieving mother as she hadn't before. The tale of desperate loss was personal. 'Oh yeah. I've dealt with loss before and it definitely brought up a lot of that stuff when I was researching. I have to say I am proud of this one.'

Her choices since have been eclectic. She appears with Jude Law in the comedy *I Heart Huckabee's* for *Three Kings'* David O. Russell and produced and stars in John Curran's adultery drama, *We Don't Live Here Anymore*. Curran permitted her to take any role she wanted; she chose the passive instigator of an affair because the other female, played by Laura Dern, 'is much more explosive and dramatic and I felt like I'd just done that in *21 Grams*'. Then there's the sequel, *Ring 2*, for director Hideo Nakata, in which she co-stars with her friend Simon Baker.

In four swift years, Watts's choices have expanded dramatically. She capitalised on them. 'I feel like I try to do whatever speaks to me. People try to instruct this is what you should do and you have to be linear but I don't want to follow the rules, you want to be someone that can bend the rules, shape things in your own way. It's about creating a balance of doing things that are a bit more commercial so you can get your dark twisted ones made that only appeal to a small audience. There's not too much planning but doing whatever speaks to you at that particular time and even if you've done it before, do it again.'

Lord of the Rings director Peter Jackson handed Watts a role for which there was no choice – the lead in his remake of *King Kong*. He says his Kong will treat the fantastical story of a giant ape seriously – 'That's the lesson we've learnt off *Lord of the Rings*,' he says. So for what 'everyone calls the Fay Wray role', Jackson wanted a 'real' actress. 'We didn't want a sort of blonde bimbo screaming her head off, we wanted somebody who can bring a great deal of depth and emotional honesty to the role and Naomi is one of the great actresses of today. We've actually been great fans of hers and when the idea of Kong came up, we just thought she'd be perfect right from the word go.'

Many directors and producers now feel Watts is perfect for their films yet Watts won't slow now she's attained financial security and professional credibility. 'Look, nothing lasts forever, I'm very aware of that and yes I do have a lot of energy because I had so much time not working and it's very hard to say no to a good role. But I am fully aware that it will only hold my interest for however long it does. I think I'll always want to act but not at quite the same speed I've been going in the last couple of years and I will start to trust a little bit that it's not going to go away tomorrow.'

While there is self-doubt, there is great self-awareness. Her Australian peers know she is the most dogged of their bunch, one who wouldn't concede, and she continues to show a savvy adaptability and resolve that remains cloaked under her serene public persona. As someone who didn't have success flung their way too quickly, her path has been full of wisdom gained

'Nothing lasts forever, I'm very aware of that'

rather than lessons learned. She knows to keep her 'deadpan, dry, acerbic humour' at bay because 'it doesn't translate to the reader'. Or Americans, as it turns out. 'In fact when I moved over there I learned pretty quickly to dilute it but years later, once I got my confidence up a bit, I thought, no, that's not me, don't dilute your personality, don't cancel it out just because you're afraid of offending someone. Be yourself and make them take it on the chin, teach them to understand your humour. It's not all Americans, though, just particularly in that city.'

Yet Watts has few qualms about making 'that city', Los Angeles, her home. 'That's where the work is,' she says with focus. 'But that's just me and it doesn't matter what surroundings I'm in, I'll always be like that. You can't have a city define you.'

'I've had my feelings about that place change and contradict themselves all along the way and they will continue to do so,' she adds. 'Your happiness is built within your own life and a city will never dictate that; it's been kind to me lately but I'm very aware of what I've had to go through to earn that recognition and that place. I'm really grateful now.'

Much is made of the unofficial Australian support group in Los Angeles. 'It's just that with the new label of "Australian invasion" it seems suddenly there's a lot of that. But there's always been, ever since I went there, quite a few.' Watts's support group is a fairly stable one: Kidman and Rebecca Rigg (wife of *The Guardian*'s star, Simon Baker) chief among them. She admits in 'a work town', without family, 'you stick together with people who've had similar experiences'.

And rather than ask for encouragement from her peers, now Watts feels she can give it. 'I do encourage people who are in pursuit of a dream. I'll always encourage that because I knew what my dream was and I'm still trying to create it. That's the thing, you can't go, I got praised for one film and the second film did really well and that's it. There's that great quote: "Trust those who are seeking the truth, not those who have found it", meaning just because a couple of things have worked for you doesn't mean you've learnt everything and you've succeeded in everything. It's about using that and going, yes, that was a good experience, and turning to something else that's going to elevate you and teach you new things.'

> 'I knew what my dream was and I'm still trying to create it'

The journey's been torturous but perhaps she needed the time to grow. Says Miller, 'She was beautiful then, now I think she's enchanting. She's grown into being this beautiful woman.' The euphoria she felt upon her Oscar nomination in 2004 was palpable. 'I've reached a place that's far beyond what I ever dreamed.'

16
heath
ledger

Pivotal Projects

The Brothers Grimm (2004), Ned Kelly (2003), A Knight's Tale (2001)

The Patriot (2000), Two Hands (1999), 10 Things I Hate About You (1999)

Paws (1997), Blackrock (1996)

heath

'There's little anyone can do to prepare you for how you're going to feel and how you're going to react to all this.' Heath Ledger knows. He had his 'How are you going to react to this?' moment in a boardroom at Columbia Pictures headquarters in Culver City, Los Angeles in 2000. The leading man could have cried but he didn't – leading men don't cry. Instead the 21 year old sat, intimidated, by a bevy of cloying studio publicists and marketing experts. 'It really freaked me out [listening to] all these people talking about how they were planning to promote me as a product,' he recalls.

Ledger slips on a shonky American accent: 'OK, kid, we've got nine countries around the world and covers of this magazine, covers of that, and we want to do these TV shows – do you want to do those shows?' He didn't know. This was only his third Hollywood movie and yet he was being told he was to be the face of Columbia's *A Knight's Tale*. Ledger also understood he was being positioned as a new Sony star (the Japanese conglomerate owns Columbia), and henceforth would shoulder some responsibility for its success.

After being bombarded with information for two hours he was asked what he thought. The usually reserved actor stood up, pushed his chair out and said, '"I have to go to the bathroom" … And when I got to the bathroom, I shut the door and just sat there and started to shiver. I wanted to burst out in tears,' he says. On returning to the boardroom, he announced he had to leave before dragging his agent outside and asking him to finish the meeting. Welcome to the big time, baby.

Still in his mid-twenties, Heath Ledger has lived a Hollywood life in full. He even came to Los Angeles skint. Then, his rapid ascent to leading-man star status was swifter than for any other Australian before him. And he knows it. But he readily admits he wanted it, so there are no complaints. Not that it was entirely clear he wanted to be an actor when he was young.

Despite being named after *Wuthering Heights'* male protagonist, Heathcliff, there was nothing melodramatic about Ledger's childhood. Born and raised in Perth, Australia's isolated city on the Indian Ocean, Ledger showed only a passing interest in acting until his older sister Kate lured him to the Globe Shakespeare Company. Slowly, an intrigue became an interest and Heath was cast in local theatre productions such as *Peter Pan, Name of the Father* and *Bugsy Malone*. His parents, who divorced when he was ten, showed little enthusiasm for their kids' theatrical interests; his father pushed him towards sport, particularly hockey. His teachers were even less involved.

At sixteen, Ledger left school and embarked on an adventure of a lifetime. With his best mate, Trevor DiCarlo, he drove the width of Australia to Sydney. His parents were mortified but knew they couldn't stop him. The boy wanted to prove something.

He soon did, quickly earning occasional commercials work and a role in the angsty teen film *Blackrock*. That led to the more challenging role of gay cyclist Snowy Bowles in the ABC's TV series *Sweat*, which ran for one season.

Other work came, including a small role in the children's movie *Paws*, and an unheralded stint on the long-running

Australian soap *Home and Away* (his future girlfriend, Naomi Watts, had previously done six weeks on the series herself). 'I had a total of six working days there that ended up being like 20 episodes,' he laughs. The show doesn't trumpet him as a former star. 'They probably didn't even notice me,' he smiles.

Then came the break. Ledger was cast as the lead in the mythological fantasy TV series for the US Fox Network, *Roar* (produced by former teen idol, Shaun Cassidy). Ledger finally had a career – but not the one he wanted. 'I hadn't done anything in Australia, really.' He describes his early roles as 'typecasting'. 'On *Home and Away* [I was] the blonde beach boy who came in to have sex with Sally [Kate Ritchie] for the first time,' he chuckles.

He obtained enough work in Australia to live comfortably because 'I don't need that much money to survive'. Satisfaction was harder to come by. According to director Gregor Jordan, 'Heath was never a normal 18 year old, he was worldly, articulate and not overwhelmed by things at all.'

In 1997 he moved to Los Angeles. Ledger says coyly, 'I just went over there, I'd met a girl and moved over here with her and I just hit the auditioning scene.' The girl was Lisa Zane, his 36-year-old *Roar* co-star. It was a personal and professional journey. 'It was half and half [for me] because I didn't expect to get any work but I thought, what the fuck, while I've got the opportunity ...'

Ledger's cause was aided considerably by one LA-based Australian, who advised Ledger to strike while the iron was hot. He did. Despite not wanting a manager, nor foreseeing a future with one, Ledger thought he initially needed a middleman. 'I couldn't get on the phone myself and say, "Hey, I think I'm pretty great",' he smiles. 'Especially when you don't [think you're pretty great] – at that time, anyway. You have to be a certain type of person to do that, I guess that's why you have managers.' But once you have an agent, your manager is super-fluous. 'Your manager just makes you feel good and drives you to parties and stuff,' Ledger laughs.

His manager proved invaluable and was probably the reason why Ledger didn't flounder like so many other young Australian actors. Nevertheless, finding an agent was problematic; the Australian saw through their insincerity: 'They're excited by everyone who walks through the door.' And agents' inducements can be exciting. 'You'd go to meetings and they'd bring out sodas or cookies, stuff like that, or they'd ring before you got there and ask, "What does he like?"' Thankfully, Ledger had someone else taking the calls, telling them, 'I dunno, croissants?' 'And you'd turn up and there'd be sugar-coated croissants on the table!'

Ledger met six agents, but none felt right. Too much bull-shit. He settled eventually on 'a younger guy who had no clients', Steve Alexander at CAA. Alexander had produced movies (1994's *Café Society*) 'and he just had a fire in his belly'. A leap of faith? Undoubtedly, but Ledger contends, 'I just did-n't like the rest of the people I'd met. They were just, I don't know, have you ever seen *Swimming with Sharks*?' Not only did the dark Hollywood satire of a tyrannical, bombastic agent mirror Ledger's experience, but Alexander had produced the movie. Ledger's still with him, as are Wes Bentley, Jared Leto and Shannyn Sossamon (his *A Knight's Tale* co-star). 'As [our] crew moved up so did he; now he's got an office with a win-dow,' he laughs. 'He's out of the broom closet.'

Ledger's next break was unlikely. He was cast as the lead in *Two Hands*, Gregor Jordan's debut feature. Australia might have forgotten him but Jordan hadn't. *Two Hands* producer Marian Macgowan says, 'He was known around town but never made that impact in the early days.' Macgowan and Jordan suspected Ledger had the 'star quality' to carry the film. Jordan took a punt and flew to meet Ledger in LA. 'The thing that distinguishes people like him is their complete determination and focus,' Macgowan says. 'He has a very clear sense of himself, he's very mature and that's what he projects on screen – clarity, determination, focus. He knows who he is. I remember one casting agent saying years ago "He's not a great actor but he's a star".' Hollywood soon noticed. At least the team behind the teen parody of Shakespeare's *The Taming of the Shrew, 10 Things I Hate About You*, did.

A self-confessed poor auditioner, Ledger concedes he was bamboozled by the way Hollywood worked. 'But I never really worried because you can't let them intimidate you; you just have to realise they're human beings and they once shat in their pants as well,' he notes dryly. 'If you take them off their pedestals and treat them like normal people, they sit back and treat you like a normal person. Australians have an incredible knack of being able to do that to people, bring them down to their level, disarm them.'

It was a necessary tactic with the 'really cocky' director of *10 Things*, Gil Junger. At the audition's conclusion, Junger, noticing a nervous Ledger, asked him about the 'Theatresports' on his resume. On being told it was acting games and improvising, Ledger says Junger 'sat back and said, "I want you to sell me the pair of shoes I'm already wearing".' That's not improvising so much as an example of Hollywood's penchant for repackaging. Ledger still laughs at the ludicrous notion. 'So I had to get off my chair and sell him his shoes. And he bought them!'

To this day the actor finds auditions 'humiliating', even if he's in the enviable position of only needing to audition for a role 'if I really want to go after it', he says. 'There's something about auditions where you don't feel like you're performing. [In fact] you're not, you're being judged and tested. It does something to your state of mind – for me anyway – in terms of how much you relax and how much you're breathing.' He says directors only see 'a crack-shattered' image of the actor. 'I've fucked up a lot of auditions. Who cares? I think everyone feels that way somewhat.'

After nabbing the co-lead role in *10 Things*, Ledger returned to Sydney to shoot *Two Hands*. Days later, he flew back to the US to make *10 Things*. His first Hollywood shoot wasn't too different from his first lead role in Australia, chiefly because the US$18 million film wasn't that 'big'. And he was allowed to retain his Aussie accent. He soon encountered one striking difference though.

'It was weird because I [was] straight from an industry where pretty much the actors and the crew all get paid the same. There's no separate unions for grips and make-up artists and at any point crew members can walk up to an actor who's out of line and say, "Listen, mate, stop acting like a little cunt." And the actor will go, "All right". Also, Australian actors will pick up gear and help them move to get a shot done because they're running out of time. Then you come up on a set [in Hollywood] where there are 14-, 15-year-old kids who have this sense of entitlement, they've been earning this huge amount of money since they were ten or something.'

At one point Ledger offered to fetch coffee for some crew members: 'Nothing special, that's what you do.' While he was at the coffee machine with the order, an assistant director came over and 'literally slapped my wrist and said, "You're not allowed to do that, you can't do that, just get back to your trailer" ...I couldn't believe it. All of a sudden I [understood] the machine that creates the monster in actors.' He saw how such pampering produced actors who 'start believing they're special'.

'The people who treat them like that then turn around and call them arrogant actors but it's the hand that rocks the cradle.' That said, 'There's probably been one actor I've worked with who's been fairly difficult. The guys on *10 Things* were all lovely. When I look back, they weren't bad, they weren't really rude, it was just the way they held themselves. It's merely a difference between [Hollywood] and how we hold ourselves back home.'

Still, many of the cast of *10 Things* have remained just that – kids. Only Ledger and his co-star Julia Stiles have progressed to more substantial film careers. Ledger cracks that his portrayal of shy teen Patrick Verona was 'a pretty amazing performance, wasn't it?' It was more than many could have hoped for though; the film earned US$38 million at the US box office. Ledger earned close to US$100 000 and when he returned to Australia to promote it in 1999, he was the Hollywood leading man his homeland had never heard of.

While publicising *Two Hands* in Australia soon afterwards, publicist Amanda Huddle says Ledger transformed from a shy kid into a seasoned pro. 'A lot came at once and he handled it so well, better than someone like Colin Farrell seems to be [doing] today.' He was still malleable; he didn't have an Australian agent and he came from the US unaccompanied. The *Two Hands* distributor took advantage. 'Now he wouldn't do the things we made him do in a million years, nor should he,' admits Huddle, who pushed him through an arduous schedule of interviews and promotional appearances. 'At times he acted like he was 75 and had been doing it for years, at others like he was a 20-year-old kid.'

Ledger's co-workers suspect his father Kim is the font of sage advice and the affirmation that keeps him grounded. He needed that advice during *Two Hands'* successful Australian launch, when Ledger hid the fact that he had just been cast as Mel Gibson's son in the US$110 million historical epic *The Patriot*. His career was rocketing. Ledger demurs. 'Things just don't quickly accelerate because after the movies were finished, it still took them eight months to come out. Eight months of sitting around scratching your bum.' During this period only two films 'were thrown my way'. Both were teen flicks, nothing interesting. 'I wanted to be in rooms with bigger directors contending bigger roles in bigger projects.'

Macgowan says, 'Another thing that distinguishes people like him is the choices they make. He made the right choices.' Yet only a few years later his choices nearly stalled his career. Ledger admits, 'I sat on my arse for over a year' as a 'beach bum', surfing the California coast and living in Laurel Canyon (a suburb of Los Angeles) with a mate. 'It was a good break because I'd been going for a while,' he adds. He wasn't perturbed about being unemployed. 'I didn't care because the beauty about being an Australian in Hollywood is we've got this sense of fearlessness that comes

'[Australians in Hollywood have] got this sense of fearlessness that comes from knowing we can always go home'

from knowing we can always go home. It's not a bad fucking back-up plan. It's a beautiful country with work, if you have to. So I thought, fuck it, I might as well stick it out and try and do something I'm proud of rather than just cash in quickly.'

He could be proud of *The Patriot*. He admits it 'saved' him but 'I had to fight for it'. Five auditions and a screen test with the Godfather of Australian actors, Mel Gibson, were 'nerve-wracking'. Ledger concedes his auditions were terrible, yet producers Dean Devlin and Roland Emmerich chose Ledger over Ryan Phillippe.

It was his first Hollywood movie with an American accent. Unfortunately, he was left to find the accent himself because he wasn't provided with a dialect coach. 'It's a US $150 million movie, massive, but they just kinda forgot about a couple of tiny things that I really wanted. There were times before I started shooting where I was banging my head against a wall saying, "How can I get out of this?" But I think that about every job I do: "I've gotta get out of this now. I was just lying, I can't act, I was just fooling you guys".' Even today, panic attacks haunt him before every job. Other actors, including Nicole Kidman, talk of similar self-doubts. Now he believes it's part of his method.

'People have got their own processes for preparing – you need to summon extreme amounts of confidence,' Ledger explains. 'At some point you've got to get to the place where you just have to give in to it. My way of getting there is by beating the shit out of myself first and just saying, "I'm hopeless. What am I doing here? I can't act" ...Then you get to a place where you're like, fuck it, this is a challenge and I have to turn it around, I've got to be strong now, I can do this. But it's a long process, I usually don't feel like that until after the first day.'

He had to master much more before *The Patriot* began filming. 'I'd done a bit of horse-riding before,' he says with understatement. 'Generally, before you work – even if you've been riding since you were two years old – they still insist on teaching you how to trot, how to get on the horse, how to get off. Every time they take you back to basics and you tell them, "Honestly, I'm OK getting on", but they say, "No, we've got to teach you".'

The Patriot signalled Ledger's real step up in commercial and audience popularity. He played Gibson's son, a patriotic warrior in what he describes as 'a big American flag-waving bonanza ... They love that shit, so all of a sudden I was the kid that was *The Patriot* to America and, honestly, it was the last thing I'd want to do.' Yet the movie exemplified Hollywood's globalisation; it starred two Australians and was directed by a German. Ledger says, 'That was kind of a joke on set.'

Another quiet spell followed. His lead role in a soccer movie called *Calcio*, set in Italy, disappeared upon the film's late cancellation and he missed the Ewan McGregor role in *Moulin Rouge!* Then his life changed forever. The studio behind *The Patriot*, Columbia, wanted to make Ledger a star with a lead role in *A Knight's Tale*. 'Actors are just products to studios, no different to what this lighter is to Bic,' he says, picking up his disposable lighter. 'The studio finds someone and goes, "I think this could be a good product that we could invest money in. So once we've built him and turned him into something, let's offer him a bunch of movies at Columbia and we'll keep pumping him up and he'll become our guy and we'll start to make money off him".'

Ledger concedes he was seduced by the notion of not having to audition for the medieval romp. 'Then I began to feel the weight and pressure of the machinery. I began to feel like a cog,' he says. The promotional posters made obvious who Columbia had invested in. They were filled with Ledger's face and the tagline 'He will rock you'. It was the kind of vanity promotion usually reserved for Tom Cruise but Ledger lacked the vanity. He almost self-combusted in that boardroom meeting mentioned earlier. 'It scared me so much I said, "I can't, I just don't want to do any of it, don't want to be part of it".' Eventually, a compromise was reached. Ledger's responsibilities halved. 'Now I understand it a little more but at the time it was such a culture shock,' he says. With hindsight, he says he panicked because 'no-one had really explained this side of the business to me'.

'I began to feel the weight and pressure of the machinery. I began to feel like a cog.'

Ledger felt it most in the following months. His industry 'anointment' was landing the cover of US *Vanity Fair* in August 2000. 'It's funny, it was an anointment but it isn't as organic as people think. You are something people have invested in.' So you lose power? Not necessarily, Ledger believes. 'You gain power and you lose it. You lose control [of] your life, where it's going and the stages in which you live. This lifestyle is so inconsistent. Every movie that comes out presents you another level, whether it's bad or good, and it's an extra $40 million worth of publicity invested in you. You gain power if you're in it for the right reasons. It gives you the opportunity to work with inspiring people.' Ledger consciously reminded himself to keep his head and 'stay cool'. 'But then you get to the point where you think, oh fuck it, my head ain't going anywhere so stop worrying about it and get on with life.'

Someone suggested media training to the actor but he passed. 'Ultimately there is nothing you can do to prepare anyone for how your life's gonna change, how the way you've been living it for the past 20 years changes...I flew myself to America to get into this position so it's no-one else's fault but my own. I can only be grateful for what I have and just put up with the rest.' Not that he expected such success although 'I believed that I had just as good a chance as anyone else in this city'.

Confidence helps. As an Australian who worked with Ledger on *10 Things* says, 'Even then, he definitely had that "thing" that makes them actors. He's tall, has that deep voice and knows exactly when to smile or charm people, as good actors do.' Macgowan agrees. 'You take away his voice and he was just another good-looking young actor, albeit an action hero who can act.' Ledger realises confidence is a requisite due to the constant put-downs. 'There has to be something inside you, whether it's pride or dignity, that says, "I'm going to keep going". I don't know what it is though.'

'There has to be something inside you, whether it's pride or dignity, that says, "I'm going to keep going"'

Perhaps it is resilience, coupled with the Aussie trait to 'not give a shit'? Ledger agrees. 'We come from an empty nation, so we are grateful for things, in a sense. I was just grateful to be here, let alone be out at meetings in LA. The other thing is we have something to fall back on, we can always go home. And we're spawned from a hugely modest society, not self-promoting, so that's a quality people pick up on when you're in the room. They don't see us sitting there trying to market ourselves saying "Bling bling, buy us!"'

Most of the current generation of Australian actors have shown enormous resilience. Ledger still sees them come and go, his Los Feliz house is 'an Aussie hostel for actors'. Most stay two or three months before the task overwhelms them or they run out of money. 'It takes time and patience just to lay the foundation,' he says. There is no particular cachet in being an Australian in Hollywood. Americans might think Australians quaint but 'they think everyone's quaint'.

His homeland isn't necessarily as welcoming though. Sure, Ledger has felt the plaudits and pride from his countrymen and he shares the excitement any Aussie feels when another Australian achieves on the world stage. Yet the Australian media also cuts them down. Ledger's felt it, although the blows are softened when they come from 11 000 kilometres away. 'The media love to promote but then they've got a sense of humour about how they cut people down. They're like: "You're great, you're fantastic" and then when you're not look-ing, they go "snap", cut you down, sit around and giggle and crack a beer and say, "Yeah, we taught him a lesson".'

Ledger's love life, his apparently petulant behaviour, even his appearances on US talk shows, have become grist for the Australian media's mill. 'Just any tiny little thing they'll jump on and go, "Did you see that, that sign of 'something'?"' he laughs. He will return home one day. He misses too much:

'Friends, family, the weather, surf, the beaches. Quite a lot. Even the bread's shit [in LA]. It's all sourdough, although we found a meat pie shop in Santa Monica that also does custard tarts.' His grin is huge.

'Maybe once you move back [home] and people get over the fact you've moved back, it'll settle down and people will let me be. I know that in the general public people are more chilled out and if they do come up to you it's more the "Good on ya, mate, good luck to ya" or "God, what's it like?" There's this general curiosity and it's more genuine than from people over here. In LA, no-one gives a shit, everyone acts like a star so you wouldn't know who's who!'

Before then, a career awaits. Despite experiencing so many of Hollywood's tribulations, Ledger is still a freshman. His choices of the last three years emphasise that; a number of misfires – *The Sin Eater (The Order), The Four Feathers* – distracted many from Ledger's fine, and AFI Award-nominated performance in *Ned Kelly*. Ledger attracted bright notices, even if the film didn't. It was the one professional high in two years of lows. The lows barely seem to matter. In less than 18 months in 2003–4, Ledger was to juggle *The Lords of Dogtown* for Catherine Hardwicke, *The Brothers Grimm* for Terry Gilliam, *Casanova* for Lasse Hallstrom and the role of a gay cowboy for Ang Lee in *Brokeback Mountain*.

'I am someone who likes to learn from my mistakes,' Ledger says. 'But I generally try not to regret anything. Who cares? [If I did] I wouldn't be sitting here now.'

the
pioneers

pioneers

The current influx and influence of Australians in Hollywood is not a new phenomenon, only a substantially larger one. But most of the Australian actors and directors who did search for success overseas did so in desperation. The Australian film industry at various times during the twentieth century just wasn't sustainable.

Australians were crucial participants in the pioneering days of the new medium. A year after Parisians paid to watch the Lumière brothers' first films in 1895, American magician Carl Hertz projected a film at the Melbourne Opera House in August 1896. Two months later, the Lumières shipped an early version of their revolutionary product to Australia; it recorded a Manly steam ferry on 25 October 1896 and the Melbourne Cup. Australians appreciated the wonder of this new technology. The next 100 years showed them to be adept at its use and development.

The embryonic Australian film industry grew at the turn of the twentieth century. Local producer Ernest Jardine Thwaites filmed local vignettes in 1897 as the Salvation Army and Queensland government both began making instructional or educational films. Production was mostly confined to amateurs and enthusiasts, with little formal organisation before 1910. Nevertheless, in 1906 Charles Tait filmed *The Story of the*

Kelly Gang, now widely regarded as the world's first full-length feature film – although only fragments of it remain. No bother; another fourteen bushranger films were made before 1912, when the New South Wales government banned them for their subversive influence – or perhaps through sheer boredom.

Between 1906 and 1912 Australia led Britain and the US in producing feature-length narrative films, many focusing on gold prospecting, convict life and horseracing. The bushranger ban proved debilitating, though, and production waned. Consequently many actors drifted back to live theatre or ventured overseas in search of further opportunities. They wouldn't be the last.

The first notable batch of expats landed in Hollywood during, and immediately after, World War I, a time in which Hollywood production began its inexorable thrust around the globe. The lure was obvious and many Australian actors succumbed, although few replicated their homeland triumphs in the US. Worse still, some left gaping holes in the nascent Australian industry.

One of the first to emigrate, vaudeville performer Clyde Cook, arrived in the US during World War I, making a name primarily in the silent film era with more than 100 roles. Tasmanian-born Arthur Shirley also earned many roles upon his move but enjoyed little success until he wrote and directed *The Mystery of a Hansom Cab* and *The Sealed Room* in 1925–26, before returning home. Another vaudevillian, Snub Pollard, managed to work with Harold Lloyd.

Coming to the US at the age of twenty-four, New Zealand-born Australian repertory theatre actor Rupert Julian began his career as a stage and screen actor but turned to directing in 1915. He was a journeyman who replaced the fired director Erich Von Stroheim on 1923's *Merry-Go-Round*. Julian worked with Cecil B. de Mille's Producers Distributing Corporation as his career peaked with 1925's *The Phantom of the Opera* starring Lon Chaney, but he, like many, struggled after the advent of sound.

John Gavin made and starred in bushranger shorts such as *Thunderbolt* and *Moonlite* before travelling to the US in 1918. He too was shunned as an actor until he founded his own Hollywood production company and cast himself in his own westerns, with some success.

Other early emigrants included Sydney's Sylvia Breamer, New Zealand-born Elsie Wilson and Western Australia's Enid Bennett, who played Maid Marian in Douglas Fairbanks's *Robin Hood*. All three forged notable, if brief, Hollywood careers from World War I into the 1920s, with Bennett most prominent.

Louise (Carbasse) Lovely was the inspiration for many expats. The child star grew with aplomb, following her Australian film successes with a move to America and a contract with Universal Studios. Studio chief Carl Laemmle reportedly noted when seeing her screen test: 'She's lovely in her work and in herself. Call her Louise Lovely...' Thus Louise Carbasse was 'Hollywooded' and became a minor star with Universal, making 50 films between 1911 and 1925 before she left the studio acrimoniously. Universal threatened legal action if she used the name 'Louise Lovely' while working for any other studio. She returned to work in Australia.

Sydney's champion swimmer, Annette Kellerman, was the most successful of the first batch. Her success was destined after being arrested in Boston in 1907 for wearing a one-piece bathing suit then considered in violation of decency standards. She was made for Hollywood's fame machine. 'The Diving Venus' went to the US after a European tour and swiftly became a major US star despite no previous experience. She only returned to Australia in 1970.

Until the 1920s, there was a chance Australia would create a sustainable film industry. An energetic, if not wholly successful, period spawned backblock farces, bush westerns and social issues films. Occasional triumphs such as Kenneth Brampton's *Robbery Under Arms* and Raymond Longford's *A Sentimental Bloke* in 1919 and *On Our Selection* in 1920 showcased a competent industry. But a wave of substandard films and uncompromising Hollywood distribution halted any momentum. Also, Australia willingly accepted those with Hollywood credentials – including F. Stuart-Whyte, Lawson Harris and Yvonne Pavis – often to its detriment, American Norman Dawn's big-budget flop, *For the Term of His Natural Life*, being the infamous example.

In 1927, a Royal Commission into Australian cinema estimated the industry employed 20 000 people but the inability to adapt to 1928's introduction of sound, both financially and technically, coupled with the Depression, resulted in film production sinking rapidly. This pre-World War II period is regarded as a dire time for Australian film yet many movies continued to be made. Ken G. Hall directed 17 features between 1932 and 1940 alone, including the successful Rudd family films. Even England's Ealing Studios tried to establish an outpost here in the 1940s. Nevertheless, Europe and the US were then the established film industries, magnets for Australia's best and most ambitious.

Lotus Thompson arrived in Hollywood in 1924 as an 18 year old whose reputation extended only to her legs. She worked unwillingly as a leg model before she deliberately disfigured her limbs by pouring acid over them. Suddenly she was considered an actor and enjoyed some triumphs, including Cecil B. de Mille's 1930 classic, *Madam Satan*.

O.P. (Oliver Peters) Heggie arrived in 1928, becoming a character actor best remembered for his blind hermit who befriends Boris Karloff's The Creature in *Bride of Frankenstein* (1935). Sportsman Snowy Baker flirted with five Hollywood features before becoming a trainer for Valentino and Fairbanks.

Alan Marshal, despite his limited attributes, was the prototype of the macho Australian leading man now dominating Hollywood. The handsome actor became a heroic, if shallow, star in *Lydia* and *In the Grade of Allah* and did enough to hold his end up against icons including Greta Garbo and Irene Dunne in late 1930s romantic dramas.

As Australian actors became more prominent in Hollywood, directors and producers toiled to build a local film industry back home. Despite the many successes of Raymond Longford, Beaumont Smith, Kenneth Brampton and Franklyn Barrett, and later Charles Chauvel and Ken Hall, almost to a man (as it was) these directors remained in Australia while losing crucial actors like Judith Anderson.

The Adelaide-born stage actress moved to Los Angeles in 1918 and then New York after de Mille told Anderson her face was unsuitable for the screen. She became a treasured actress on Broadway (famous for her Lady Macbeth) who nevertheless remained damned as a character actress, albeit a highly regarded one, on screen due to her unconventional beauty. After her stunning debut as an alluring nightclub owner in 1933's *Blood Money*, she toiled in a number of dour roles, topped by her Academy Award-nominated performance as Mrs Danvers in Alfred Hitchcock's *Rebecca* (1940).

A number of faux Aussies surfaced in Hollywood before World War II, actors who could conceivably have called other nations their home. South African-born Brit Cecil Kellaway moved to Australia as a 27 year old. The much-loved comedy and character stage actor performed in three notable Australian films, including *It Isn't Done*, from which his performance as a squatter earned him a Hollywood contract.

Soon, he became disgruntled by his inability to secure anything beyond gangster bit parts although that changed in 1939
when William Wyler offered him a part in *Wuthering Heights*.
The film spawned a prolific period in the 1940s as a Paramount
contract player. He delivered his best performance as Lana
Turner's husband in *The Postman Always Rings Twice* (1946)
and was nominated for Best Supporting Actor Academy
Awards in two other roles: in 1948's *The Luck of the Irish* (playing a leprechaun) and 1967's *Guess Who's Coming to Dinner*
(playing a priest). He appeared in more than 100 films until
1970, although he is just as famous for a role he declined, that
of Santa Claus in *Miracle on 34th Street*; he apparently told his
son, 'Americans don't go for whimsy.'

Merle Oberon was the most fantastic of the faux-
Australians, a star whose studio publicists claimed she was
born on a ship passing by Tasmania, in order to hide her true
identity, that of a Eurasian born in India. She moved to
London in her late teens and toiled in many small roles until
producers began to groom her for more in the early 1930s.
After her portrayal of Lady Marguerite Blakeney in 1934's *The
Scarlet Pimpernel*, she moved to Hollywood, where she
promptly snaffled an Oscar nomination for Best Actress as
Kitty Vane in 1935's *The Dark Angel*. She shone in many more
films, including 1938's *The Divorce of Lady X* and *Wuthering
Heights*. Eventually, she retired the charade; nevertheless, the
southern island state hosted a reception in her honour in 1979,
the year before she died.

Another Tasmanian, of sorts, Errol Flynn, became one of
Australia's most celebrated exports. The swashbuckling leading man with the swaggering sexual peccadilloes claimed he
was born in Tasmania; others suggest Northern Ireland. He did
spend his troublesome childhood and school years in Australia
before moving to England where he lurched from job to job.

His first break came when, while in Australia, he was asked to perform in Charles Chauvel's first 'talkie', *In the Wake of the Bounty*. His expressionless performance as the mutiny leader, Fletcher Christian, barely hinted at the cavalier performances he would later deliver, although the fact that his mother, Marrelle Young, was a descendant of an HMS *Bounty* midshipman hinted at his seemingly predetermined path.

On returning to England, he kept acting and was spotted by American agents who signed him to a contract with Warner Brothers. His athleticism and handsome stature meant he was a solid bet when he replaced Robert Donat in the title role of *Captain Blood* (1935). His journey to stardom as the undisputed king of swashbuckler films, a title inherited from Douglas Fairbanks, was swift. He became the hero in *The Charge of the Light Brigade*, *The Adventures of Robin Hood* and *The Sea Hawk*, earned the moniker 'The Baron', and did 31 movies before 1948, partnering Olivia de Havilland in seven of them.

He was as much an insouciant, carousing rebel off screen as he was on screen. By indiscriminately indulging in his passions — drinking, fighting, boating and sex — a phrase was coined in his dubious honour: 'in like Flynn'. In his prime, in films such as 1938's *The Dawn Patrol* opposite David Niven and Basil Rathbone, he was indisputably a star but his libido was a destructive influence. His career somehow managed to survive an acquittal of rape charges in 1942 and later tax problems, but after World War II, Flynn sank into a creative and personal morass, resorting to playing drunks as his looks faded. Incredibly, before his death Flynn was rejuvenating his career but sadly the legend of Flynn focuses more upon his off-screen exploits.

World War II moved the balance of filmmaking power further towards the United States. Australian feature film production halted during the war and actors returned to the stage, if they could, or fled overseas. Shirley Ann Richards wanted to stay on screen. Her two-year contract with Sydney's Cinesound, secured after *It Isn't Done*, was rescinded when Cinesound abandoned production for the war effort. She was then Australia's leading female film star, so she moved to Hollywood, changed her name to Ann Richards so as not to be confused with actress Anne Shirley, and won roles in a number of major films, including King Vidor's *An American Romance*, before retiring in the early 50s.

The cruel circumstances of World War II incongruously gave Australia its first Academy Award winner. Cameraman Damien Parer was in the first official Australian team of war correspondents sent to the Middle East. He quickly established a reputation as an uncompromising, humanist documenter of the war through his newsreels, particularly his work from the front line in New Guinea. Ken Hall suggested Parer record a personal introduction to a collection of that footage. The result, *Kokoda Front Line*, an edition of the Cinesound Review newsreel, screened internationally and won Parer the 1942 Academy Award for Best Documentary. In 1943, Paramount secured his services for newsreels but Parer was killed while filming frontline action on Peleliu in the Caroline Islands in 1944.

After the war, Hollywood's lustre grew even brighter as Australian production withered further. In fact, America contemptuously exploited Australia, utilising funds frozen after wartime for US productions in Australia such as *Kangaroo* and *Long John Silver*. By the end of the 50s, Australian feature film production was negligible due to a recession, the introduction of television and the inability of locals to secure exhibition or distribution. Consequently, the industry could no longer groom stars; they'd have to become stars elsewhere. Most moved to the UK.

Some, including Allan Cuthbertson, Lloyd Lamble, John McCallum and Grant Taylor, first took to the English stage. Cuthbertson arrived in Britain in 1947 and starred on London's West End, his film persona limited to military roles including *The Guns of Navarone* and even as Colonel Hall in a 1975 episode of *Fawlty Towers*, while Lamble only secured bit parts in mediocre British fare including two *St Trinians* movies. Taylor, a star in Chauvel's *Forty Thousand Horsemen*, couldn't crack a lead film role in England after shunning an expected move to Hollywood but McCallum had a number of notable starring roles in English films before returning home in the mid-50s to act and produce (including launching the *Skippy* TV series).

Charles 'Bud' Tingwell and Guy Doleman trod similar paths to the UK. Doleman realised Australia's slim pickings weren't enough, despite winning roles in many of the American films made in his homeland, including *The Kangaroo Kid*, *Kangaroo* and *On the Beach*. On moving to England he prospered in many character roles in films including *Thunderball*, *Dial M For Murder* and the recurring role of Colonel Ross in Len Deighton's spy thrillers, beginning with *The Ipcress File* in 1965. He returned to Australia in the early 80s. Tingwell forged a prolific UK film career in the 50s, working for the Hammer and Rank studios, among others, and gaining notoriety as Inspector Craddock in four *Miss Marple* mysteries. He returned to Australia in 1972. Leo McKern moved to the UK after the war and worked solidly, the highlight of his career being his iconic characterisation of the *Rumpole of the Bailey* for BBC television.

Edward Ashley (Cooper) became a leading man in the UK prior to World War II, before turns as a supporting player in 40s and 50s US films including *Gay Blades* (1946).

Broken Hill-born Ron Randell broke through when he

starred as Charles Kingsford Smith in Ken Hall's *Smithy* (1946). Columbia Pictures signed him soon after, contracting him until 1951 and providing leading man roles, most notably playing Cole Porter in *Kiss Me Kate* (1953). He also featured in the 1955 British production of *I Am A Camera*.

Chips Rafferty bettered Randell's run as the archetypal screen Aussie. During the Australian production drought of the 40s–60s, Rafferty was the one constant in Australian film. Such was his stature, and intent, he established Platypus Productions and then Southern International in the early 50s – desperate acts to keep his native film industry alive. Rafferty finally succumbed to the lure of more regular work in the United States in the 60s, scoring many character actor roles in films such as *The Wackiest Ship in the Army* (1960) and *Mutiny on the Bounty* (1962) and in television series including *Gunsmoke*, *Tarzan* and *The Monkees*. He remained stridently Australian though, maintaining his base here and preferring international films made in Australia, including *They're A Weird Mob*.

Later, Rod Taylor assumed the mantle of 'international Aussie'; the bullish, sunburnt male left in 1955 after starring in two Australian films. He constructed a prosperous, if limited, international career, beginning with British films and television before attracting supporting roles in the US. He worked his way up to leading man status, performing charmingly in high profile pics as diverse as *The Time Machine* (1960), *The Birds* (1963) and *Sunday in New York* but his career reached some sort of zenith when he was considered for 1968's *Planet of the Apes* until trumped by Charlton Heston. He spent the tail end of his career in mediocre American TV shows, with an occasional surprising role such as playing an American in the 1976 Australian production, *The Picture Show Man*, or popping up in Stephan Elliott's *Welcome to Woop Woop*.

Peter Finch returned to his birthplace, London, in 1949 after establishing himself as one of Australia's leading actors. Despite his Oberon–Flynn-like right to call himself Australian (he grew up in France and India before Australia), he came to epitomise the typical Aussie in many roles, from his first, as a young farmer in 1938's *Dad and Dave Come To Town*, to an alcoholic husband in 1946's *A Son Is Born*. After war service and on the urging of Laurence Olivier, Finch moved to the UK where, infamously, he had an affair with Olivier's wife, Vivien Leigh. Stage fright killed his theatre ambitions although his transition to international films was smooth, first as Aussie-for-hire and then as a talented character actor. He returned to Australia for the last time to star in two British adaptations of novels, *A Town Like Alice* in 1956 and *The Shiralee* in 1957. Across three decades, Finch built a Flynn-like reputation for his drinking and womanising. His screen legacy remains robust, though, due to five BAFTA award wins, an Oscar nomination for his performance as a homosexual Jewish doctor in *Sunday, Bloody Sunday* (1971) and a posthumous Academy Award for his over-the-top performance as a TV presenter in 1976's *Network*.

Diane Cilento's journey was not dissimilar to Finch's, although her theatrical training was in the US and England. She starred in many British movies of the 50s and 60s and won an Oscar nomination for her performance as Molly Seagrim in 1963's *Tom Jones*. She returned to Australia in the mid-70s after divorcing Sean Connery.

Similarly, accomplished stage actress Coral Browne worked primarily on the British stage. She brightened many pictures though, most specifically 1973's *Theatre of Blood*, in which she co-starred with Vincent Price. They married in 1974, so Browne continued a sporadic relationship with Hollywood, most notably in 1972's *The Ruling Class* and as the heavenly voice in *Xanadu*.

Frank Thring took his advance to Hollywood with a grain of salt. The son of a major theatre and film producer, Thring Jr was a stage actor who saw film as an amusement. Like Finch, he befriended Laurence Olivier, who suggested he try Hollywood. He barely did but what he did do there was memorable, delivering extravagantly camp performances as Pontius Pilate in *Ben Hur* and as Herod, the man who dropped the hankie, in 1961's *King of Kings*.

A similarly melodramatic international career, or at least collection of roles, was Robert Helpmann's. The dancer and choreographer was a prominent feature in British productions *The Red Shoes* and *Henry V* and American films, *The Iron Petticoat* (1956) and *Chitty Chitty Bang Bang* (1968). Despite his revered reputation in dance, Helpmann was just as much an international film actor, only performing in Australian films at the end of his career, to the detriment of his reputation.

John Meillon's stint abroad was as brief and eventful as Thring's. The stage and film character actor worked in the UK for five years (1959–64), featuring in a number of notable British films including *Billy Budd* and *The Running Man* before returning to a largely government-induced blossoming of the Australian film industry in the early 70s where he starred in seminal works including 1974's *The Cars That Ate Paris* and, later, *Crocodile Dundee*.

Radio and stage actor Michael Pate left in 1950 after making a name for himself in Charles Chauvel's *Sons of Matthew* in 1949. He worked in American television and film for 17 years at a rate that couldn't be done in Australia. He was a stunning character actor who specialised as a gunman in *A Lawless Street*, *Reprisal* and *Westbound* but also played an Indian chief, Vittorio, in *Hondo* (1953, with John Wayne). Incidentally, *Hondo* was directed by an Australian whose career took place entirely in the US, John Farrow. Farrow, the father of Mia Farrow, arrived in Hollywood in the late 20s and in 1942 became the first Australian to be nominated for Best Direction at the Academy Awards, for *Wake Island* (he won in 1956 for his screenplay of *Around the World in 80 Days*).

Pate's career blossomed in films such as Sam Peckinpah's *Major Dundee* and in guest roles on TV series such as *Maverick*, *Gunsmoke*, *Mission: Impossible* and *Batman*, and as the screenwriter of *Escape from Fort Bravo* and *The Most Dangerous Man Alive*. He returned to Australia in 1968, spending time in all facets of film and television.

It is easy to dismiss George Lazenby's international career. After all, he was the infamous James Bond who barely was, replacing Sean Connery for one film only, *On Her Majesty's Secret Service*. After moving to the UK in 1969 and nabbing that prized role after performing only in commercials, Lazenby fashioned a career, albeit a minor one, in Hollywood. His roles were as diverse as the *Emmanuelle* film series to Hong Kong action films and from *Hawaii Five-O* to *Baywatch*.

Given the sunburnt, swaggering males Australia became infamous for producing, from Randell and Flynn through to Rafferty and Finch, it's difficult to reconcile that five of the first six Oscars won by Australians were by the costume designers Orry-Kelly and John Truscott. The tradition has continued with recent wins for Lizzy Gardiner and Catherine Martin for *The Adventures of Priscilla, Queen of the Desert* and *Moulin Rouge!*, respectively.

Orry-Kelly (real name John Kelly) is an enigma, with little detail known of his life, nor much celebration of his achievements. After studying art in Australia, he sailed to New York to become an actor. He moved to Los Angeles in 1932, where his old New York flatmate, Cary Grant, introduced him to the head of wardrobe at the prolific Warner Brothers studio, who promptly hired him. His high fashion consciousness and subtle style worked on everything from Busby Berkeley musicals to gangster movies for many more studios, including Universal, RKO and MGM. He came into his own winning Academy Awards for his costume design on *An American in Paris* in 1952, *Les Girls* in 1957 and *Some Like It Hot* in 1959. He was also nominated for *Gypsy* in 1962. A favoured designer of Ingrid Bergman, Marilyn Monroe and Bette Davis, who called him her 'right hand', Orry-Kelly remains Australia's greatest Oscar winner.

John Truscott's stature as a theatre director and administrator in his hometown Melbourne is considerable — the Victorian Arts Centre foyer is named in his honour. His brief foray into Hollywood was extraordinary as he won 1967 Academy Awards for his costume design and art direction on *Camelot*, his first Hollywood movie. His free-spending methods meant he only worked on one other Hollywood film, the gaudy *Paint Your Wagon*.

The opportunities for today's actors, directors, designers and others involved in film production were made far brighter by such expats. Today, a Hollywood career is attainable; for the pioneers, it was a gamble that had to be taken due to the fickle state of the Australian film industry.

bibliography

A note on the research

This book is based on author interviews with the subjects of each chapter conducted in 2003–04 and with others who are specifically quoted. Every effort has been made to corroborate subjects' recollections. In the course of secondary research, the authors also used a significant number of articles from Australian publications, including: *The Sun*, *The Daily Mirror*, *The Daily Telegraph*, *The Sunday Telegraph*, *The Sun-Herald*, *The Sydney Morning Herald*, *The Age*, *The Australian*, *The National Times*, *TV Week* and *The Bulletin*. International magazines used include *Variety*, *Premiere*, *Vanity Fair*, *GQ*, *Movieline* and *Interview*.

Books consulted

Australian Film Commission, *Get The Picture*, 6th edn, Sydney, 2002

Raffaele Caputo and Geoff Burton (eds), *Second Take*, Allen & Unwin, Sydney, 1999

Raffaele Caputo and Geoff Burton (eds), *Third Take*, Allen & Unwin, Sydney, 2002

Tim Cawkwell and John M. Smith (eds), *The World Encyclopedia of the Film*, Galahad Books, London, 1972

Peter Coleman, *Bruce Beresford: Instincts of the Heart*, Angus & Robertson, Sydney, 1992

Gail Kinn and Jim Piazza, *The Complete History of Oscar*, Black Dog & Leventhal Publishers, New York, 2002

Leonard Maltin (ed.), *Leonard Maltin's 2004 Movie & Video Guide*, Signet, USA, 2003

Leonard Maltin, Spencer Green, Luke Fader and Cathleen Anderson (eds), *Leonard Maltin's Movie Encyclopedia*, Plume, USA, 1995

Brian McFarlane, Geoff Mayer and Ina Bertrand (eds), *The Oxford Companion to Australian Film*, Oxford University Press, South Melbourne, 1999

Scott Murray (ed.), *Australian Film 1978–1994*, Oxford University Press, Melbourne, 1995

Andrew Pike and Ross Cooper, *Australian Film 1900–1977*, Oxford University Press, Melbourne, 1998

James Sabine (ed.), *A Century of Australian Cinema*, Australian Film Institute, Port Melbourne, 1995

Andrew Sarris, *"You Ain't Heard Nothing Yet": The American Talking Film History & Memory, 1927–1949*, Oxford University Press, New York, 1998

David Thomson, *A Biographical Dictionary of Film*, Andre Deutsch, London, 1994

acknowledgements

The authors would like to thank their agent Annette Hughes for believing in the concept, publisher Sue Hines for having a dip and editors Clare Emery and Jo Jarrah for their hard work and patience. And in no particular order: Ismail Merchant, John Badham, Ang Lee, Anthony Minghella, Peter Jackson, David Elfick, Bill Bennett, Barrie Osborne, Patricia Rozema, John Landis, Marion Macgowan, George Miller, John Duigan, Matt Carroll, Leonard Hill, Ann Churchill-Brown, Jessica Carrara, Rob Marsala, Emma Cooper, Fiona Searson, Neil Bell, Catherine Jefferey, Jillian Bowen, Lauren Bergman, John Palermo, Bruce Pollack, Paul Getto, Jane Cameron, Wendy Millyard, Heidi Schaeffer, Wendy Day, Trish Coffey, Annabel, Sarah and David at BVI; Danielle, Gillian and Tom at Roadshow, Charlie and Di at UIP; Sarah Ritson, Alan Ladd Jr, Tony Bill, Beatriz Sequeira, Miranda Culley, Richard Harris, Jack Thompson, Deb Fryers; Michael and Fiona Sheridan for the beachhouse; Peter Lalor, John K. Davies, Peter Holmes à Court, Bobbie Whiteman, Rachel Newman and Dino Scatena for advice and encouragement; Alan Finney for enthusiasm; our parents Diane and Tony, Anne and Rodger for encouraging us to read; the Australian film producers who so generously permitted us to use photos from their films; and the subjects of this book who, in good faith, told their stories with such heart.

photographic credits

Permission to reproduce copyright material has been sought and the authors wish to acknowledge the following photographers and other copyright holders:

Picture section 1

page 1
top & bottom: Kennedy Miller, Nicole Kidman

page 2
Jane Scott, Geoffrey Rush

page 3
Robert McFarlane, Geoffrey Rush

page 4 & 5
Paul Hogan

page 6
top: Eric Bana, Michele Bennett
bottom: Robert McFarlane, Gillian Armstrong

page 7
top: Bryan Brown
bottom: Bryan Brown, South Australian Film Corporation

page 8
top: David Parker, Phillip Noyce, Hilary Linstead
bottom: Stavros Kazantzidis

Picture section 2

page 1

Latent Image Productions Pty Ltd

page 2

Lance Reynolds

page 3

top: Robert McFarlane, Samson Productions
bottom: Takashi Seida, Samson Productions

page 4

top: Lisa Tomasetti, Robyn Kershaw
bottom: Jan Chapman

page 5

top: Robert McFarlane, Samson Productions
bottom: Fred Schepisi

page 6

Roadshow, Coote and Carroll

page 7

Marian Macgowan, Heath Ledger

Still supplied from *The Adventures of Priscilla, Queen of the Desert*
courtesy of Latent Image Productions Pty Limited is not to be
interpreted as an endorsement of the material or views contained herein.